# Police Practices in Global Perspective

# Police Practices in Global Perspective

Edited by
John A. Eterno and Dilip K. Das

ROWMAN & LITTLEFIELD PUBLISHERS, INC.
*Lanham • Boulder • New York • Toronto • Plymouth, UK*

Published by Rowman & Littlefield Publishers, Inc.
A wholly owned subsidiary of The Rowman & Littlefield Publishing Group, Inc.
4501 Forbes Boulevard, Suite 200, Lanham, Maryland 20706
http://www.rowmanlittlefield.com

Estover Road, Plymouth PL6 7PY, United Kingdom

British Library Cataloguing in Publication Information Available

**Library of Congress Cataloging-in-Publication Data**

Police practices in global perspective / edited by John A. Eterno and Dilip K. Das.
   p. cm.
Includes bibliographical references and index.
ISBN 978-1-4422-0024-1 (cloth : alk. paper) — ISBN 978-1-4422-0026-5 (electronic)
1. Police. 2. Law enforcement. 3. Transnational crime. 4. Terrorism. I. Eterno, John, 1959– II. Das, Dilip K., 1941–
HV7921.P57154 2010
363.2'3—dc22
                          2009019441

Printed in the United States of America

# Contents

# Introduction

## John A. Eterno

In the endless struggle between law enforcement and those who commit illegal behavior, advances in technology have far-reaching consequences—from knives to bombs, from handguns to weapons of mass destruction, from local crime families to international networks. Law enforcement needs to recognize these changes and adapt. It cannot use outdated tactics; rather, it needs to be innovative and adjust quickly, as criminals and terrorists are quick to take advantage of new technologies. Just as many in France before World War II felt impregnable with the Maginot Line, law enforcement cannot simply depend on old, traditional practices such as preventive patrol, reactive policing (rather than proactive policing), and policing sectors. Exacerbating the problem of these outdated practices is a police culture that can stymie investigative efforts through practices such as not sharing information with other agencies. Criminals and terrorists adapt and evolve—so too must law enforcement.

The speed with which these changes are taking place is astronomical. Is law enforcement ready for the challenges ahead? Sociologist Emile Durkheim suggests that rapid social change will bring anomie (i.e., normlessness), leading to deviant behavior. Have the rapid technological changes led to anomie? Cultures and subcultures, including law enforcement, are having difficulty adjusting to the fast-paced world in which we live. Indeed, the world's legal codes are often woefully inadequate to handle many of these new global threats. In many jurisdictions we do see new codes for computer fraud, computer tampering, terrorism, and the like. Yet these laws are slow to develop. Furthermore, they fail to address the international reach of a criminal/terrorist working in, say, another continent and using the Internet to commit fraud or other criminal activities. Adding to these complicated issues, at least in democratic society, are questions with respect to the extent to which law enforcement can act to capture, interrogate, and investigate possible criminals/ terrorists. In many democratic nations courts are the first to write the rules of criminal procedure (laws that influence those working in the criminal justice system). Courts are very slow and reactive. This leads to confusing laws that can lead to abuse or noncompliance. To the extent possible, courts and other policymaking bodies need to be clear and consistent in their direction to law enforcement (see, for example, Eterno, 2007).

Local law enforcement seems ill equipped to handle many new threats such as bioterrorism, weapons of mass destruction, and other threats that are global in nature. Technological advances allow the unscrupulous to murder, steal, and enslave across government boundaries with few or no repercussions. Criminals, always ready to exploit a weakness, have taken advantage of new technologies: pedophiles using the Internet to attract victims, terrorists using airliners, drug smugglers taking advantage of every trade route and technology to transport their illegal goods, terrorists setting up global networks, and so forth. Law enforcement must adapt. What strategies are they using? How are different governments adapting? This book examines how different countries are handling these international threats. Our method of examining this is to invite experts in their respective countries to write about their perceptions and understandings. Making this book unique, we examine countries from nearly every continent—Australia, Brazil, China, India, Nigeria, the Russian Federation, and the United States. Each country adds a unique aspect to the book. Each sees the global issue through the lens of its local culture and history.

We begin our journey in the United States—familiar ground for many readers. Here the focus is on balancing rights with the need for law enforcement to have the tools to fight crime. Also, we discuss the idea of understanding Islamic terrorism as a global East-meets-West phenomenon.

In strong contrast to the first chapter, Verma in his chapter unleashes his views on India. He is very critical of the United States, especially for helping Pakistan. Verma's views are very important and show some of the cultural hurdles that law enforcement must overcome to fight international criminals/ terrorists.

Next, Wong discusses a historical and cultural understanding of China and terrorism. Wong points out that to the Chinese the idea of terrorism is new. He suggests that a threat to the political order is a threat to the cosmic order or the "mandate from heaven." Again, this is an understanding that law enforcement authorities working beyond national boundaries must learn to work with.

Next the reader is exposed to Brazil. Here Dellasoppa relates crime to the social conditions of Brazil. He suggests that Brazil has rarely, if ever, attained a monopoly on the use of legitimate violence and that this is a source of crime and instability. Additionally, he talks about poverty and corruption by public officials and how this exacerbates the aforementioned problems. One of his main themes is that collusion among various legitimate and illegitimate powers is one way to understand the complicated processes involved in establishing some type of order in Brazil. Due to this collusion, police are just one of many entities that use legitimate force in Brazil. He relates this collusion to the rising and illegal power of militias in everyday society as well as other legitimate and illegitimate entities that use force in Brazil. He concludes by asking whether this complicated arrangement is actually a strategy being used by the government.

In Australia, James and Warren discuss many issues, such as the growth of Australian Federal Police. Again, the contrast with the United States, which has a decentralized system, is evident. They suggest a need for international criminal law but suggest it as unlikely.

We conclude our countries with the Russian Federation and Nigeria. In both countries there is a deep concern with corruption. Further, Gilinskiy talks explicitly about corrupt officials in the Russian Federation and gives graphic descriptions of horrid crimes. Dambazau talks about how criminal networks are more organized in other parts of the world. He also talks about loosely structured groups that exist in Nigeria. Interestingly, he also brings up the issue of the country being surrounded by French-speaking nations. Language is clearly a barrier to international efforts.

In the final chapter, Sciarabba and Sullivan focus on the law and begin to develop a worldwide understanding by discussing the four legal systems of the world. They talk about corruption and discuss how countries might begin to properly handle transnational crime and terrorism.

I ask the reader to keep an open mind as he or she travels on a worldwide journey examining how each country handles transnational crime and terrorism. The reader is left to make her/his own conclusions. Nevertheless, there are two particular points that I will highlight. These are the two initial steps that need to be taken before any progress can be made on fighting global crime and terrorism. First, law enforcement and governments need to remove corruption from within before any success will be met. In my view, this is the single most important aspect to successfully implementing democratic reforms and eventually fighting crime and terrorism. Second, we are fighting a new criminal. This new criminal compels us to examine our methods of law enforcement. Sharing information will be critical in this new world. This requires trust. The civilized world will need to unite and share information if we are to fully take control of the horrific behaviors of terrorism and global crime that we have witnessed. Some organizations such as INTERPOL and the United Nations have made substantial efforts. These efforts need to be re-inforced and supported by every civilized country.

I recently had the privilege of interviewing Odd Berner Malme (former second in command of Norway's police and now attached to the Norwegian Mission to the United Nations) and also saw his presentation at the fifteenth annual meeting of the International Executive Police Symposium held May 12–16, 2008, in Cincinnati, Ohio. He suggests that strong treaties and organizations among nations will be helpful in fighting these criminal activities. He then suggests Norway's alliances with other nations are an excellent example of this. I agree. As a start, we need to understand one another: legal systems, methods of law enforcement, strengths and weaknesses, and so on. This book, covering a wide range of countries, is a step in that direction. The understandings that are developed from this book are a necessary beginning in the ever more complicated fight against global criminals/terrorists.

## REFERENCE

Eterno, John A. 2007. "Understanding the Law on the Front Lines: The Need for Bright-Line Rules." *Criminal Law Bulletin*. 43 (5): 706–25.

## ACKNOWLEDGMENTS

My wife, JoAnn, and two daughters, Julia and Lauren, are my love and inspiration. I want to thank them for all they do. I also want to thank all at Molloy College, including faculty and staff for their help—especially Maureen Stea and Samantha Modik. Thank God for all of you.

*Chapter One*

# Policing in the United States

## *Balancing Crime Fighting and Legal Rights*

### John A. Eterno

Policing in any nation is an inextricable and essential aspect of the existing government. The government of the United States is an elected democracy. It is a tripartite system including legislative, executive, and judicial branches. Essentially, the legislature creates the laws, the executive is charged with enforcing laws, and the judiciary interprets the laws. At the federal level these branches are the president, Congress, and federal courts (the highest court being the United States Supreme Court). Because the founding fathers of the U.S. (the authors and supporters of the Constitution of the United States) feared tyranny, no branch of government has unlimited power. That is, the branches of government check and balance one another. As James Madison writes in *The Federalist Papers* (No. 48), "An *elective despotism* was not the government we fought for; but one which should not only be founded on free principles, but in which the powers of government should be so divided and balanced among several bodies of magistracy as that no one could transcend their legal limits without being effectually checked and restrained by the others." Americans, taken as a whole, cherish these limits and the freedoms that come with them.

The checks and balances and freedoms built into the American Constitution can make policing in the United States an arduous task. There is a strain between the limits and freedoms guaranteed by the Constitution and the task of police to enforce the criminal laws. Additionally, law enforcement is generally considered to be a function of the executive branch. However, the other branches of government have an enormous impact on police because of the tripartite nature of the U.S. government. Police have the power to enforce the laws but they must follow the law while enforcing it.

In fact, a wide range of factors contribute to the complex nature of law enforcement in the United States. First, police are limited in power in the U.S.

5

They must work with the law while they enforce the law. This means follow-ing all the laws including those made by other branches of government. In particular, the complexity and ambiguity of the procedural laws (those laws that explain and limit police power generally explicated by the courts) com-plicate the situation for law enforcement. Police are often faced with an array of guidelines issued by various courts and legislatures that, at times, make lit-tle or no sense.[1]

Second, there exists a decentralized policing system with many overlap-ping jurisdictions. At times, several jurisdictions have authority to investigate and make an arrest for the same crime. This can create tension and competi-tiveness that hinders the efforts of law enforcement. Third, there is a large criminal population that includes many illegal drug users. With such a large criminal element, policing can be very arduous. Fourth, a sophisticated and advanced communications and transportation system makes it easier for crim-inals to cross jurisdictional boundaries. Finally, the large size and diversity of the country presents various challenges to police. Simply getting to some of the more remote areas presents problems.

The U.S. is a vast country with a landmass of over 9 million square kilo-meters (3.7 million square miles). It has a population of 300 million people who speak hundreds of languages. Nevertheless, the main language is En-glish with a significant Spanish-language population. In fact, some areas of the country are bilingual. In 2004, those who identified themselves as being of Hispanic origin exceeded 40 million people (Bernstein, 2005).[2] The growth in the Hispanic population accounted for nearly half of the growth in the U.S. population from July 1, 2003, to July 1, 2004 (Bernstein, 2005).

Many of the people—approximately 80 percent—are descended from a wide variety of European countries. About 13 percent of the population is African in origin, 4 percent Asian, and 1 percent indigenous (American Indian). Most of the population is Christian—a majority of whom are Protestant—with about a quarter of the population identified as Roman Catholic. There is a fairly sig-nificant group who identify themselves as atheist (about 10 percent), 2 per-cent are Jewish, and the remaining 4 percent identify themselves with other religions including Islam, Hinduism, and so on.

This diversity makes policing difficult but, at the same time, this diversity can also help American police—if they properly work with the communities they serve. In most of the large cities, officers will need to familiarize them-selves with a wide variety of cultures. A movement toward community polic-ing as the dominant philosophy of American law enforcement has made knowledge of various communities that agencies serve mandatory. In fact, 66 percent of police departments in the U.S. are using community policing and 100 percent of those agencies serving jurisdictions with over 1 million people are applying community-policing methods (*Sourcebook Online*, 2002: Table 1.48: 49). It can be described as a revolution in American policing. Community policing entails developing partnerships between the police and the communities they serve. Together, the police and the community identify issues that the police must deal with. Once the problems are identified, the police engage in problem-solving exercises bringing to bear all the resources needed—including those outside the police such as child welfare agencies and libraries—to solve the identified issues. The shift to community policing means that police must be less reactive, merely responding to emergency radio calls for help, and more proactive, developing strategies and engaging problems before they become emergency situations.

The diversity of the country has also led to other policing issues. Informal social control mechanisms such as laughter, smiles, and gossip tend to be very weak. Americans, therefore, rely heavily on formal social control such as the police to suppress criminal behavior. While diversity makes policing difficult, it is also an advantage in that Americans are exposed to a variety of ideas and cultures. While there is a checkered past of police relations with other cultures, based on the lessons of the past police today are trained in various cultures and tend to be fairly tolerant of those whose racial/ethnic/religious backgrounds are different.[3]

Another difficulty for police in the U.S. occurs when more than one police agency has the authority to enforce the law in the same area. This is termed overlapping jurisdictions. This is a fairly regular occurrence in the U.S. for two main reasons. First, the government has many agencies with law enforcement powers. Sometimes more than one agency is given law enforcement powers in the same region. For example, in the New York City area, there is a Metropolitan Transit Authority (MTA) Police Department, which has police powers throughout New York State. They are charged with policing the transportation system in and around the city. If something occurs, say, near a train in New York City, both the MTA Police and the New York City Police Department would have jurisdiction (i.e., their jurisdictions overlap).

A second reason for overlapping jurisdictions is due to the parallel nature of the government in the U.S. The federalist system divides the government into national, state, and local levels. Each operates fairly independently of the others. At the state and local level, as of the year 2000, there were 17,784 state and local law enforcement agencies employing over 708,022 sworn officers. Additionally, there were 88,496 federal law enforcement officers with 60 percent of them working in various agencies such as the Immigration and Naturalization Service, Federal Bureau of Prisons, U.S. Customs Service, and the Federal Bureau of Investigation (Bureau of Justice Statistics, 2000).[4] These jurisdictions often overlap. For example, if a person robs a bank in Floral

Park, New York, the following agencies, at a minimum, have jurisdiction: Floral Park Police, Nassau County Police, and the New York State Police. If it is discovered that the suspect may have robbed a bank in the nearby state of Connecticut, then the Federal Bureau of Investigation would also have jurisdiction as well as the Connecticut police (including any local jurisdictions in Connecticut).

A good example of overlapping jurisdictions is the Washington-area sniper case. John Allen Muhammad and Lee Boyd Malvo went on a killing spree in which ten people were killed in several jurisdictions in 2002. After their arrest, even the officers were unsure of where they were to be taken for processing: "As John Muhammad and Lee Malvo sat handcuffed at a rest stop off Interstate 70 in Myersville after their arrest in the early morning of Oct. 24, the first question was who should take custody of them. They had been captured by the FBI, the Maryland State Police, and the Montgomery County police. They were being arrested on federal warrants. And they were in a jurisdiction patrolled by the state police, who had been first on the scene" (Horwitz and Ruane, 2003: A1).

Policing in the United States is also difficult due to the fairly high crime rate (although the rate has decreased in recent years) and the methods employed by American police to fight crime. American police have attempted to control crime through a variety of methods such as community policing. Nevertheless, American police tend to use formal social control such as arrest and/or summons to handle problems so that the numbers can be reflected in the agency's statistics. Such tactics combined with "get tough on crime policies" have led to enormous increases in the number of people under the supervision of corrections.

These policies are reflected in statistics that show an enormous increase in the number of adults incarcerated, on probation, or on parole in the U.S. In 1980 there were 1,840,400 adults in this category; by 2006, the number had increased to 7,211,840 (Sourcebook Online, 2002: table 6.1.2006). This represents a 292 percent increase in the adult population under correctional supervision. One can only imagine the Herculean efforts needed to place nearly 7 million people under the supervision of the criminal justice system and keep them there. It is possible that these policies have helped reduce crime in the U.S. to historically low levels. Nevertheless, the U.S. still has the highest homicide rate compared to other Western nations (Stephens, 2005). Further, the U.S. remains the largest consumer of illegal drugs in the world (Country Watch, 2005). Lastly, the U.S. has the dubious distinction of having the highest prison population rate in the world (Walmsley, 2003). Certainly the U.S. has chosen, for whatever reason, to handle much of its crime problem via formal sanctions. Whether these policies are successful or not remains the subject of debate. For police who must deal with the large volume of people considered criminal, these policies present difficulties.

One of the difficulties with such a strong focus on crime control is that police must work within the law to enforce the law. If police in the U.S. were in a police state, then crime control would be a simple matter. For example, one could simply make a draconian law in such a state that directs "all people caught stealing will have their hands chopped off." Such a law would undoubtedly deter thieves. Crime control is easy in such a horrid, tyrannical environment. The key to law enforcement in a democracy, however, is to control crime while, at the same time, respecting basic human rights. This is the dilemma for police in democratic societies; they must work within their legal authority. In the above example, chopping a thief's hands off would be intolerable in the U.S. due to the Constitution's Eighth Amendment prohibition against cruel and unusual punishment.

The U.S. is a free government and its Constitution contains basic rights granted to all citizens. These rights are specifically stated in the Bill of Rights, the first ten amendments of the Constitution. All police officers in the U.S. must swear an oath to support and defend the Constitution. The Constitution is the foundation for the procedure law. The procedure law is aimed at granting and limiting the powers of those who work in the criminal justice system. While its roots are in the Constitution, the procedure law is also explicated in many state constitutions, statutes, and, most importantly, in court cases.

All officers are responsible for learning and properly applying procedural laws that place limitations on their authority. This can, however, get very complicated. In order for officers to understand what is expected of them legally, they must learn a confusing array of court cases that interpret federal and state constitutions, laws, and statutes at each level of government. The courts have been particularly ambiguous in that area of the law that affects police, such as "search and seizure" and "stop and frisk" laws. Judge Harold Rothwax (1996: 40–41) writes, "The problem is, the law is so muddy that the police can't find out what they are allowed to do even if they wanted to." Many other scholars and commentators have elaborated on this issue for police in the U.S. (e.g., Amsterdam, 1974; Goldstein, 1992; Grano, 1982; LaFave, 1972; Reinharz, 1996).[5]

The remedies for police officers not obeying the procedure law vary. In extreme cases, officers have been arrested and convicted.[6] Generally, however, the remedy is exclusion of illegally obtained evidence. That is, if an officer does an illegal search, the remedy is to disallow illegally obtained evidence from being used in court against the defendant. Other remedies may also be applied. Most jurisdictions have some form of civilian complaint system in which people can complain about an officer's behavior. Punishment for civilian complaints can involve the loss of the job. Civil suits (torts) have also been used quite frequently as a remedy to illegal behavior by officers. That is, civilians can sue an officer or department in civil court for such behaviors. This can lead to a judgment against an officer or a department, which ultimately may mean a monetary award for the plaintiff. Most police departments also have an internal affairs unit or something similar that investigates illegal activity by officers. Additionally, the officer's supervisor should be cognizant of the legal criteria officers must obey and discipline those officers who stray.

Another aspect of the U.S. that creates difficulties for law enforcement is the comparatively modern infrastructure, including transportation and communications systems. This infrastructure makes it very easy to conduct illegal business enterprises across jurisdictional boundaries. Since the U.S. is generally policed by local authorities, the ease with which criminals can move and communicate across boundaries makes enforcement difficult. To combat this, many local agencies are developing partnerships with federal authorities. For example, many areas partner with an arm of the federal government called the Drug Enforcement Agency, creating joint task forces in an attempt to control narcotics trafficking.

Complicating this issue further is the local nature of laws and enforcement. The laws vary, sometimes drastically, by jurisdiction and area of the country. This system can easily be abused by criminals involved in gun running, money laundering, and other such crimes. For example, in the South it is fairly easy to purchase a firearm, while in the Northeast and in most urban areas there are strict laws against the purchase of firearms—especially concealed firearms. Gun runners can purchase firearms in the South and easily transport them through a variety of methods to areas where it is illegal to sell and/or own them without permits.

Overall, policing in the U.S. is complex. The large size of the country, overlapping jurisdictions, the large criminal population, limited police powers, and a modern infrastructure are just a few of the difficulties that American police must contend with. The country is a politically stable democracy and economically prosperous—two important facts that are helpful to police. However, American police, like no other in the world, are closely scrutinized, not only by Americans, but also by worldwide authorities. Policies developed by flagship police departments such as New York City are emulated throughout the democratic world (e.g., Silverman, 1999, with respect to the Compstat process). Additionally, the U.S. is a multicultural society (especially in urban areas) that relies heavily on formal social control (i.e., government law enforcement). This is one reason that the U.S. has a very high number of people in prison. The philosophy of community policing is prevalent but some departments are becoming overwhelmingly "crime control"–oriented, often minimizing the importance of protecting freedom and the Constitution of the U.S., which is their main mission (see, for example, Eterno and Silverman, 2006). Overall, law enforcement in the U.S. is a complex endeavor, especially when police officers are mandated to know and follow the principles of a free society.

## TRANSNATIONAL CRIME

The complexity of the American system of policing is further challenged by the international nature of some crimes. The international drug trade, international terrorism, cybercrime, and organized crime are just a few examples of illegal activities that transcend national boundaries. We must understand the nature and extent of transnational crime in the United States before we can discuss the mechanisms, or lack thereof, to combat it.

Modern technology has led to globalization. National boundaries are increasingly meaningless. Criminals can transport goods, communicate, and travel as easily as anyone else, particularly in free societies. Certain crimes, such as identity theft, can be accomplished quite easily using information freely available on the Internet, from outside national boundaries. In fact, identity theft is increasingly a problem in the United States. Just how much identity theft and, for that matter, transnational crime is occurring in the United States is far from clear.

Law enforcement in this area, including statistical information gathering on international crime, is still in its infancy. In the United States, the Federal Bureau of Investigation still relies on local law enforcement to supply crimes known to them in order to report their figures in *Crime in the United States* (i.e., the uniform crime reports [UCR]). The crime index in the United States is used to calculate the amount of crime that occurs. A crime rate can then be calculated to determine the amount of crime in an area by factoring in the population. The crime index includes the following crimes: murder/nonnegligent manslaughter, forcible rape, burglary, arson, grand larceny, aggravated assault, robbery, and motor vehicle theft.

Many crimes, especially those of an international nature, will not be recorded using such a system. This is because many crimes, such as drug trafficking, identity theft, copyright infringement, and so on, transcend national and local boundaries. Indeed, local law enforcement generally does not consider such crimes their responsibility. Even if a victim of, say, identity theft shows up at a police station, the police are likely to turn the victim away without taking a report unless the entire crime, or a major part of it, took place in their jurisdiction.[7]

The second nationwide method for counting crime, the National Crime Victimization Survey (NCVS), is no better. Both the UCR and the NCVS concentrate on local street crimes. White-collar crimes and organized crimes (many of which are transnational crimes) will not be captured by these American crime-counting instruments. Certainly, if these crimes are not measured by local law enforcement and information about them is not readily available (it is not), then the ability to properly combat those crimes is diminished. Indeed, little concrete information is known about the scale of transnational crimes.

This problem is not limited to the United States. According to the United Nation's Office for Drug Control and Crime Prevention, Centre for International Crime Prevention (1999: chapter 9, paragraph 8),

> although governments are responding to transnational criminal organizations and transnational criminal activities, they are doing too little too late. Efforts need to be expanded especially in the area of reliable and uniform data collection. More sophisticated methodologies need to be devised and greater use made of the information available in the private sector. As a matter of urgency a central clearing house needs to be established with a focus on illicit market activities of all kinds and a recognition of the cross-linkages and synergies that are being developed.

We can, however, using various sources, establish that the level of transnational crime affecting the United States is not inconsequential. As a start we can examine statistics from U.S. Customs and Border Protection under the U.S. Department of Homeland Security (formerly the U.S. Customs Service under the U.S. Department of the Treasury). Of interest to us are the statistics on drug seizures. With respect to drugs, based on the number of seizures and the quantity of illegal drugs being seized, the general tendency indicates an enormous amount of illegal drugs are entering the country. Heroin, for example, increased from 245 seizures for a total of 277.7 pounds in 1977 to 916 seizures for a total of 3,622.4 pounds in 2001. Similarly, there was a dramatic increase in cocaine seizures from 1,025 seizures for a total of 952.1 pounds in 1977 to 2,698 seizures for a total of 190,856.4 pounds in 2001. Not every drug saw an increase, but the sheer amounts are staggering. The Customs Service, for example, did 14,587 seizures for a total of 1,503,940.8 pounds of marijuana in 2001 alone (Sourcebook Online, 2002: table 4.43, p. 393). With such staggering numbers of illegal drugs seized by the Customs Service, one can only speculate that transnational crime with respect to illegal drugs in the U.S. is out of control.

Another estimate of transnational crime comes from the Federal Trade Commission. The Federal Trade Commission sponsored a survey conducted by the company Synovate to examine identity theft. Using random digit dialing, respondents were contacted by telephone in March and April 2003. Ultimately a sample size of 4,057 adults was attained (Synovate, 2003: 3).

One pertinent finding is that a staggering 10 million Americans reported being a victim of some form of identity theft within the last year (Synovate, 2003: 4). Only 25 percent of victims reported the crime to the police (Synovate, 2003: 9). Six percent of the victims stated that a person who worked at a company or financial institution that had access to the information on them stole that information (Synovate, 2003: 29). Additionally, 85 percent of victims reported having their accounts misused with 3 percent of victims indicating it was done over the Internet (Synovate, 2003: 33). With many American companies outsourcing services conducted by telephone or computer to other nations, the possibility of having one's identity stolen outside the nation is markedly increasing. At a minimum, this survey indicates that this crime is susceptible to crossing state and local boundaries, but the possibility of international criminal organizations and terrorists getting such information presents a credible danger as well. Anecdotal information is widely available on the high level of transnational crime in the United States. Liddick (2004) collates and discusses many of these events, for example, the music industry losing $5 billion a year because of stolen materials; terrorist attacks in Bali, Indonesia, killing more than 180 people; several arrests for selling the illegal drug ecstasy worth $40 million on the street with the most likely origin of the drug being in the Netherlands; drug smuggling and money laundering operations run by the Italian Mafia covering thirteen countries; the largest child smuggling operation in U.S. history recently exposed by the U.S. immigration; and there are countless others (Liddick, 2004: 3–6). These are just a small sampling of the events that we are aware of; unfortunately, what is not known must be enormous.

Liddick (2004) also points out the main groups that he believes to be a problem with respect to transnational crime for the U.S. today: La Cosa Nostra, outlaw motorcycle gangs, the Yakuza, Chinese triads, Russian gangs, and Colombian and Mexican drug cartels.[8] One needs to add international terrorists, especially fundamentalist Islamic groups such as al-Qaeda, as well as other gangs with international reach such as Mara Salvatrucha (MS13). Of course, there are many other groups with international ties that are a viable threat. Unscrupulous corporate leaders should be seen as possible problems for law enforcement. For example, one could add Kenneth Lay and other executives at Enron as well as Bernard Madoff, all of whom were involved in white-collar crime, to the list of transnational criminals influencing America. Using Liddick's listing of problem groups, we will explain each of them.

The Federal Bureau of Investigation (2005) considers La Cosa Nostra (which means "our thing") "the foremost organized criminal threat to American society" (History of the La Cosa Nostra, paragraph 1). La Cosa Nostra is not a simple alliance of criminals. Rather, it is arranged by "families" or groups generally by geographic region. They maintain their numbers through fear, strict obedience to a hierarchy, loyalty to family members, and "'omerta'—the code of silence" (Liddick, 2004: 19).

The FBI traces the history of La Cosa Nostra back to the late 1800s. However, the form of La Cosa Nostra has evolved over the years. Today it is unquestionably transnational in scope. It is currently involved in a wide range of illegal activities such as "murder, extortion, drug trafficking, corruption of public officials, gambling, infiltration of legitimate businesses, labor racketeering, loan sharking, prostitution, pornography, tax fraud schemes, and most notably today, stock manipulation schemes" (FBI, 2005: History of the La Cosa Nostra, paragraph 8).

La Cosa Nostra are generally expert at camouflaging their illegal activities—sometimes the legitimate and the illegitimate are so well mixed that it is nearly impossible to distinguish the two. In the U.S., according to the FBI, they are most active in New York, Philadelphia, New England, Detroit, and Chicago. Of course, their activities extend elsewhere as well. While an accurate count of their membership is impossible, one estimate indicates that there are twenty-five Italian-dominated crime families, with 1,700 made men and another 17,000 associates (Siegel, 2004: 420). However, given the ambiguous nature of La Cosa Nostra such estimates should be considered very tentative.

Motorcycle gangs are the second category of concern with respect to transnational crime in the United States. The National Alliance of Gang Investigators Associations (NAGIA) reports that there has been a resurgence of motorcycle gangs in the U.S. due to law enforcement efforts concentrating on street gangs, illegal drugs, and other activities. Some of these gangs have become international in scope. As stated by Tretheway and Katz (1998, paragraph 2) of NAGIA, "The international problem has become clearer through Interpol's 'Project Rockers,' which demonstrated that American-based motorcycle gangs such as the Bandidos, Hell's Angels and Outlaws (three of the larger gangs) use their networks to spread criminal activity overseas. Indeed, at least six motorcycle gangs in the United States now have chapters outside the country's borders. The Hell's Angels gang alone has chapters in 20 countries and is expanding so rapidly that it's difficult to keep up with prospective new chapters. By moving outside the United States, biker gangs can enhance their international criminal connections through involvement with the Italian Mafia, Colombian cartels and other organized crime enterprises."

Many types of illegal activities are associated with these motorcycle gangs. While illicit drugs are generally associated with them, other illegal activities include "murder for hire, prostitution, the operation of 'massage parlors,' international white slavery, kidnapping, burglary, theft, gambling, truck, hijacking, arson, forgery of government documents, extortion, the fencing of stolen goods, theft for U.S. military bases, assault, and rape" (Liddick, 2004: 23). The larger groups are much more organized and they generally have hundreds of members with many chapters around the world.

Another group listed by Liddick is the Yakuza. The Yakuza are the equivalent of organized gangs in Japan. They are mostly male adults who, compared to American gangs, enjoy some acceptance from the population. As Kersten (1993: 278) states, "in Japan the location of the local *boryokudan* (organized crime group) offices is well known to many ordinary citizens." There are a very large number of members of the Yakuza in Japan. According to Kersten (1993: 288), there are 88,000 registered members of the Yakuza. This compares well with Liddick's estimates, which range from 60,000 to 110,000 members (Liddick, 2004: 27).

Japanese crime is considered fairly low by American standards. Kersten (1993), however, suggests this may be due to some complicity by authorities with the Yakuza. Nevertheless, many reported serious crimes may be attributed to the Yakuza. Crimes that they get involved in include illegal gambling, prostitution, and other areas of illegal sexual activity such as sex workers (Kersten, 1993: 290). With respect to the U.S., major illegal activities involve illegal importation of American handguns and amphetamines. The Yakuza are also able to launder illegal money in the U.S. by the "purchase of legitimate businesses to launder and repatriate its illegally earned revenues" (Liddick, 2004: 28).

Chinese triads are, numerically, among the largest known criminal organizations in the world. Liddick (2004: 28) states that there are over 100,000 members. The triads each have their own organizational structures. According to the U.S. Department of State, currently, there is no known centralized authority controlling the triads. However, many individual triads have been active in the U.S.—some for well over one hundred years. Some examples of those investigated by the FBI include 14K Triad, Four Seas Gang, King Yee Triad, Hung Mun Triad, San Yee On Triad, Wo Hop To Triad, Wo Lee Kwan Triad, Wo On Lok Triad (also called Shui Fong), Wo Shing Wo Triad, Wo Shing Yee Triad, United Bamboo Gang, and Yee Kwan Triad, and there are other gangs and groups (Mahlmann, n.d.). The East Asian heroin trade is very lucrative to the triads, bringing in profits estimated at $200 billion (Liddick, 2004: 29). Many of the senior members of the triads are quasilegitimate businessmen (Mahlmann, n.d.). The international network allows the

Chinese triads to conduct sophisticated international crimes. Their loose organization and sophistication also make them difficult to penetrate and uproot. All this, combined with the transnational nature of their crimes, makes the Chinese triads a source of significant concern for authorities in the U.S.

Russian gangs represent another significant threat to the U.S. According to Liddick (2004: 29), "more than one hundred Russian organized crime gangs are thought to operate in forty-four countries around the world." With the collapse of the Soviet Union, organized crime has filled the power vacuum left behind. It is very powerful. Indeed, Liddick (2004) suggests that nearly half of the former Soviet economy is affiliated with organized crime.

In the United States, it has been suggested that Russian gangs rival and even surpass the threat of traditional organized crime. Although Russian gangs tend not to use "indiscriminate violence, they will use the amount of violence necessary to further and protect their illegal enterprises" (Rush and Scarpitti, 2001: 537). Additionally, Rush and Scarpitti (2001: 538) suggest that "Russian organized crime groups will present a greater overall threat to American society than the traditional Italian-American crime families ever have (U.S. Congress, Senate, 1996; Cilluffo, 1997; Sterling, 1990)." They believe this is due to Russian organized crime having a "higher level of sophistication." Liddick (2004) suggests that there are hundreds of members in the U.S. with ties to the former Soviet Union. Profit seems to be their main motive. Of major concern is the possibility of nuclear material from the former Soviet Union being sold to terrorist groups. While a nuclear bomb is always a concern, many consider such a scenario less likely since its delivery to the U.S. would be difficult. A more likely scenario in the U.S. is a "dirty-bomb"—a traditional bomb laced with nuclear material that has the potential to murder millions of innocent people and, at the same time, possibly make a large area uninhabitable to human life.

Another major area of concern for policing in the United States is the Colombian and Mexican drug cartels. Liddick (2004) reports that the Colombian drug trade alone is $5 billion annually. With such enormous amounts of money at stake, it is unlikely that the drug cartels will discontinue their illegal activities anytime soon.

Currently, Colombia and Mexico supply over 80 percent of illegal heroin entering the U.S. (Forero and Weiner, 2003: 1). One major concern is that the organizations seem to be working together. According to Forero and Weiner (2003), Colombian heroin dominates in the eastern U.S., while Mexican heroin dominates in the west. Such an arrangement does not appear to be due to happenstance.

The scourge of illegal drugs in the U.S. has always been associated with high crime rates and violence. Gang activity surrounds the illegal drug trade.

The countries to the south of the United States, including Colombia and Mexico but others as well, have given birth to some of the most notorious gangs involved in many types of international crime. One of the most violent, and a major concern to law enforcement, is MS13. They have over 80,000 members in Central America and approximately 10,000 in the U.S. They were founded in El Salvador. They are best described as follows: "Hardened by years of warfare in their home country, and attacks by other gangs in America, MS-13 has emerged as an ultra-ruthless group of street toughs whose members kill, steal, rape, and deal drugs without the slightest fear of cops or rivals" (Baram and Hamilton, 2003: 9). One of the greatest concerns to law enforcement is the possible link between such gangs and terrorists.

## TERRORISM

For the American people, the scourge of terrorism is an evil they are confronting, and, unfortunately, an evil they have come to know well. Most of the world is familiar with the attacks of September 11, 2001, on the World Trade Center in New York City and at the Pentagon in Washington, D.C. In New York, two hijacked planes piloted by suicide bombers slammed mercilessly into the twin towers. The Pentagon was similarly hit. The final act of fanatical Islamic terrorists was to murder thousands of innocent people. Countless others were touched: children lost parents; relatives who simply went to work never returned; neighbors who attended parties the day before were now dead; firefighters and law enforcement officers went tragically to their deaths trying to help. Such calamity cannot be measured; the pain and suffering caused by these horrid acts seems endless.

This particular band of terrorists use a sick and perverted religious ideology called fundamentalist Islam to brainwash some of their own into believing that God wants them to murder innocent people and take their own lives in the process. While people of understanding and wisdom know that such an ideology violates the most basic principles of goodness including those of Islam—not to mention the Judeo-Christian understanding of God's Ten Commandments—namely, respect for human life, or "thou shalt not kill."

These terrorists have been linked to Osama bin Laden's al-Qaeda organization. Al-Qaeda had many of its training camps in Afghanistan. After 9/11 a coalition of forces led by the U.S. overran the ruling regime of Afghanistan at the time, called the Taliban. The Taliban, a fundamentalist Islamic regime, allowed al-Qaeda to operate the training facilities freely in the country. The free world could not allow such camps to exist. It is in such camps that the ideology and the training of terrorists take place. Some type of training is necessary to properly "indoctrinate" (brainwash) recruits. Without such training facilities, it is much more difficult to indoctrinate people to the point where they are willing to kill themselves "for the cause." Because of the large threat that such terrorists present, it is likely that the U.S. and its allies will continue to attack any such training camps throughout the world. In particular, any facility that provides a total institution where recruits will—twenty-four hours a day, seven days a week—be indoctrinated into the sick ideology of the terrorist organization is a target. Without such facilities, it is much more difficult for terrorists to train recruits to overcome basic human instinct (survival) and other appropriate controls that most people have developed at some time in their lives (e.g., feelings of guilt when killing innocent people). That is, getting a person to murder innocent people and commit suicide at the same time requires a great deal of effort and training, even for a person who is predisposed to agree with the terrorist ideology. It generally requires a total institution in which a person can be immersed into the evil logic that the fundamentalist Islamic terrorists preach.

Some other acts of international terror directly aimed at Americans and accomplished by fundamentalist Muslims include the bombing of the USS *Cole*. This occurred on October 12, 2000. The ship was in the process of refueling in Yemen. Two suicide bombers from Osama bin Laden's terrorist organization approached in a small boat filled with explosives. They blew it up near the refueling destroyer, killing themselves in the process.

Another incident of terror occurred at the World Trade Center on February 26, 1993. Islamic extremists placed a bomb in a rented truck and parked it in the garage of the North Tower. The bomb exploded, killing six people and injuring over one thousand others. According to the Anti-Defamation League, quick action by the Joint Terrorist Task Force (JTTF) (a combined group of law enforcement officers from the Federal Bureau of Investigation and the New York City Police Department) led to the arrests of four terrorists, with each doing 240 years in prison. The quick action of the JTTF did help restore confidence in American law enforcement and helped allay many concerns. However, the vigilance that was warranted by the successful attack, unfortunately, did not take place to the extent necessary to prevent 9/11.

Other direct attacks on American interests familiar to most Americans include the bombings of the U.S. embassies in both Kenya and Tanzania. On August 7, 1998, the simultaneous bombings of both embassies—in Nairobi, Kenya, and Dar es Salaam, Tanzania—occurred. Both used car bombs. In Nairobi, 213 were killed and over 4,000 injured. In Dar es Salaam, 12 were killed and 85 wounded (White, 2009). Few Americans were killed in the attacks and many of those responsible have been brought to justice. Nevertheless, Osama bin Laden remains free and currently there is a $50 million reward for his capture (Koelbl and Simons, 2004).

Recent attacks on mass transit systems in London and Madrid leave no doubt that international terrorism is an awful evil that the modern world must confront. Madrid signaled a change in strategy by al-Qaeda. On March 11, 2004, ten bombs exploded on Madrid's rail system. As a result, 191 people were killed and over 2,000 were wounded (White, 2009). Within a month, fifteen people had been arrested, with Islamic fundamentalist groups bearing responsibility. Similarly, attacks on the London underground and bus system were conducted by Islamic terrorists. On July 7, 2005, four bombs exploded killing 56 people and injuring an additional 700. Later in the month on July 21, 2005, an additional four attempted bombings occurred but only the detonators exploded, resulting in no fatalities or injuries. Closed-circuit television (CCTV) images installed in much of London's transportation system were one of the keys to unlocking the mystery as to who was responsible. Police were able to capitalize on the mistake and make numerous arrests of the perpetrators and their accomplices. Of concern to authorities is that some of the perpetrators were not known terrorists and, in fact, had no history of such activity. Additionally, some of the accomplices were women. Since the attacks, it has been reported that the London police are engaging in racial profiling. As Harrington (2005: A23) writes, "Police make no bones about who they are targeting . . . Ian Johnston, chief constable of the British Transport Police, put it more bluntly on Sunday: No use searching 'old white ladies,' he told reporters." However, conflicting statements came from British Home Office Minister Hazel Blears, who advised police "not to use racial profiling as a basis for conducting stop-and-search operations in the wake of the July bombings of London's transport network. I don't think you should be ruling out anybody in terms of how you exercise stop-and-search powers. You can equally have white people who could be the subject of intelligence, so I don't accept [that it] is right to target groups."

In the U.S., it is less likely that racial profiling will be conducted—at least on a widespread basis.[9] Americans are all too aware of the pitfalls this brings. For example, most Americans know about the U.S. government's internment of those with Japanese ancestry during World War II. War hysteria led to the shameful act of incarceration of 100,000 people based solely on national origin. U.S. society is multicultural and the police must act to join all segments of society, including those of the Islamic faith. Indeed, cooperation from that segment would seem essential, and not alienating the Islamic community is helpful to law enforcement; rather, law enforcement's goal is to work with the Islamic community to root out those who have evil intent.

While racial profiling is very controversial in the U.S., most would argue, based on experience, that the evil face of terrorism in the U.S. is not simply the Islamic terrorist—that is, a Middle Eastern young male. The aforementioned acts conjure up images of Osama bin Laden and Afghanistan training camps with fanatical young Middle Eastern men being trained to kill the innocent. However, there are several important facts that serve as reminders that anyone is potentially a terrorist and that authorities must use intelligence to make reasonable decisions rather than broad, unreasonable decisions that could have lasting consequences for our people.

First, the British caught several female accomplices who do not fit the profile. This should be considered a first warning sign. Given the adaptability of the enemy, one should assume that if law enforcement adopts a public policy of racial profiling, the terrorists will be aware of that fact and adapt their strategy accordingly.

Another reason for concern is that an American was captured among the Taliban in Afghanistan. The American who was captured is John Walker—a most unlikely Taliban. He is a twenty-year-old white male who was baptized as a Roman Catholic and lived in an affluent suburb of San Francisco. After high school Walker felt a spiritual need. He found some Internet sites and eventually attended mosques in the San Francisco area. He converted to Islam and studied in Yemen and Pakistan, eventually becoming tied to the Taliban. There is no reason to believe that unscrupulous Americans of any ethnicity or religion might not attempt terrorist activity ("American Taliban," 2002).

Americans are also quite aware of acts of terror that occurred domestically—some of them apparently based on ethnic hatred. Timothy McVeigh, assisted by Terry Nichols—both American and white—did the most heinous act of domestic terrorism recorded in the United States. They bombed the Alfred P. Murrah Federal Building in Oklahoma City on April 19, 1995, killing 191 men, women, and children (Eterno, 2005). A page from the novel *The Turner Diaries* by recently deceased William Pierce (a leader of a neo-Nazi hate group in the United States called the National Alliance) under the pseudonym Andrew McDonald was found on McVeigh at the time of his arrest for the bombing. The book is about angered white supremacists conducting a series of terrorist attacks against the federal government.

White supremacist groups are a concern in the U.S. (Eterno, 2005). These groups attach extreme significance to skin color and make the baseless claim that the white race is somehow better than other races. Although there are no firm figures on the number of supremacists in the U.S., the Southern Poverty Law Center has identified five hundred groups that they classify as white supremacist. These groups are generally placed into four categories: the Ku

Klux Klan, neo-Nazis, the Christian Identity church movement, and the militia movement. As stated, the neo-Nazi group known as National Alliance was headed by William Pierce, who wrote *The Turner Diaries*. Other neo-Nazi groups, such as skinheads, are transnational and have thousands of members in the U.S. One theme among these groups is that the federal government (as well as the media and the economic system) is controlled by Jews or what they call ZOG, the Zionist Occupation Government. Somehow these groups see the Jews as a threat to the white race.

Of course, the white supremacist movement is not the only movement to espouse hate and the use of terror in the U.S. For example, the Black Liberation Army in the 1960s and 1970s used terrorist actions and violence to change what they saw as the white establishment. They are likely responsible for a number of violent deaths of police officers in the U.S. among other violent acts.

From this law enforcement in the U.S. generally realizes that no group or individual is to be selected in or selected out as a possible terrorist without evidence. Of concern to society is guarding against ethnic, racial, and/or religious hatred, which appear to be commonalities in both domestic and international terror. That is, both appear to be fueled by irrational hatred of those who are different—in the case of the domestic terrorists, those who are not white, and in the international cases, those who are not of the fundamentalist Islamic faith. Rather than embracing diversity, terrorists are willing to kill themselves and others using indiscriminate violence in a feeble attempt to show that their way of life or they themselves are somehow superior. Thus, law enforcement and the American culture is trying to embrace diversity and multiculturalism. For these reasons, American law enforcement is less likely to use indiscriminate racial profiling. This leads us to how law enforcement in the U.S. is responding to these threats.

## POLICE/JUSTICE RESPONSES

Due to the complexity of the American system, the response by law enforcement to transnational crime and terrorism is multifaceted. First, I will discuss recent changes made to laws to combat these crimes, since the law is the foundation upon which other modifications are based. Some aspects of these laws are very controversial and touch upon issues that strike at the very heart of democracy. I will focus on the USA PATRIOT Act among other changes at the federal level and also discuss some changes in state laws, using New York as an example. The next area of change that I will discuss is the organization and tactics of law enforcement agencies. To that end, I will first describe the fairly new Department of Homeland Security at the federal level in the United States. I will then talk about changes in the preeminent local agency (which was vastly affected by 9/11), the New York City Police Department—now considered to be far ahead of all other local departments with respect to combating transnational crime and terrorism. Last, I will discuss the use of task forces as a tool to combat these crimes.

The U.S. is working with many other nations to fight these horrid menaces to civilization and democracy. For example, the U.S. signed the United Nations (UN) Convention Against Transnational Organized Crime on December 13, 2000, at Palermo, Italy. The U.S. also works closely with INTERPOL, whose mission is "to be the world's pre-eminent police organisation in support of all organisations, authorities and services whose mission is preventing, detecting, and suppressing crime" (INTERPOL, 2005: Mission). INTERPOL also has a longstanding agreement with the UN (made official in a 1996 cooperation agreement that both signed) in an attempt to deal with the changing and complex nature of transnational crime and terrorism. INTERPOL has a separate "Public Safety and Terrorism Sub-Directorate (PST) [that] deals with matters relating to: Terrorism, Firearms and explosives, Attacks and threats against civil aviation, Maritime piracy, and Weapons of Mass Destruction" (INTERPOL, 2005: Terrorism). After 9/11, such international cooperation seems mandatory to most Americans.

There is much more controversy surrounding changes in general policy and domestic laws: the value of preemptive war, the use of the military (particularly in Iraq), violation of civil liberties, immigration issues, and many others. The public is fairly divided on many of these issues. For example, in December 2001, a *New York Times*/CBS News poll asked, "What worried them more—that the government would fail to enact strong antiterrorism laws or that the government would enact new antiterrorism laws that excessively restrict the average person's civil liberties?" (Eterno, 2003: 1). Responses to this indicated that Americans were equally concerned with both.

One of the most controversial laws passed by the national legislature is the USA PATRIOT Act. It was signed into law on October 26, 2001, right after 9/11. The more controversial aspects of the law are suggested by O'Meara (2002: 69–70).

> The law allows for indefinite detention of noncitizens who are not terrorists on minor violations. It minimizes judicial supervision of telephone and Internet surveillance by law-enforcement authorities in antiterrorism investigations and in routine criminal investigations unrelated to terrorism. The act expands the ability of the government to conduct secret searches—even in criminal investigations unrelated to terrorism. It gives the attorney general and the secretary of

state the power to designate domestic groups as terrorist organizations. The new law grants the FBI broad access to sensitive medical, financial, mental-health and educational records about individuals without having to show evidence of a crime and without a court order. The act allows searches of highly personal financial records without notice and without judicial review, based on a very low standard that does not require the showing of probable cause of a crime or even relevance to an ongoing terrorism investigation. It creates a broad new definition of "domestic terrorism" that could allow a police sweep of people who engage in acts of public protest and subject them to wiretapping and enhanced penalties. And this law allows the sharing of sensitive information in criminal cases with intelligence agencies, including the CIA, National Security Agency, Immigration and naturalization Service and the Secret Service.

O'Meara is essentially arguing that the U.S. is becoming tyrannical or unlimited in power—lacking checks and balances. Civil liberties, she feels, are so eroded by the act that the terrorists can claim a victory in extracting our freedom.

On the other hand, O'Beirne (2003: 76–79) argues that the USA PATRIOT Act has been a success; it is a "key weapon in the fight against terrorism." She argues that the Justice Department must report to Congress twice a year with details on the implementation of the Patriot Act. This provides some checks and balances that critics suggest are not there. She argues that critics are exaggerating their case and that the law is necessary and being prudently used to fight specific cases of terrorism. This is a difficult issue. Law enforcement needs the power to stop such atrocities—but how much power is enough? Recent so-called random searches of commuters in New York City have led to a lawsuit against the city by the New York Civil Liberties Union. Although these searches were upheld (see *McWade et al. v. Kelly*, 2006), such privacy issues will certainly be debated in the future.

At the state level, laws have also changed. In New York State, the penal law has been changed to reflect the terrorism threat. Article 490 on terrorism was recently added. It includes acts of domestic and international terrorism. The death penalty can be invoked for some of the more heinous terrorist crimes (although the death penalty is currently unconstitutional in New York State [see *People v. LaValle*, 2004]). Some of the new laws include soliciting or providing support for an act of terrorism, making a terrorist threat, crime of terrorism, hindering prosecution of terrorism, and criminal possession of a chemical weapon or biological weapon. These new laws seem to be a logical step for states. Certainly, previous laws are not adequate to deal with this new threat, and having laws that specifically address these crimes will make it easier to prosecute suspected terrorists and keep them from harming the public.

Laws are not the only area in which the justice system of the U.S. has responded to the threat of transnational crime and, more critically, terrorism. Another area is the organization and tactics of law enforcement. At the federal level, the most critical change is the creation of the Department of Homeland Security (DHS). The creation of the DHS involved transforming twenty-two federal agencies with approximately 180,000 employees. These agencies were brought under the control of the new DHS, established on November 25, 2002. Recently, the mission of the department was, "We will lead the unified national effort to secure America. We will prevent and deter terrorist attacks and protect against and respond to threats and hazards to the nation. We will ensure safe and secure borders, welcome lawful immigrants and visitors, and promote the free-flow of commerce" (DHS, 2005, Our Mission). However, the department is constantly evolving and this mission statement can no longer be found on their website.

The current secretary of the DHS is Janet Napolitano. She is President Barack Obama's choice for secretary, replacing Michael Chertoff. The department has been restructured several times since its formation. A six-point agenda was developed in 2005 to guide the future of the Department (see http://www.dhs.gov).

1. Increase overall preparedness, particularly for catastrophic events
2. Create better transportation security systems to move people and cargo more securely and efficiently
3. Strengthen border security and interior enforcement and reform immigration processes
4. Enhance information sharing with our partners
5. Improve DHS financial management, human resource development, procurement and information technology
6. Realign the DHS organization to maximize mission performance

According to the DHS website, there are currently sixteen major department components (see http://www.dhs.gov).[10] The Directorate for National Protection and Programs attempts to minimize risks. Under this office are Cyber Security and Communications, Infrastructure Protection, Intergovernmental Programs, Risk Management and Analysis, and US-VISIT (using technology such as digital fingerprints to identify possible terrorists/ criminals). The next major department is the Directorate of Science and Technology. It provides state and local officials with technology and also is involved in research and development. The Directorate for Management is responsible for funding. The Office of Policy attempts to coordinate offices and work on long-term planning. The Office of Health Affairs specializes in medical issues.

Of critical importance is the Office of Intelligence and Analysis, which gets information from multiple sources and attempts to use that information in the most appropriate way to protect the homeland. One pertinent point is that two critical intelligence agencies do not come under the secretary of the DHS: the Federal Bureau of Investigation and the Central Intelligence Agency. Both agencies conduct independent investigations and gather their own intelligence. Since they are separate from DHS, there is still some concern that they will not share information.

Other offices include the Federal Law Enforcement Training Center, the Domestic Nuclear Detection Office, the Transportation Security Administration, United States Customs and Border Protection, United States Citizenship and Immigration Services, United States Immigration and Customs Enforcement, the United States Coast Guard, the Federal Emergency Management Agency (FEMA) (after the internationally viewed debacle in New Orleans with Hurricane Katrina, FEMA has been markedly restructured), and the United States Secret Service (which guards the president and other high-level officials and has responsibilities in investigating counterfeiting money, other financial crimes, and computer-based attacks).

In the U.S. the individual fifty states are responsible for state and local responses. They should be coordinating that response with federal agencies and with each other. Due to the complexity of the American system of policing, especially involving numerous law enforcement agencies with many overlapping jurisdictions, coordination is difficult. With respect to investigations agencies, rather than sharing information, often compete with one another. Even worse, in larger agencies, one unit will not share information with another. At the federal level, the DHS is supposed to help prevent the failure of agencies to share information. At the state and local level, this can be more difficult.

One of the most advanced local agencies with respect to intelligence and terrorism is the New York City Police Department (NYPD). The NYPD has made enormous strides since 9/11. They have created a Counterterrorism Bureau with over one thousand officers assigned to it. This bureau is responsible for counterterrorism operations, training and exercises for NYPD personnel, and risk assessment and critical infrastructure protection of key sites within New York City. The Deputy Commissioner of Intelligence also has an expanded role. NYPD officers are now deployed worldwide as they no longer completely rely on the federal government for protection. As Finnegan (2005: 61) states, "there was a strong feeling that federal agencies had let down New York City, and that the city should no longer count on the Feds for its protection." The Intelligence Division also handles Nexus (a program that handles terror-sensitive business, financial investigations, cyberintelligence, and various undercover operations [Finnegan, 2005]).

Today NYPD is much more involved in direct terrorist investigation and prevention. They have been very proactive in this area compared to other local and state agencies. The NYPD deploys Hercules teams throughout the city to protect sensitive or possible targeted locations of terrorists. These teams include heavily armed officers, canine units, and armored vehicles.

NYPD now has officers on the scene at locations around the world, giving them information on terrorist incidents around the world quickly and efficiently. For example, officers in London gave Police Commissioner Raymond W. Kelly information on the London Underground (i.e., subway) attacks that few had access to. Indeed, Commissioner Kelly gave information about the materials the bombs were constructed of to the press, to the anger of some British officials. Nevertheless, the NYPD has a very good relationship with most police around the world. This is due, in part, to the professional image of the NYPD as well as a camaraderie among law enforcement officers around the world that should not be underestimated. Further, many agencies identify with the NYPD due to 9/11.

While the NYPD has generally been thought of as the epitome of law enforcement agencies, there are some areas of concern, particularly with their emphasis on crime reduction. Compstat is the NYPD's management tool to lower crime. It involves precinct commanders being held strictly accountable for crime in their assigned areas. At Compstat meetings precinct commanders must present what is happening in the precincts with an emphasis on crime—particularly index crime. Commanders are, at times, publicly berated at these meetings for failing to reduce crime. Indeed, commanders have lost commands for failing to reduce crime numbers. Such a scientific management approach is not necessarily conducive to successful policing. Why? Because it can alienate the community the department is trying to serve (which it has, especially in minority communities that may have information on potential terrorists), alienate midlevel managers (those considered part of a team rather than being berated are more likely to be forthcoming with information and innovative ideas), and fail to motivate the vast majority of officers (see Eterno and Silverman, 2006; Cowper, 2000). It is suggested that the NYPD could benefit from being more community friendly (thinking of themselves as "service oriented" rather than simply "crime fighters") and fostering a human relations–management approach. While this does present a challenge to the NYPD (they are essentially a top-down bureaucracy at the current time), the potential benefits (e.g., getting intelligence to stop a future attack; officers willing to be innovative and proactive in their efforts rather than passively obeying orders) outweigh the difficulties. Even with these issues, NYPD is still the preeminent police agency in the U.S. with respect to combating terrorism.

One nationwide tool that is very effective in the fight against terrorism and transnational crime is the establishment of joint task forces. These task forces bring together local and federal authorities. Rather than competing with each other for valuable leads and resources, the efforts of the agencies in the task force are combined. Federal agencies often bring a variety of resources and leverage that local agencies may not have. Local agencies often know the neighborhoods and have local connections and sources of information that federal authorities lack. These task forces are a critical tool in law enforcement in the U.S.

One example of the success of the task force is on Long Island in New York. In 1999, with gang violence rising, the United States Attorney's Office–Eastern District helped create the Long Island Gang Task Force. Agents and officers are from numerous jurisdictions: the Federal Bureau of Investigation; Immigration and Customs Enforcement (ICE); the New York State Police; Nassau County Corrections; and the Nassau County, Hempstead, Freeport, and Port Washington police departments. As an added part of this task force, local district attorneys have been cross-designated to prosecute on both the federal and state levels. At least forty convictions of members of the notorious international gang MS13 are due to the efforts of this task force. Two were recently convicted in violation of the federal Violent Crimes in Aid of Racketeering (VICAR) statute among other crimes. (Racketeering statues have been used very successfully by law enforcement in these types of organized transnational crimes. The Racketeer Influenced and Corrupt Organizations statute [RICO] is another example of such a statute.) Eighteen members, including two critical leaders, also plead guilty to federal racketeering charges. An additional twenty were convicted on various other charges (nonracketeering) such as robbery, firearms possession, and immigration crimes (see United States Attorney's Office, 2005).

## FUTURE/CONCLUSIONS

The battle against terrorism and transnational crimes is sure to continue well into the future as these menaces are threats to the civilized world. As a first step, we must understand the dynamics of these incidents. Why do they occur? What purpose do terrorists and criminals have? Typical criminal behavior, at least to some extent, is easier to understand. Most criminals (although there are, of course, exceptions) want money, power over others, or have some other tangible goal. Terrorists, on the other hand, have more elusive goals (in some cases one can question whether a reasonable goal exists for them)—often to change a government, change its policies, or to change an entire society. In any case, terrorists are fanatics. They often believe in what they are doing—even though, ironically, they are doing just the opposite of what they think. That is, they do great evil, sometimes brainwashed into thinking they are actually doing good (or the "will of God"). Such attitudes are difficult to battle against. Terrorists are unlikely to see, or want to see, the other side's point of view. Such dogmatic and stubborn people often cannot be reasoned with. Nevertheless, developing an understanding of the enemy is a first step.

To most Americans, fanatical Islamic terrorists are very foreign and very evil. Nothing is worse than taking the lives of innocent people for whatever reason one might have. Law enforcement is being trained in understanding fundamentalist Islamic terrorists. Training includes learning about Islam and how perverted the terrorists' view is. Because the U.S. is a multicultural society, Americans have excellent sources of information on just about any culture in the world, including various Islamic cultures.

Americans are also familiar with hate or bias crimes, which terrorist ideology is based on (irrational hate of Americans, their allies, and/or their government). The history of the U.S. is an uneasy one with respect to ethnic and racial bias. The U.S. had to fight a civil war to end slavery. Even so, one hundred years after the U.S. Civil War, many still did (and do) discriminatory acts against blacks and other minorities. The U.S. is not perfect, and no place in the world is. Americans, however, have learned from their past that to survive one must be tolerant of others and their views. In the U.S., if people were not at least somewhat tolerant, the society could not function. Tolerance is something that terrorists do not understand. In the worldwide community, there is a general consensus that the radical extremist dogma of terrorists as well as their actions are wrong.

One way to understand Islamic terrorists is through the use of criminological theory. Sociologist Emile Durkheim's theory of anomie is an excellent tool. Durkheim, who wrote in the late 1800s and early 1900s, saw a stark contrast between agricultural society and industrial society. In the older agricultural society, people understood their roles—they knew what they were supposed to do. There was a strong consensus among the people about right and wrong. Durkheim calls this mechanical solidarity. In such a society there is a strong collective conscience. In industrial society, however, there is a division of labor. The collective conscience is initially weakened. However, in a normally developed industrial society people realize how dependent they are on one another and develop a new social bond that Durkheim terms organic solidarity. If change happens too rapidly you get a situation in which you have "anomic" division of labor or "anomie"—normlessness. This leads to a weakened, or even a lack of, collective conscience.

Fundamentalist Islamic terrorism can be seen as a clash between Western society and the fundamentalist Islamic version of Eastern society (indeed, other terrorist acts can also be seen as a struggle between ideologies and sometimes cultures, especially when one group is much stronger than the other, generally leading the weaker group to resort to terrorist acts [e.g., Irish Republican Army, Black Liberation Army]). Due to advances in technology, communications, and transportation, society is becoming a global village. The ideology of fundamentalist Islamic militants comes from Eastern society. As Western ideas take hold (e.g., freedom of religion, equal protection for women), some will undoubtedly reject them—especially those in power, such as the former ruling Taliban in Afghanistan. As the East tries to cope with the social change that modern Western society brings, the strong collective conscience that once existed is breaking down. The social order and the collective conscience are weakened. The change is happening very rapidly—perhaps too rapidly for some. It is possible that in some cases subcultures have become anomic, leading to a lack of a collective conscience, irrational ethnic hatred (especially against Americans and their allies, who represent the Western ideal), and eventually a lashing out at Western society through terrorist acts.[11]

To combat terrorism, it is very important for the U.S. to maintain high moral standards and respect for other cultures. Some terrorist groups, in an attempt to defend their actions (recall they are conducting their violence in the name of "God"), will try to rationalize what they are doing by pointing to any actions the U.S. does that seems contradictory or evil. Much of what America is doing around the globe is in the name of defending freedom—certainly a noble goal—but sometimes is not perceived that way by others. Americans have been seen as exploitive, fighting for oil, and imperialist. This, however, is not what most Americans feel they, or their government, are doing.

Americans believe, for example, in religious freedom—that you can worship in whatever way you deem appropriate without government interference—a very tolerant view. They believe that others who feel differently from you have the right to meet, speak, and even protest against the dominant view. Americans believe in equal protection of the law (groups should not be treated differently), in due process (if the government is going to take something, you have the right to a fair hearing), and in checks and balances (that no branch or person in government should have unchecked power—the government is limited). No system of government is perfect, but Americans generally feel that ultimately, there is nothing better. Winston Churchill in a speech to the House of Commons on November 11, 1947, captures the essence of Americans' feelings: "Many forms of Government have been tried, and will be tried in this world of sin and woe. No one pretends that democracy is perfect or all wise.

Indeed, it has been said that democracy is the worst form of Government except all those other forms that have been tried from time to time."

Fundamentalist Islamic terrorists are fighting for a cause that Western civilization patently rejects: tyranny and worship of God in one way—their way. Such an ideology is as hopelessly doomed as are the terrorists. The U.S. needs to better portray these ideals such that they are not perceived as imperialists. Globally, the U.S. must understand its leadership position and better sell the ideals of its society. Unfortunately, the controversial war in Iraq, prisoner abuse scandals, support given to various corrupt regimes, and other such policies have not boded well for the U.S. internationally.

Nevertheless, years of battles and death stand behind democracy and tolerance of others. As Abraham Lincoln (arguably one of the greatest American presidents) stated in his Gettysburg address, a speech after a pivotal battle in the American Civil War, "that these dead shall not have died in vain . . . that this nation, under God, shall have a new birth of freedom . . . and that government of the people . . . by the people . . . for the people . . . shall not perish from the earth." The stark contrast between terrorists and the U.S. government could not be clearer. The U.S. stands for freedom and democracy, while the terrorists are, simply put, intolerant murderers. The U.S. must, to the extent possible, demonstrate that its society is a better way of life, that the cause of terrorists and other criminals is an evil cause, and that the Bill of Rights (including freedom of religion, freedom of the press, freedom from unnecessary government searches and seizures, etc.) is an enduring and meaningful part of the Constitution and our way of life that many Americans are willing to die for (and that some have already died for).[12]

Within the U.S., we need to also understand that the harm that occurs from acts of terrorism and transnational crimes come not only from the destruction and murder committed but also from the reactions (or overreactions or underreactions) to the criminal acts or the threat of possible future acts. Unquestionably, the global community must continue to work together to eradicate these crimes. The U.S. is a leader in this effort. As such, the U.S. has a great responsibility.

As a first step, the U.S. and its law enforcement agencies must understand that protecting the U.S. Constitution while, at the same time, stopping terrorists and criminals, is their primary mission. Crime control (terrorism control) is *not* the highest mission of police; rather, it is crime control (terrorism control) joined with respect and dignity of human rights. This means law enforcement must respect people's constitutional rights. People have a right to speak their views, to assemble, and so on, as long as they do not endanger others or trample on other's rights. One area of concern is that fear of a terrorist incident—especially from a weapon of mass destruction (WMD)—

could lead to erosion of civil liberties to the extent that the society is no longer free. However, freedom is what we are fighting for. We cannot allow our fears to overwhelm us. As Franklin Delano Roosevelt (another eminent American president) stated, "We have nothing to fear but fear itself." Fear of an attack can cause a nation to take unnecessary and draconian actions in the name of fighting terrorism. The internment of the Japanese at the beginning of World War II during the war hysteria after Pearl Harbor is an example.[13] How free democratic society remains in the future will be directly related to the actions that we take in our own defense. These actions need to be based on reason and not fear. What can be done to maximize safety and minimize intrusions on civil rights?

Law enforcement officers need to be given appropriate guidance by legislatures and policymakers. To that end and to the extent possible, bright-line rules should be composed so that officers understand the extent of their power. Research indicates that bright-line rules help front line practitioners work within the limits of their authority (see Eterno, 2003). Furthermore, without such rules, policymakers are relinquishing their responsibility by pushing it down to the lowest ranks. Leaders must give guidance and not shirk responsibilities.

Checks and balances on law enforcement's power need to be carefully reviewed. The exclusionary rule, civil suits, arrest (although rare), civilian complaint review boards, and internal review by police agencies are just a few of the remedies for police excess. We need to determine whether these remedies are sufficient given law enforcement's expanding role. We could, for example, certify officers on a national basis. That is, officers would have to earn a national license to be police officers anywhere in the U.S. That license or certification could be removed for improper behavior (see, for example, Goldman and Puro, 2001). Additionally, we need to revisit the exclusionary rule and determine whether it is appropriate in all circumstances. Say a police officer does an illegal search and finds a nuclear device. Should the evidence be excluded? Perhaps, but should any action be taken against the perpetrators? These are truly questions for the future of our democracy.

Law enforcement agencies need to recruit the best and the brightest into their ranks. Currently the best and the brightest often shy away from law enforcement, often due to inadequate remuneration. However, these professions are some of the highest callings in a democratic society, particularly since law enforcement officers are at the front line of democracy in action. It is a very difficult job, if done properly. Officers must balance the need for safety and fighting crime with protecting constitutional rights. They, and their leaders, need to understand the complexities that this balancing presents to law enforcement.

Police agencies must work as a team: do not disrespect those of lower rank; think service. Officers who have worked under a top-down management style will likely become discontent and not work efficiently. Indeed, my own research in New York City indicates that Compstat (a top-down management approach) motivates very few officers to make arrests and write summonses. It is more efficient to work as a team than to berate lower ranks. This has the effect of motivating more officers to work, being more efficient, and getting more innovative ideas from the rank-and-file (see Eterno, 2003; Eterno and Silverman, 2006).

Agencies need to work with communities and not alienate people. Today, this especially means working with and not alienating those of the Muslim faith. Ask and willingly receive the assistance and cooperation of all peoples. Emphasize being proactive in law enforcement but also that officers, as representatives of the government, are there to serve people.

Officers need to be trained in the adverse influence of the police culture. In particular, car stops seem to be an area where officers are abusing their authority due to the influence of other officers (Eterno, 2003). Enhanced supervision and the use of video and audio as well as training would seem to be prudent steps. The success of video (CCTV) in the London Underground bombings seems to indicate that its use should be expanded. However, this should be done carefully so as not to trample on people's rights.

The government and police agencies must allow the media to have limited access to operational commands. Let them report on what is or is not happening. An open, candid discussion can bring new ideas and agencies should welcome some criticism. In fact, some criticism is good and can lead to constructive change.

Agencies and the public need to be open to reasonable change and ideas, allowing debates about key issues such as whether the war in Iraq is justified, are we fighting for oil, are we expanding democracy, is the Patriot Act a threat to civil liberties, should we allow officers to use racial profiling, and so on.[14] Open dialogue is necessary and to be embraced. This will allow the U.S. to capitalize on its strengths. Also, the diversity of people in the U.S. will allow for a very informed discussion. The U.S. needs to consult its best and brightest on these weighty issues.

## NOTES

1. See especially Eterno (2006) for an interesting discussion on the need for bright-line rules for police.

2. The U.S. Census Bureau advises that Hispanics can be of any race.

3. Although there is a need to be ever-vigilant of police abuse of authority. Examples abound of police misuse of their authority, including incidents such as that of Abner Louima, where a Haitian immigrant had a stick placed in his rectum by a police officer who had him in custody. The police officer, Justin Volpe, is currently serving a thirty-year sentence for his actions.

4. The Immigration and Naturalization Service has merged into the Department of Homeland Security. U.S. Immigration and Customs Enforcement (ICE) and U.S. Customs and Border Protection (CBP) are components of Border and Transportation Security (BTS) within the Department of Homeland Security (DHS).

5. See Eterno (2003) for more information on this issue.

6. Lieutenant Patricia Feerick of the New York City Police Department is one example.

7. For example, the UCR did not factor in the terrorist attacks in New York City when calculating the crime rate for the city in 2001 (although the murders were reported with a footnote explaining them).

8. Liddick adds "Italian-based transnational crime groups" and "other" groups as well.

9. For an interesting debate on racial profiling with respect to terrorism see Simonson (2001) and Clegg (2001) in Balkin (2005).

10. As recently as 2005, there were nine components, four of which were directorates. This structure has completely changed in the span of several years.

11. This is based on Emile Durkheim's anomie theory. A complicated array of political, economic, and numerous other pressures are also likely responsible for terrorist acts. This is one way to try to understand such terrible acts of violence. There are, of course, many other ways. For example, modern (post-enlightenment) versus old (pre-enlightenment) philosophies. There are many other examples such as Brown (2007); Rees and Aldrich (2005); Kudryavtsev, Luneyev, and Petrishchev (2005), and many others (see also Verma's chapter in this book).

12. Most Americans would not commit suicide attacks (at least in the sense that terrorists do) as such acts are considered the ultimate in evil (taking innocent life) but also in violation of cultural norms that all life—including one's own—is precious.

13. Franklin Delano Roosevelt was the president at this time and was ultimately responsible for the internment.

14. These questions are debated in Balkin (2005).

## REFERENCES

"American Taliban." (2002). Retrieved August 3, 2005, from http://www.pbs.org/newshour/extra/features/jan-june02/walker_john_1-2.html.

Amsterdam, A. (1974). "Perspectives on the Fourth Amendment." *Minnesota Law Review*. 58: 349–439.

Anti-Defamation League. (n.d.). "The World Trade Center Bombing." Retrieved August 3, 2005, from http://www.adl.org/learn/jttf/wtcb_jttf.asp.

Balkin, K. F. (Ed.). (2005). *The War on Terrorism: Opposing Views*. Farmington Hills, MI: Greenhaven.

Baram, M. and Hamilton, B. (2003, June 1). "Roughest of Toughs: Bloodthirsty Latin Gang Invades N.Y." *New York Post*. p. 9.

Bernstein, R. (2005). U.S. Census Bureau News Release. Retrieved June 13, 2005, from http//www.census.gov/Press-Release/www/releases/archives/population/005164.html.

Brown, C. (2007). "The New Terrorism Debate." *Alternatives: Turkish Journal of International Relations*. 6 (3/4): 28–43.

Bureau of Justice Statistics. (2000). Law Enforcement Statistics, Summary. Retrieved June 20, 2005, from http://www.ojp.usdoj.gov/bjs/lawenf.htm.

Ciluffo, F. J., ed. (1997). Russian Organized Crime. In Rush and Scarpitti (2001). Washington, DC: Center for Strategic and International Studies, p. 538.

Churchill, W. (1947, November 11). Speech to the House of Commons. In James, R. R. (Ed.). (1974). *Winston S. Churchill: His Complete Speeches, 1897–1963*. Vol. 7, p. 7566.

Clegg, R. (2001). "Racial Profiling Is Not a Threat to Civil Liberties." In Balkin (2005), pp. 84–87.

Country Watch. (2005). United States. Retrieved June 21, 2005, from http://www.countrywatch.com.

Cowper, T. J. (2000). "The Myth of the 'Military Model' of Leadership in Law Enforcement." *Police Quarterly*. 3 (3): 228–46.

Department of Homeland Security (DHS). (2009 and 2005). DHS website. Retrieved April 1, 2009, and August 8, 2005, from http://www.dhs.gov on.

Eterno, J. A. (2007). "Understanding the Law on the Front Lines: The Need for Bright-Line Rules." *Criminal Law Bulletin*. 43 (5): 706–25.

Eterno, J. A. (2005). Criminal justice entries, including "The Oklahoma City Federal Building Bombing" and "White Supremacist Movement." Draft for Min, P. G. (Ed.). (2005). *The Encyclopedia of Racism in the U.S.* Westport, CT: Greenwood.

Eterno, J. A. (2003). *Policing within the Law: A Case Study of the New York City Police Department*. Westport, CT: Praeger.

Eterno, J. A. and Silverman, E. B. (2006). "The New York City Police Department's Compstat: Dream or Nightmare?" *International Journal of Police Science & Management*. 8 (3): 218–31.

Federal Bureau of Investigation. (2005). "Investigative Programs: Organized Crime." Retrieved July 18, 2005, from http://www.fbi.gov/hq/cid/orgcrime/lcn/lcn.htm.

Finnegan, W. (2005, July 25). "The Terrorism Beat: How Is the NYPD Defending the City?" *The New Yorker*. pp. 58–71.

Forero, J. and Weiner, T. (2003, June 8). "Latin American Poppy Fields Undermine U.S. Drug Battle." *New York Times*. p. A1. Retrieved from Lexis-Nexis July 27, 2005.

Goldman, R. L. and Puro, S. (2001). "Revocation of Police Officer Certification: A Viable Remedy for Police Misconduct?" *Saint Louis University Law Journal*. 45: 541–75.

Goldstein, J. (1992). *The Intelligible Constitution: The Supreme Court's Obligation to Maintain the Constitution as Something We the People Can Understand.* New York: Oxford University Press.

Grano, J. D. (1982). "Rethinking the Fourth Amendment Warrant Requirement." *American Criminal Law Review.* 19 (1): 603–30.

Hamilton, A., Madison, J. and Jay, J. (1787–1788). *The Federalist Papers.* Reprinted with an introduction by Clinton Rossiter. (1961). New York: The New American Library.

Harrington, M. (2005, August 3). "Putting Up with the Profiling." *Newsday.* p. A23.

Horwitz, S. and Ruane, M. E. (2003, October 9). "Jurisdictions Vied to Prosecute Pair." *Washington Post.* p. A1.

INTERPOL. (2005). Retrieved from http://www.interpol.com/Public/Icpo/default.asp on August 9, 2005.

Kersten, J. (1993). "Street Youths, *Bosozoku*, and *Yakuza*: Subculture Formation and Societal Reactions in Japan." *Crime and Delinquency.* 39 (3): 277–95.

Koelbl, S. and Simons, S. (2004, August 16). "Saber Seven." *New York Times.* Retrieved May 13, 2009, from http://www.nytimes.com/2004/08/16/international/europe/16SPIEGEL.html.

Kudryavtsev, V., Luneyev, V. and Petrishchev, V. (2005). "Terrorism and Organized Crime under Globalization Conditions." *Social Sciences.* 36 (3): 84–94.

LaFave, W. (1972). "Warrantless Searches and the Supreme Court—Further Ventures into the Quagmire." *Criminal Law Bulletin.* 8 (1): 9–30.

Liddick, Donald R., Jr. (2004). *The Global Underworld.* Westport, CT: Praeger.

Lincoln, A. (1863, November 19). "Gettysburg Address." Retrieved August 11, 2005, from http://libertyonline.hypermall.com/Lincoln/gettsburg.html.

Mahlmann, Ning-Ning (n.d.). "Chinese Criminal Enterprises: Excerpt from 'Asian Criminal Enterprise Program Overview: A Study of Current FBI Asian Criminal Enterprise Investigations in the United States.'" Department of State, United States. Retrieved July 18, 2005, from http://usinfo.state.gov/eap/Archive_Index/Chinese_Criminal_Enterprises.html.

*McWade et al. v. Kelly and City of New York.* (2006). U.S. Court of Appeals, 2nd Cir., Docket No. 05-6754-cv.

O'Beirne, K. (2003). "The USA PATRIOT Act Does Not Threaten Civil Liberties." In Balkin (2005), pp. 75–79.

O'Meara, K. P. (2002). "The USA PATRIOT Act Threatens Civil Liberties." In Balkin (2005), pp. 67–74.

*People, State of New York v. Steven LaValle* 3 N.Y. 3d 88 (2004).

Rees, W. and Aldrich, R. J. (2005). "Contending Cultures of Counterterrorism; Transatlantic Divergence or Convergence?" *International Affairs.* 81 (5): 905–23.

Reinharz, P. (1996). "The Court Criminals Love." *City Journal.* 6 (1): 38–48.

Roosevelt, F. D. (1933). "First Inaugural Address." Retrieved December 27, 2006, from http://www.gettyimages.com/detail/2017-634/Archive-Films?esource=feed _google_video.

Rothwax, H. J. (1996). *Guilty: The Collapse of Criminal Justice.* New York: Random House.

Rush, R. J., Jr., and Scarpitti, F. R. (2001). "Russian Organized Crime: The Continuation of an American Tradition." *Deviant Behavior: An Interdisciplinary Journal.* 22: 517–40.

Siegel, L. (2004). *Criminology: Theories, Patterns, and Typologies*, 8th edition. Belmont, CA: Thomson-Wadsworth.

Silverman, E. B. (1999). *NYPD Battles Crime: Innovative Strategies in Policing.* Boston: Northeastern University Press.

Simonson, P. G. (2001). "Racial Profiling Is a Threat to Civil Liberties." In Balkin (2005), pp. 80–83.

Sourcebook of Criminal Justice Statistics Online. (2002). Bureau of Justice Statistics. Retrieved July 10, 2008, from http://www.albany.edu/sourcebook/index.html.

Stephens, G. (2005). "Global Trends in Crime." In Victor, J. L. and Naughton, J. (Eds.). *Annual Editions: Criminal Justice*. (pp. 16–20). Dubuque, IA: McGraw-Hill/Dushkin.

Sterling, C. (1990). "Octopus: The Long Reach of the Sicilian Mafia." In Rush and Scarpitti (2001). New York: Simon and Schuster.

Synovate. (2003, September). *Federal Trade Commission—Identity Theft Survey Report.*

Tretheway, S. and Katz, T. (1998). "Motorcycle Gangs or Motorcycle Mafia?" National Alliance of Gang Investigators Associations. Retrieved July 18, 2005, from http://www.nagia.org/Motorcycle_Gangs.htm.

United Nations Office for Drug Control and Crime Prevention, Centre for International Crime Prevention. (1999). "Global Report on Crime and Justice." Retrieved June 29, 2005, from http://www.uncjin.org/Special/GlobalReport.html.

United States Attorney's Office—Eastern District of New York. (2005, July 26). "Ms-13 Gang Members Convicted on Federal Racketeering Charges Stemming from Long Island Shootings." Press release. Retrieved from http://www.usdoj.gov/usao/nye/pr/2005jul26.htm.

U.S. Congress, Senate. (1994). *International Organized Crime and Its Impact on the United States*. Hearing before the permanent Subcommittee on Investigations of the Committee on Governmental Affairs. United States Senate, 104th Congress, 2nd Sess. S. Hrg. 103-899. Washington, DC: Government Printing Office.

Walmsley, R. (2003). *World Prison Population List, Fifth Edition*. Research, Development, and Statistics Directorate. Home Office, London. Retrieved June 21, 2005, from http://www.homeoffice.gov.uk/rds/pdfs2/r234.pdf.

White, J. R. (2009). *Terrorism and Homeland Security*. Belmont, CA: Wadsworth.

*Chapter Two*

# Policing in India

*Response to Transnational Crime
and Terrorism*

Arvind Verma

Modern independent India was born in blood and turmoil. The departing British rulers partitioned the country on religious grounds and established Pakistan as the home for South Asia's Muslims. However, the partition left a large proportion of Hindus and Muslims as minorities on the wrong side of the border. This led to bloody attempts by the majority communities to push the minorities into the other territory and the desperate efforts of these people to cross the border for safety. Perhaps 10 million people were displaced and around a million were killed in gruesome pogroms. The bitterness that developed from this partition between Hindus and Muslims and between Pakistan and India has colored the history of South Asia ever since. It has led to communal riots between the two communities in India and Bangladesh, where a small population of Hindus still exists. In Pakistan, Hindus have been completely obliterated, but strife between the Sunni and Shia factions of Muslims has turned bitter. The creation of Bangladesh on the basis of Bengali revolt against Pakistan's Punjabi dominance and the intra-Muslim strife raging in Balochistan and northwest territories have all demonstrated that religion is not the binding factor in whose name the land was partitioned. Rather, culture, language, and regional affiliation are more important than religious sentiments. However, this lesson is yet to be learned and religious strife continues unabated in the region.

Unfortunately, a good proportion of transnational crime and terrorism existing in South Asia, particularly in India, is linked to this part of history. The enmity between India and Pakistan has led to four wars between them, a nuclear race, and animosity that transcends all relations and erupts even in sporting events. A cricket match between India and Pakistan is seen as a war between the two nations and emotions run extremely high. Despite sharing a long border and common culture, there is little exchange amongst the people. Moreover, India, a larger and secular nation, has been able to strengthen its democratic institutions, which is now resulting in rapid economic progress and development of the country. Pakistan, established in the name of Islam, has not been able to unshackle itself from its religious moorings, which have prevented the growth of modern liberal institutions.

Taking advantage of Pakistan's vulnerability, the Pakistani military staged a coup in 1952 and basically since then has been the ruling force. Despite small periods of elected governments, Pakistan has largely been ruled by military dictators. The present leader is Pervez Musharraf, who staged a coup in 1999. To preserve its power, the Pakistani military has attempted to keep close to American foreign-policy objectives in this region of the world. It played a major role in nurturing the Islamic militants on behalf of the Americans to fight the Soviet Union when it invaded Afghanistan. In return, Pakistan received substantial military and economic aid, which has been used to wage four wars with India. Pakistan has actively supported terrorism from its soil including the direct involvement of its military personnel. The objectives of the Pakistani army in maintaining its grip over the governance and policymaking of Pakistan and in its attempts to battle India form the basis of terrorism and related dangerous crimes in the region. This chapter will examine the nature of transnational crime and terrorism in India and argue that Pakistani involvement and American complicity is a major factor in these crimes.

## TRANSNATIONAL CRIME

India, like most other countries, has not been able to escape the scourge of transnational crime, such as human trafficking, drugs, and crimes committed through the Internet. As an open democratic society where police are guided and controlled by the rule of law, India is vulnerable to organized criminal syndicates that use the freedom and reduced surveillance to establish themselves and operate without restrictions. A country of more than a billion people lying on the geographical pathways of the Golden Crescent and Golden Triangle, India is not only attractive for organized syndicates as a transit point but also for the sale and consumption of illegal goods and services. The economic boom, growing contact with the West, and the entry of young people into the lucrative job market has fueled social experimentation that is similar to that seen in Western nations. Lifestyles involving wanton consumption, fashionable clothes, brand names, and fast cars are within the reach of a new entrepreneurial middle class that does not hesitate in experimenting with drugs, sexual promiscuity, and adventurous lifestyles. The economic boom is fueling a vast churning of Indian society in which traditional restraints are breaking down. Prostitution, pornography, and drug intake are growing in the country, especially in major urban centers. Consequently, transnational crimes are establishing their roots in Indian society. Below we describe some of these that are affecting the society.

## CYBERCRIMES

India is emerging as a software giant and the hub of high-tech industries. In particular, the growth of India's information technology (IT) industry has been phenomenal. Beginning in the 1990s, India's IT industry has seen growth reaching almost 400–500 percent and now it ranks second only to that of the United States. The growing middle class is also encouraging a spurt in the growth of Internet and computers, and it is estimated that more than 200 million users exist in the country. Indian companies like Infosys, Wipro, and Tata Consultancy Services are now ranking high in Forbes' list of major companies of the world. India has also emerged as the hub of backroom services, and almost every major company in the world has outsourced its services to India. Call centers where millions of Indian youth are engaged in providing services ranging from help lines to technical assistance, accounting, medical and legal services, and education are new landmarks in major metropolitan cities of the country. Consequently, "Cyber Crimes are a new and emerging class of crimes which are rapidly expanding due to extensive use of computers, Internet and electronic equipments" (National Crime Records Bureau [NCRB] 2006: 513).

In order to deal with cybercrimes effectively the government of India enacted the Information Technology (IT) Act, 2000, which specifies the behaviors that are now punishable in a court of law. The objectives of this act are:

(1) To provide legal recognition for transactions carried out by means of electronic data interchange and other means of electronic communication, commonly referred to as "electronic commerce," which involve the use of alternatives to paper-based methods of communication and storage of information;

(2) To facilitate electronic filing of documents with government agencies; and

(3) To amend the Indian Penal Code, the Indian Evidence Act, 1872, the Bankers' Books Evidence Act, 1891, and the Reserve Bank of India Act, 1934, to enable the environment for commercial use of information technology.

The act gives recognition to the legality of transactions carried out by means of electronic data interchange and other means of electronic communication. These transactions are known as "electronic commerce," which involves the use of alternatives to paper-based methods of communication and storage of information. This can now facilitate electronic filing of documents with government agencies. Two specific rules have been introduced to give teeth to the legislation. The Information Technology (Certifying Authorities) Rules, 2000, describe issues concerning digital signatures. These rules specify how digital signatures are to be created and authenticated. More importantly, they lay down security guidelines for certification authorities, violation of which is deemed a crime.

The government has also specified the procedures relating to the Cyber Regulations Appellate Tribunal in the notified Cyber Regulations Appellate Tribunal (Procedure) Rules, 2000. These rules lay down proceedings that have to be conducted by the tribunal in case of a dispute or complaint. The government, by another notification of October 17, 2000, has also constituted the Cyber Regulation Advisory Committee. The committee acts as the watchdog for the government and comprises the minister of information technology, various secretaries of related ministries, representatives from different trade bodies and technical bodies, the director of the Central Bureau of Investigation, police chiefs from the states, and the controller of certifying authorities.

Through this act India has made it possible to do business in electronic format. It is now possible to retain information in an electronic format. Electronic contracts have been recognized to be legal and binding. Additionally, a new set of crimes have been defined and made punishable in law. Cybercrimes like hacking, damage to computer source code, publishing of information which is obscene in the electronic form, breach of confidentiality and privacy, and publishing digital signature certificates false in certain particulars and for a fraudulent purpose are all deemed to be criminal behavior.

India is still developing its IT industry, and so the act attempts more to create an enabling environment for businesses than to take a punitive view. Thus, there are many deliberate omissions in the legislation. At present, many offenses related to cyberspace are still covered by the Indian Penal Code (IPC),

1860, with the legal recognition of electronic records and the amendments made in several sections of the IPC via the IT Act, 2000. We get a picture of these crimes through the National Crime Records Bureau, which presents them under two categories: (a) offenses registered under the Information Technology Act, 2000, and (b) offenses registered under the standard IPC codes.

Thus, during the year 2005, 179 cases were registered under the IT Act, which constitutes a significant increase of 163.2 percent over 2004. Of the total 179 cases registered under IT Act 2000, about 50 percent (88 cases) were related to obscene publications/transmission in electronic form, normally known as cyber pornography. There were 125 persons arrested for committing such offenses during 2005. There were 74 cases of hacking of computer systems during the year wherein 41 persons were arrested. Further, during the year 2005, a total of 302 cases were registered under IPC sections, as compared to 279 such cases during 2004, thereby reporting an increase of 8.2 percent in 2005 over 2004. The crimes fall under two categories, namely criminal breach of trust or fraud, totaling 186, and counterfeiting of currency/stamps, numbering 59. Though these offenses fall under the traditional IPC crimes, the cases involved use of computers, the Internet, or its related aspects and hence they were categorized as cybercrimes. Most of the offenders involved in these crimes were below the age of forty-five years (NCRB 2006: 513). Details of these crimes are given below in tables 2.1 and 2.2.

Reports indicate that cybercrimes are beginning to pose a serious threat to the country. It is expected that with the continuing growth of the IT industry and an increasing number of users cybercrimes are going to increase. The Indian police are taking special steps to combat this growing threat and have embarked upon special training to equip officers in dealing with IT-related cybercrimes. A special cell has been created at the Central Bureau of Investigation, and the National Police Academy is also offering specialized training in handling such crimes.

## DRUGS

Drug consumption in the country to get a "high" and for medicinal purposes has been a tradition for thousands of years. Several plants that are used as drugs, such as cannabis, poppy, khat, and datura, are common to Indian terrain. Cannabis is processed into three main products, bhang, ganja (marijuana), and charas, before it is consumed (Chopra and Chopra 1990). Opium

**Table 2.1.   Incidence of Cases Registered and Number of Persons Arrested under Cybercrimes (IT Act + IPC Section) during 2005 (All India)**

| Sl. No | Crime Head | Cases Registered | Persons Arrested |
|---|---|---|---|
| (1) | (2) | (3) | (4) |
| | **A. Offenses under IT ACT** | | |
| 1. | Tampering computer source department (Sec. 65) | 10 | 10 |
| 2. | Hacking computer systems | | |
| | a. Loss/damage to computer resource (Sec. 66[1]) | 33 | 27 |
| | b. Hacking (Sec. 66[2]) | 41 | 14 |
| 3. | Obscene publication/transmission electronic form (Sec. 67) | 88 | 125 |
| 4. | Failure | | |
| | a. Of compliance/orders of certifying authority | 1 | 0 |
| | b. To assist to decoy or interception by gov't (Sec. 69) | 0 | 0 |
| 5. | Unauthorized access to access-protected computer (Sec. 70) | 0 | 0 |
| 6. | Obtaining license by misrepresentation of fact (Sec. 71) | 0 | 0 |
| 7. | Publishing false digital signature (Sec. 73) | 0 | 0 |
| 8. | Fraud digital/signature (Sec. 74) | 1 | 3 |
| 9. | Breach of confidentiality/privacy (Sec. 72) | 5 | 13 |
| 10. | Other | 0 | 0 |
| | **TOTAL (A)** | **179** | **192** |
| | **B. Offenses under IPC** | | |
| 1. | Public servant offenses (Sec. 167, 172, 173, 175) | 0 | 0 |
| 2. | False electronic evidence (Sec. 193) | 0 | 0 |
| 3. | Destruction of electronic evidence (Sec. 204, 477) | 0 | 0 |
| 4. | Forgery (Sec. 463, 465, 466, 468, 469, 471, 476, 477A) | 48 | 71 |
| 5. | Criminal breach of trust/fraud (Sec. 405–6, 408–9) | 186 | 215 |
| 6. | Counterfeiting | | |
| | a. Property/mark (Sec. 193, 482–485) | 0 | 0 |
| | b. Tampering (Sec. 489) | 9 | 8 |
| | c. Currency/stamps (Sec. 489A to 489E) | 59 | 83 |
| | **TOTAL (B)** | **302** | **377** |
| | **Grand Total (A + B)** | **481** | **569** |

**Table 2.2. Incidence of Cybercrimes Cases Registered during 2005 (IT ACT 2000)**

| Sl. No. | State/UT | Tampering Computer Source Department (Sec. 65) | Hacking | | Obscene Publication/ Transmission in Electronic Form (Sec. 67) | Failure | |
|---|---|---|---|---|---|---|---|
| | | | Loss/Damage to Computer Resource/ Utility (Sec. 66[1]) | Hacking (Sec. 66[2]) | | Of Compliance/ Orders of Certifying Authority (Sec. 68) | To Assist to Decoy or the Information in Interception by Govt. Agency (Sec. 69) |
| (1) | (2) | (3) | (4) | (5) | (6) | (7) | (8) |
| | **STATES** | | | | | | |
| 1 | Andhra Pradesh | 2 | 3 | 9 | 0 | 0 | 0 |
| 2 | Arunachal Pradesh | 0 | 0 | 0 | 0 | 0 | 0 |
| 3 | Assam | 0 | 0 | 0 | 1 | 0 | 0 |
| 4 | Bihar | 0 | 0 | 0 | 0 | 0 | 0 |
| 5 | Chhattisgarh | 0 | 0 | 0 | 17 | 0 | 0 |
| 6 | Goa | 0 | 0 | 0 | 0 | 0 | 0 |
| 7 | Gujarat | 1 | 1 | 0 | 0 | 0 | 0 |
| 8 | Haryana | 0 | 3 | 0 | 2 | 1 | 0 |
| 9 | Himachal Pradesh | 0 | 0 | 0 | 0 | 0 | 0 |
| 10 | Jammu & Kashmir | 0 | 0 | 0 | 0 | 0 | 0 |

(continued)

**Table 2.2.** *(continued)*

| Sl. No. | State/UT | Tampering Computer Source Department (Sec. 65) | Hacking | | Obscene Publication/ Transmission in Electronic Form (Sec. 67) | Failure | |
| | | | Loss/Damage to Computer Resource/ Utility (Sec. 66[1]) | Hacking (Sec. 66[2]) | | Of Compliance/ Orders of Certifying Authority (Sec. 68) | To Assist to Decoy or the Information in Interception by Govt. Agency (Sec. 69) |
| (1) | (2) | (3) | (4) | (5) | (6) | (7) | (8) |
| | **STATES** | | | | | | |
| 11 | Jharkhand | 0 | 0 | 0 | 0 | 0 | 0 |
| 12 | Karnataka | 4 | 0 | 24 | 10 | 0 | 0 |
| 13 | Kerala | 0 | 2 | 0 | 1 | 0 | 0 |
| 14 | Madhya Pradesh | 0 | 0 | 0 | 0 | 0 | 0 |
| 15 | Maharashtra | 1 | 3 | 8 | 14 | 0 | 0 |
| 16 | Manipur | 0 | 0 | 0 | 0 | 0 | 0 |
| 17 | Meghalaya | 0 | 0 | 0 | 0 | 0 | 0 |
| 18 | Mizoram | 0 | 0 | 0 | 0 | 0 | 0 |
| 19 | Nagaland | 0 | 0 | 0 | 0 | 0 | 0 |
| 20 | Orissa | 0 | 1 | 0 | 5 | 0 | 0 |

| | | | | | | | |
|---|---|---|---|---|---|---|---|
| 21 | Punjab | 0 | 0 | 0 | 6 | 0 | 0 |
| 22 | Rajasthan | 0 | 0 | 0 | 18 | 0 | 0 |
| 23 | Sikkim | 0 | 0 | 0 | 0 | 0 | 0 |
| 24 | Tamil Nadu | 2 | 15 | 0 | 5 | 0 | 0 |
| 25 | Tripura | 0 | 0 | 0 | 0 | 0 | 0 |
| 26 | Uttar Pradesh | 0 | 1 | 0 | 2 | 0 | 0 |
| 27 | Uttaranchal | 0 | 0 | 0 | 0 | 0 | 0 |
| 28 | West Bengal | 0 | 0 | 0 | 0 | 0 | 0 |
| | **Total (States)** | **10** | **29** | **41** | **81** | **1** | **0** |
| | **UNION TERRITORIES** | | | | | | |
| 29 | A&N Islands | 0 | 0 | 0 | 0 | 0 | 0 |
| 30 | Chandigarh | 0 | 0 | 0 | 2 | 0 | 0 |
| 31 | D&N Haveli | 0 | 0 | 0 | 0 | 0 | 0 |
| 32 | Daman &Diu | 0 | 0 | 0 | 0 | 0 | 0 |
| 33 | Delhi | 4 | 4 | 0 | 5 | 0 | 0 |
| 34 | Lakshadweep | 0 | 0 | 0 | 0 | 0 | 0 |
| 35 | Pondicherry | 0 | 0 | 0 | 0 | 0 | 0 |
| | **Total (UTS)** | **0** | **4** | **0** | **7** | **0** | **0** |
| | **TOTAL (ALL INDIA)** | **10** | **33** | **41** | **88** | **1** | **0** |

use in the country takes many forms, from being blown through a water bubble pipe called a *hukka* to being brewed with tea as *bonda chai*. These drugs were never a major problem and are naturally available without restrictions. The society developed internal mechanisms to control their spread and consumption, especially amongst the youth. Ancient governments too never restricted their consumption and relied upon social disapproval to limit their use by the addicts.

Ironically, the problem of drug trafficking in the Indian subcontinent emerged from the policies of the East India Company, which traded tea with opium from China. The British expanded the trade in opium, systematically controlling its cultivation, consumption, production, and sale within the country. The profit margins were high as the production in the country did not exceed demand. Soon the local people followed, cultivating this as a cash crop to reap the huge profits. The revenue generated by the British from poppy cultivation quickly led to opium becoming a viable commodity for sale. This facilitated illicit cultivation as well as smuggling of opium across native states and from provinces to the native states (Charles 2001).

However, the real problem of drugs in the country started with the advent of Westerners, especially during the sixties when the so-called hippie movement attracted a large number of rebellious youth to India. The introduction of other drugs such as marijuana and even heroin started spreading in the country. The growing demand led to the growth of organized criminal gangs that began procuring and distributing these drugs to the tourists and even the Indian youth who followed the trend. The response of the government was to begin a variety of legislation that outlawed many drugs, including some that had been consumed traditionally. The counterresponse from the organized criminals was as expected—the network of distribution went underground, where it gained strength as drug usage became fashionable amongst the youth and demand grew.

The process of illegalization of drugs in India began with the United Nations (UN). These problems arise from the criminalization of centuries-old cultural habits in India.

The Indian government enacted the Narcotic Drugs and Psychotropic Substances Act, 1985 (NDPS), which was designed to conform to the UN convention of 1961, which the Indian government had signed in 1964. India subscribed to the international goal of eradicating all cultural uses of cannabis within a twenty-five-year period. The main elements of the control regime mandated by the act are as follows.

(a) The cultivation, production, manufacture, possession, sale, purchase, transportation, warehousing, consumption, inter-state movement, transshipment and import and export of narcotic drugs and psychotropic substances is prohibited except for medical or scientific purposes and in accordance with the terms and conditions of any license permit or authorization given by the Government (section 8).

(b) The Central Government is empowered to regulate the cultivation production, manufacture, import, export, sale, consumption, use etc of narcotic drugs and psychotropic substances (section 9).

(c) State governments are empowered to permit and regulate possession and inter-state movement of opium, poppy straw, the manufacture of medicinal opium and the cultivation of cannabis excluding hashish (section 10).

(d) All persons in India are prohibited from engaging in or controlling any trade whereby narcotic drugs or psychotropic substances are obtained outside India and supplied to any person outside India except with the previous authorization of the Central Government and subject to such conditions as may be imposed by the Central Government (section 12).

(e) The Central Government is empowered to declare any substance, based on an assessment of its likely use in the manufacture of narcotics drugs and psychotropic substances as a controlled substance (section 9-A).

(f) Assets derived from drugs trafficking are liable to forfeiture (chapter V-A).

(g) Both the central government and state governments are empowered to appoint officers for the purposes of the act (sections 4, 5, and 7).

(Narcotics Control Bureau 2006)

The act empowers enforcement agencies to control chemical precursors that could be used in the illicit manufacture of narcotic drugs as well as provide for investigation and seizure of assets made from illegal drug trade. A number of police agencies have been empowered under this act: the Department of Customs and Central Excise, the Directorate of Revenue Intelligence, the Central Bureau of Narcotics, the Central Bureau of Investigation, the Border Security Force at the central level, and state police and excise departments at the state level. Section 4(3) of the act provides for the creation of a central authority to coordinate the activities of the various central and state agencies involved in drug law enforcement, to implement India's obligations under various international conventions, and to coordinate with international organizations and authorities in foreign countries in the prevention and suppression of the illicit traffic in narcotic drugs and psychotropic substances. Under the terms of this provision, the Narcotics Control Bureau (NCB) was set up by the central government in 1986 to coordinate drug law enforcement in the country. The bureau now functions as a national coordinating center which liaisons with international agencies and functions as the nodal point for the collection and dissemination of intelligence.

The government now controls the cultivation of plants that are related to drugs covered by the narcotics act. For example, the rules provide that poppy cultivation may be licensed within stipulated guidelines by the central government. However, the act provides that no cultivator shall be granted license unless he satisfactorily proves that in the course of actual cultivation the area licensed for poppy cultivation during the previous crop year was not exceeded and that he did not at any time resort to illicit cultivation of opium poppy and was not charged in the competent court for any offense under the Narcotic Drugs and Psychotropic Substances Act, 1985, and the rules thereunder. The central government announces an opium policy each year which sets out the terms and conditions subject to which licenses for the cultivation of opium are given and describes the areas where cultivation will be allowed and the prices at which the opium crop will be purchased by the government, including stipulating the minimum qualifying yield for a license in the ensuing crop year. The crop cycle runs from October to May and, based on this policy, the narcotics commissioner of India issues licenses to individual cultivators for specified tracts of land.

This results in strict enforcement of the drug-related laws in the country. There are frequent measurements of fields permitted for licit cultivation, periodic crop surveys, and physical checks to prevent diversion. Failure to tender the entire yield to the government is treated as a serious offense and any cultivator who embezzles or otherwise illegally disposes of the opium produced by him is by the terms of section 19 of the act punishable with rigorous imprisonment for a term of between ten to twenty years and a stiff fine. In view of the strict regulation, India is the largest licit producer of opium in the world. It is both exported and used by the domestic pharmaceutical industry.

Despite the strong control and enforcement of drug cultivation and distribution in the country, the problem is, to a very large extent, the result of its geographical location between the two major opiate-producing regions of Southwest and Southeast Asia. This has rendered India both a destination and a transit route for opiates produced in these regions. The trafficking of opiates through the country consequently remains a vital element of India's counternarcotics strategy. In addition to this there are a number of other factors that drug law enforcement in India is required to address and confront. These include the possibility of diversion from the licit opium crop and the conversion of some of this diverted opium into heroin, the illicit cultivation of the opium poppy and cannabis plant, the clandestine manufacture of methaqualone (Mandrax), and the trafficking of hashish and ganja from Nepal. Further, diversion from both the domestic and international trade and the export trafficking of various drugs and precursor chemicals is a constant threat. Drug law enforcement in India thus demands a variety of measures against a wide range of illegal activities.

The other problem is that the legislation and enforcement has occurred without real public debate and research. The tradition of drug use and commercial drug suppliers in a context of widespread poverty and desperation, and in some areas political conflict, encourages the spread of heroin in the country (Charles 2001). The advent of new economic policies in 1991 opened the Indian markets to foreign goods and services. It also liberalized several sectors and reduced large inflated custom duties on precious metals that virtually stopped the smuggling of gold in the country. However, these policies have pushed the drug cartels to take to the smuggling of drugs and arms, especially through areas where internal conflicts are raging. Thus, areas of Jammu and Kashmir and the northeast have become especially vulnerable to drug smuggling. India's geographical location between the Golden Crescent (Afghanistan) and the Golden Triangle (Myanmar/Thailand), both of which have been entangled in armed conflicts for years, has also facilitated the emergence of drug trafficking. In particular, the 1981 Russian invasion of Afghanistan and the spread of extremism in Pakistan encouraged heroin smuggling networks that often doubled as arms smugglers and Islamic militants supported by Americans. The civil war in Sri Lanka also encouraged the Liberation Tigers of Tamil Eelam (LTTE) and other militant groups in drug trafficking in India.

By criminalizing culturally sanctioned drug use and supply, the new drug legislation has ironically increased the consumption and distribution of drugs in the country. Organized crime has been able to profit since drug supply has been restricted and artificially controlled. There is considerable evidence that criminals have entered elected bodies through loopholes in the electoral laws and criminalization of politics in the country. The decline of the bureaucracy and political system is a consequence of several interests linked to organized crime in drug trade (Charles 2001).

## HUMAN TRAFFICKING

India faces considerable problems of human trafficking, especially regarding women and children for the purposes of sex. A study (Bakhry 2005) commissioned by the National Human Rights Commission of the country found that the trends and dimensions in human trafficking in the country are extremely serious. India is reportedly a major sending, receiving, and transit nation. Receiving children from Bangladesh and Nepal and sending women and children to Middle Eastern nations is a common occurrence (Sleightholme and Sinha 1997). The major proportion of women and children are trafficked from four states: Andhra Pradesh, Karnataka, West Bengal, and Tamil Nadu. Among the trafficked persons, the majority are girls lured at a very young age. Further, and not surprisingly, the majority of the victims are from broken poor families and socially weaker sections of society. While most of the trafficking takes place for the purposes of sexual exploitation, children are also taken away or virtually sold by their parents to work as indentured labor in small factories, homes, and shops around the country. A large proportion, especially young boys, also fall prey to sex tourists from Europe, the United States, and other Western countries. Indeed, India has become one of the favored destinations of pedophiles from Europe and the United States (*Indian Express* 1997). It has also been reported (Bedi 1996) that a large number of foreign tourists frequent India because of its relaxed laws, abundant child prostitutes, and the false idea that there is a lower incidence of AIDS.

Some of the facts reported in the press reveal that the situation remains grim in the country. Human Rights Watch (1995) estimates that at least hundreds of thousands, and probably more than a million, women and children are employed in Indian brothels. Another report suggests that the brothels of India hold between 100,000 and 160,000 Nepalese women and girls; 35 percent are taken on the false pretext of marriage or of providing employment (Coomaraswamy 1997). Moreover, most of the girls are either sold to traffickers by poor parents or tricked into fraudulent marriages, from where they are transported to the brothels of Mumbai, Kolkata, and other major cities (Wadhwa 1998). A good number fall to traffickers on the promise of employment in towns only to find themselves sold in prostitution. These girls are locked up for days, starved, beaten, and burned with cigarettes until they learn how to service up to twenty-five clients a day. Some girls go through "training" before being initiated into prostitution, which can include constant exposure to pornographic films, tutorials in how to "please" customers, and repeated rapes (Wadhwa 1998). Friedman (1996) states that prostitution in Bombay generates millions of dollars a year in revenue but most of the money is cornered by the pimps and brothel owners while the prostitutes barely earn two dollars a day. Unfortunately, a large proportion of prostitutes in Bombay's red-light district areas are also infected with sexually transmitted diseases (STDs) and AIDS (CATW 2006), which is creating another catastrophe in the country.

Another reason for the high prostitution rates in the country is the tradition of Devadasi. In this tradition a woman is married to a god and considered to be blessed at all times. Thereafter she becomes the wife of the powerful in the community (Lambey 1997). Many girls are lured into prostitution in this manner.

Despite such wide prevalence of trafficking of women and children, the police register few crimes of this nature. In 2005, there were 5,908 cases of illegal trafficking of women registered in the country (NCRB 2006: 245). This is a declining trend, since in 2001 there were 8,796 cases registered, while in 2002 a total of 6,598 cases were registered. There is little to explain why crimes under this category are declining. One very plausible explanation is that the police are manipulating the crime statistics, since kidnapping and abduction figures are going up. In 2001 there were 14,645 cases of kidnapping while in 2005 the number had gone up to 15,750. The conduct of police in dealing with such a serious crime is lamentable, to say the least. Indian police personnel are notorious for their corrupt and brutal practices. A practice known as *hafta* or weekly collection of bribes is ubiquitous around the country. In this way, brothel owners and traffickers ensure that police do not closely look into their activities. It is commonly believed that top politicians and police officials provide protection for monetary benefits (Friedman 1996). It is also difficult to recover underage girls from brothels because the pimps and owners receive tip-offs from police about impending raids (Menon 1998). Unfortunately, Mumbai's sex industry has become a big business enterprise. Operators have developed expertise in paying off the police, in laundering the illegal profits, and in procuring women and girls from a vast network stretching across the subcontinent (CATW 2006).

A problem related to prostitution and trafficking is the growing epidemic of the HIV/AIDS virus in the country. An estimated 5.1 million Indians are currently living with HIV. Surveys in 2003 found 14 percent of commercial sex workers in Karnataka and 19 percent in Andhra Pradesh were infected with HIV. In Mysore, 26 percent of sex workers were HIV positive, according to a 2005 survey (UNAIDS 2006). Furthermore, it was learned that most prostitutes did not know that condoms prevented HIV infection. Despite efforts by government and nongovernment organizations, HIV prevalence among female sex workers has not fallen below 52 percent since 2000 (National AIDS Control Organization [NACO] 2004). In the northeast of India, HIV transmission is concentrated chiefly among drug injectors and their sexual partners, especially in areas which lie adjacent to the drug-trafficking Golden Triangle zone (UNAIDS 2006).

Several steps have been taken by the government to deal with this problem of trafficking. The Immoral Traffic Prevention Act (ITPA), passed in 1956, prohibits trafficking in persons, criminalizes sexual exploitation, and enhances penalties for offenses involving minors. The UN Convention of the Suppression of the Traffic in Persons and the Exploitation of the Prostitution of Others (1949) and the supplementary convention on the abolition of slavery, the slave trade, and institutions and practices of slavery have been signed by India. To halt child marriages, the National Human Rights Commission (NHRC) in India has recommended compulsory registration of marriages to be added as an amendment to the Child Marriage (Restraint) Act (*Hindu* 1998). Countries in the South Asian region, through their forum South Asian Association for Regional Cooperation (SAARC), signed a treaty to cooperate and deal effectively with the epidemic of human trafficking in the region. This treaty attempts to promote cooperation so member countries can develop effective action plans for the prevention, interdiction, and suppression of trafficking in women and children as well as the repatriation and rehabilitation of victims (SAARC 2002).

A major role is being played by nongovernmental organizations who are active in tracking missing women and children as well as exposing the nexus between traffickers and enforcement agents. Organizations like Saheli, Save the Children India, Sanlaap, Shakti Vahini, Prajwala, Nandi foundation, Lok Satta, and many others assist in getting the women out from brothels, help with their rehabilitation, and also get them medical assistance for treatment of HIV. They have also been seeking the assistance of industry in cooperating to prevent exploitation of women and children (*Hindu* 2004). At the very least, their efforts have raised the issue as a national concern and forced the indifferent police to take some action. A large number of women kidnapped and sold into brothels have been recovered through such persistent efforts by citizen groups. However, until the widespread conditions caused by poverty and denying education to a large number of children are properly dealt with, this crime is not likely to go away.

## TERRORISM: INTERNAL THREATS

Terrorism reared its face in the country immediately after independence, when the nation faced terrorist attacks from the Communist Party members seeking to usher Communism into the country. The "successes" in Russia, China, and Cuba appear to have encouraged the Indian Communists to pursue the line of overthrowing the state through violent means (Verma 2001). A foreign hand has always been present in terrorist attacks in the country even to this day. Apart from this threat, the failure of the government to nurture a system where grievances could be settled through independent mechanisms and where every section of the residents feel themselves to be a part of the society has also played a role in the use of violence by disgruntled groups. At present terrorism in India is fueled by Pakistan, Bangladesh, and China but also by the failure of policies and distortion in the governance of the country.

In the fifties and sixties, in the early phase of terrorism, the leftist cadres targeted the landlords, moneylenders, and the bourgeoisie in general, who were dubbed as exploiters of the working people. Around 1967, a powerful movement emerged at Naxalbari in West Bengal and Srikakulam in Andhra Pradesh (Dasgupta 1974). A number of villages were declared liberated by the Communists and scores of people were murdered in the name of revolution. In these two regions, the armed groups led by Charu Majumdar, Azizul Haq, and Kanu Sanyal picked and killed people on grounds of being class enemies. These leftist groups also began targeting people in the city of Calcutta in the beginning of seventies. The police appeared powerless against this violence which encouraged many criminal elements to spread lawlessness in the society. Extortion from business people and kidnapping and rape of women as well as destruction of property were some of the acts perpetuated in the name of overthrowing the state. A delayed but brutal police response followed with hundreds of arrests and killings of suspects in so-called false encounters. The lack of support for Communism from the people and brutal police action eventually put an end to the group led by Majumdar, Haq, and their comrades.

After their failure in Bengal, radical Maoist groups moved away to the states of Bihar, Orissa, Madhya Pradesh, and Andhra Pradesh. The failure of governance in these states, poor infrastructure, poor communications, and a politicized police force helped these groups to gain ground and strengthen their base (Verma 2001). At present, the People's War Group (PWG) operating in northern Andhra Pradesh (Ramanujan 1997), the Maoist Communist Center (MCC), Communist Party of India (Marxist-Leninist) (CPI-ML), and Party Unity groups in central Bihar are firmly entrenched (Singh 1999). These groups have targeted "feudal" elements: landlords, policemen, and those who have broken away from their party. In recent years, with the support of the Maoist party in Nepal, these groups have succeeded in establishing a long corridor from Nepal to Andhra Pradesh in South India as a vast region of operations.

There are many factions amongst these Communist groups based upon ideological and leadership differences as well as territorial supremacy. All these groups are not only in constant combat with the police and landlord-supported resistance but have also been battling amongst themselves. Indeed, in this battle for supremacy amongst the armed squads, the resistance forces organized by the farmers have assumed alarming trends with savage brutality on both sides. For instance, CPI-ML first staged violent attacks against the landowners in the districts of Bhojpur and Gaya of Bihar state. Their success in terrorizing the landowners and targeting the upper-caste people led to the creation of self-defense militia such as Ranvir Sena (Bhelari 1997). These resistance groups, consisting of upper-caste goons, began targeting the lower castes, who were aligned with the Communist groups. In the battle for supremacy countless atrocities have been perpetuated by both sides (Verma 2001).

Another virulent terrorism emerged in the Northeastern (NE) region of the country, where some members of the Naga and Mizo tribes formed guerrilla groups and attempted to wage a war of secession. The NE is largely a region inhabited by indigenous people with a history of interethnic rivalries. Even during the British period, this region was largely inaccessible and the British found it difficult to control. After the independence of the country, many tribal people demanded autonomy for themselves. In small pockets terrorist attacks on government establishments including police and army posts were carried out. Their targets were also the people who did not support their cause, who were aligned with the state, and who worked for the state. Terrorism in the NE continued for a long period of time and lasted until the mid-sixties when Laldenga, the Naga guerrilla leader, accepted peace and joined the political mainstream. This compromise with the government of India finally brought peace to Nagaland and other regions. Subsequently, Manipur and other Northeastern regions were given autonomy and created as provinces within the Indian union. This political arrangement has brought some peace to the region, though terrorist attacks by splinter groups are continuing (*Oriental Times* 1999). Since most of these splinter groups function as a regular guerrilla army, the Indian army, rather than the police, has been used to battle them. The Naga and Mizo insurgency has subsided considerably although small groups continue to target state officials and those people who refuse shelter or food to the guerrilla bands.

However, other groups, like United Liberation Front of Assam (ULFA), operating in the northern part of Assam state, have stepped up their violence. They receive assistance from neighboring countries of China, Myanmar, and Pakistan that orchestrate their support through the diplomatic missions in Bangladesh and Nepal. Victimization has not been confined only to the killing of innocent bystanders in bomb blasts or cross fire; citizens have also been deliberately targeted by these groups. For instance, ULFA kidnapped and killed a social worker, Sanjoy Ghosh. The victims of these terrorist activities have also included many of the tea planters, who have been kidnapped for ransom purposes. In one case, a leading business house of the country negotiated and got the release of one of its managers by paying a huge sum of money to the ULFA kidnappers. The company also provided medical treatment to some of the terrorists and their families. This revelation resulted in the prosecution of some of the business managers for conspiring with the terrorists (Goswami 1997).

## TERRORISM: EXTERNAL THREATS

The real serious threat of terrorism however emerged in the eighties when Pakistan, exploiting the political problems in the state of Punjab, began to get actively involved in promoting disgruntled Sikh groups to resort to terrorism in the country. A large number of Sikh terrorists found shelter in Pakistan, from where they received training, arms, and money to engage in spreading violence in Punjab. Terrorist activities of a more sinister nature and aided by Pakistan's Inter-Services Intelligence (ISI) and Afghan guerrilla groups created serious problems in the states of Punjab (Joshi 1999). Terrorism in Punjab from 1982 onwards involved considerable violence with loss of thousands of lives.

Unfortunately, the roots of Sikh terrorism came from the politics of Punjab where the Akali Dal, the political wing of the religious group, raised the theme of Punjabi Suba in the sixties to draw a distinction between the Hindus and the Sikh communities. The Congress Party had been ruling Punjab from the early years of independence. Akali Dal, due to its religious moorings, obviously did not attract non-Sikh voters. The Dal pressed for a partition of Punjab in order to carve out a domain where the Sikhs would be in a majority. Their virulent demands did force the government of India to bifurcate the state into Punjab, Haryana, and Himachal Pradesh, which made Punjab a Sikh-dominated area. However, non-Sikhs still constituted 40 percent of its population. This made it obvious that a political party aspiring to come to power would necessarily have to adopt a pluralist mode, something that did not fit with Akali Dal's basic tenets (Verma 2001). It therefore continued to project assumed Sikh grievances to drive a wedge between the two communities.

The Congress Party under Indira Gandhi also played the religious card by supporting the growth of Bhindranwale, a semi-literate wandering preacher who initially opposed the Akali Dal for various reasons. Bhindranwale adopted violent means to terrorize his opponents. Despite clear evidence against him of murder, the Congress Party ruling at the center did not arrest him and indeed exonerated him. This further emboldened him to indulge in a terror campaign against the moderate Sikh politicians. Bhindranwale and his men attacked and killed the leader of the Nirankari sect of Sikhism and yet were not charged for the crime. His violent tactics tamed the Akali Dal leadership, too, who feared for their lives. "Eventually, the government chose to act, albeit hesitatingly" (Gill 1997: 82). A prominent member of Bhindranwale's storm troopers, Amrik Singh, was arrested in July 1982 for a series of murders, robberies, and desecration in the state. Realizing that he too would be arrested, Bhindranwale moved into the Golden Temple complex and forcibly occupied some rooms that were sacred to the Sikhs. Unwilling to move into the temple for fear of antagonizing the Sikhs, the police were prevented from going after him. This enabled Bhindranwale to build a safe place for himself where he could operate with impunity. Gill (1997: 75) states, "The creed of hatred that had been propagated for decades was suddenly translated into action." A telling example of this action was the daylight murder of a senior police officer, A. S. Atwal, by Bhindranwale's men. Atwal had come to pray at the temple and was murdered in front of scores of witnesses, including his own police bodyguards and a police contingent posted outside the temple. "Such was the terror of those days, so great the demoralization of the police—crippled and constrained as they were by the political leadership—that his bodyguards simply fled; the police outpost was also abandoned, and the policemen ran and hid in the [nearby] shops" (Gill 1997: 86). As Gill pointedly states, "It was actions like these that provided the greatest fillip to violence and to the acceptance of violence as a legitimate political weapon" (87). For a full decade thereafter, violence in the name of religion became the norm in Punjab.

The government's attempts to combat this menace were also ill-planned and ill-executed. In order to control Bhindranwale, Indira Gandhi, the prime minister of the country, ordered the army to move into the temple complex. This operation was organized hastily, and although Bhindranwale and many of his prominent supporters were killed in the army operation, parts of the temple were also damaged. This roused the Sikh community, which interpreted military action as an assault on their religion. Some months later, two Sikh bodyguards of Indira Gandhi murdered her, which set off a vast reaction against the Sikh community in many parts of the country. Now the Hindus retaliated, but chose innocent Sikh citizens as their targets. In Delhi alone more than three thousand Sikhs were killed by the rampaging mobs that were led by Congress Party leaders. This time, too, the police acting at the behest of Congress Party did little to save the innocent Sikhs being butchered by the mobs. More than anything else, this pogrom against the Sikhs plunged Punjab and the country into a chaotic situation where Sikhs felt themselves alienated from the Hindus (Verma 2001).

This situation was ripe for Pakistan to exploit and avenge its "defeat" in the 1971 Bangladesh war. Since Punjab has a long border with Pakistan, it became easy for the ISI of Pakistan to provide the terrorists a sanctuary, guidance, and weapons. For many years (until a border fence was constructed) militants could run back to Pakistan after committing violent acts against selected targets in Punjab. Terrorism also provided a cover for criminals to find shelter amongst the estranged people and escape from the police. However, the citizens' support was largely exaggerated, as Gill repeatedly informs us. The largest numbers of people killed as a consequence of Sikh terrorism were Sikhs themselves, and the people who fought against them were also Sikhs.

The Sikh terrorists found it convenient to operate from Pakistan across the international border and carry out attacks on police as well as the civilian population. They planted bombs on buses and trains and exploded them in market areas to terrorize the population and cause breakdown in normal life. Specially designed transistor bombs killed sixty-nine people in Delhi (*Hindu* 2006). Prominent people were murdered, including journalists and newspaper editors who dared to write against them. Even the family members of police and army personnel were killed to break the morale of government forces and cause panic in the society. These Sikh militants received considerable support, funds, and material resources not only from Pakistan but also from Sikh communities in England, Canada, and the United States (Gill 1997). For almost ten years terrorism continued in Punjab and could only be crushed with a heavy-handed police and army action (Joshi 1993). At present, Punjab is largely at peace, but several militant groups are dormant and not totally vanquished. Even at the present time some isolated Sikh terrorist groups have been detected operating with the encouragement and assistance of Pakistan's ISI. Raman (2003) states, "Pakistan has given sanctuary to 20 principal leaders of Sikh and Muslim terrorist groups, including hijackers of Indian aircraft and trans-national criminal groups colluding with terrorists. Despite strong evidence of their presence in Pakistani territory and active operation from there, its government has denied their presence and refused to act against them. It has also ignored Interpol's notices for apprehending them and handing them over to India." Gall (2006) states that "the trail of organizing, financing and recruiting the bombers who have carried out a rising number of suicide attacks in Afghanistan traces back to Pakistan."

The terrorism in Jammu and Kashmir (J and K) has been more serious and is still continuing unabated. J and K is a predominant Muslim state and part of it has been occupied by Pakistan since the partition of the country. Three wars have been fought over this region, and the two armies continue to face each other over the line of cease-fire. The mountainous terrain has also made it difficult to launch strong military operations against the militants, who slip into the country from Pakistan or even from not-too-distant Afghanistan. Terrorism reached its peak in the mid-nineties, when many towns, including the capital city Srinagar, were seriously affected by violent attacks. Many tactics were used to terrorize the population and provoke the armed forces into retaliation, in which a large number of people have been killed. The militants targeted the Hindu minority population in particular and attempted a form of ethnic cleansing. A very large proportion of Hindus have been driven away to seek shelter in other parts of the country (Kashmir Information Network, 2001). These militants also burned down the Hazratbal mosque, which is considered sacred to the Muslims, in order to provoke violent clashes. During the visit of President Clinton in 1999, these terrorists killed thirty-nine Sikhs living in the Kashmir valley (Punjabilok 2000). Pakistan-supported terrorists have perpetuated vicious attacks in other parts of the country also. They have killed foreign tourists trekking in the Himalayas and attacked an army camp in New Delhi. They used powerful explosive devices to damage the Air India building and the stock exchange in Mumbai, killing a large number of people. They also hijacked an Indian Airlines plane from Kathmandu and killed one of the passengers. None of these offenders could be arrested, as they found shelter in Pakistan.

As the above brief narrative suggests, while the West has discovered terrorism only after the advent of al-Qaeda and, in particular, the events of September 11, 2001, India has been facing terrorism in various forms for several decades. Since the eighties Pakistan has virtually been waging a proxy war through various terrorists created, trained, controlled, and equipped by Pakistan's ISI, the secret intelligence agency of Pakistan's armed forces. ISI-controlled terrorists have operated in Punjab and Kashmir and are now spreading across different parts of the country. Terrorist strikes in the country include an attack on the Parliament of India; the planting of bombs in buses, trains, and marketplaces; and attacks on security forces and vital installations. More than sixty thousand citizens have been killed in J and K in terrorist-related violence. Indeed, the level of terrorist violence in India is perhaps equal to what the West has faced collectively over several years. Though the suicide attack on the World Trade Center was the most dramatic terrorist attack, in terms of continuous temporal span, numbers, and ferocity, the terrorist attacks on Indian soil are unprecedented in the world. "For a long time, outsiders viewed India's warnings as a crude attempt to divert attention from internal problems. Today, however, it is the foreign press and foreign governments who are reiterating what India has always maintained" (SAPRA 1996). These terrorist attacks are no longer the handiwork of misguided youth influenced by misconstrued ideology. Most such attacks are for the purpose of furthering the foreign and domestic policies of Pakistan and taking revenge against India for her victory over the Pakistani army in the 1971 Bangladesh war (Haqqani 2005). Pakistan's army, with training and material assistance from the U.S., which was fighting a proxy war against the Soviet Union in Afghanistan, has spawned a Frankensteinian monster that is now threatening the entire world. Raman (1999) states that the nature of terrorism changed when sovereign nations like Pakistan began assisting terrorist groups, such as Markaz Dawa Al Irshad (the Center for Preaching) and its armed wing the Lashkar-e-Taiba (the

Army of the Pure), in Kashmir and other parts of India for its own agenda without directly getting involved. In this telling article, Raman (1999) writes:

> Pakistani State-sponsorship of insurgencies and terrorism against the Govt. of India dates from 1957. Initially, this was confined to support for the Naga and Mizo insurgencies. Then, it was extended to the Sikh extremist groups in the Punjab and the Kashmiri extremists in J&K. This has now been further expanded to cover assistance to any alienated group in India. Whereas in the pre-1990 period, Pakistan's tactical repertoire consisted essentially of training and arms assistance to indigenous insurgent and terrorist groups in India, since 1990, it has been infiltrating Pakistani and other foreign mercenaries in large numbers into Jammu & Kashmir, initially to beef up the indigenous groups and, subsequently, to marginalize them and take over the leadership from them. What we are facing in Kashmir today is not indigenous terrorism, but undeclared incremental invasion from across the border.

An overview of terrorist attacks in 2006 reveals that, up to October 1, 2221 people have died (Sahni 2006). This review suggests that nearly 45 percent of all such fatalities occurred in J and K, while 23 percent occurred in insurgencies in the Northeast. Approximately 32 percent of fatalities resulted from left-wing extremism (Maoist/Naxalite) in some areas of the states of Chhattisgarh, Andhra Pradesh, Maharashtra, Orissa, West Bengal, Uttar Pradesh, Jharkhand, Bihar, and Karnataka (Sahni 2006). Although the number of terrorist attacks in J and K has come down from previous years as a result of Pakistan scaling down its support after September 2001, the fact remains that almost one hundred people are killed every month as a consequence of this Pakistani-inspired proxy war.

There is now considerable evidence to link Pakistan directly to a large number of terrorist groups that are operating not only against India but also against the Western countries (Gall 2006). The review of terrorism suggests a number of disturbing trends. Sovereign nations are not averse to the use of terrorism to fight their proxy wars and harm other countries. During the Cold War, both the Soviet Union and the United States armed militias, dictators, and mercenaries to wage wars and indulge in violence for their foreign-policy objectives. Whether it was in Vietnam or Namibia or South America, the arms and funds given by America led to instability and violence on an unprecedented scale. The Middle East conflict was largely a proxy for the two nations during the Cold War period. Nations were pitted against each other and hundreds of thousands were killed as a consequence. The Middle East has become explosive largely due to the arms and funds pumped by the U.S. and Soviets. In the fifties, the U.S. used Pakistan to station and operate its spy plane U-2 against the USSR. Pakistan also played a major role in facilitating

Henry Kissinger's secret overtures to China. In return, the U.S. provided considerable economic and military assistance to the country. The armed forces of Pakistan were built by the U.S., which provided sophisticated Sabre jet fighters and Patton tanks. Even though Pakistan used these arms against India in the 1965 and 1971 wars, the U.S. has continued to arm Pakistan and to ignore Indian protests.

This became even more intensified when the U.S. found an opportunity to repay back the Soviets in Afghanistan for what they had done to them in Vietnam. In 1980 when the USSR invaded Afghanistan, Pakistan again became actively involved in the covert war and the U.S. gratitude knew no limits. In return for training and operating Afghan Jehadis against the Soviet forces, the U.S. let all arms and assistance, including Stinger missiles, flow through Pakistani hands. The United States, as is now well known, armed and funded mujahideens to fight the Soviet forces in Afghanistan. Even deadly arms, like Stinger missiles to down airplanes, were provided. What is less well known is the process that led to the destabilization of Afghanistan. Pakistan was recruited for training, arming, and controlling these mujahideens, and all assistance was routed through the Pakistani army. General Zia-ul-Haq, the Pakistani dictator, became a willing supporter in exchange for the U.S. not stopping his attempts to acquire nuclear weapons clandestinely (Haqqani 2005). The consequences were that Pakistan acquired nuclear weapons and Khan, the Pakistani metallurgist who headed this secret attempt, became the conduit for giving nuclear assistance to Iran, Libya, and North Korea (Linzer 2005). Norris and Kristensen (2005), two respected atomic scientists, state about the U.S. role that "achieving short-term foreign policy goals took precedence over preventing widespread nuclear proliferation." Afghanistan and the bordering region of Pakistan became flush with weapons and Islamic suicidal militants. Once the Americans withdrew, the region turned into a Wild West, with the Taliban and al-Qaeda establishing the terror base with assistance from Pakistan.

The decade-long conflict wrecked Afghanistan, but the Americans succeeded in driving the Soviets out of that country. However, once the Soviets left, the Americans too withdrew and left the region embroiled in the aftermath. The millions of dollars worth of aid and arms/ammunition given to Islamic militants turned many parts of that region into the biggest marketplace of arms, which were openly sold in major cities like Peshawar. It also left a large number of trained fighters who needed another conflict to sustain them. The Pakistani army took advantage of this situation and turned to these mujahideens to fight its proxy war in the J and K region of India. From 1990, the terrorist attacks in Kashmir escalated rapidly and led to virulent terrorism that wrecked the valley and turned the beautiful region into a war zone. What is more poignant is the fact that these mujahideens found a leader in bin Laden, who found shelter in Afghanistan and turned them into a well-equipped terrorist organization. Thus was born the al-Qaeda, which operated from Afghanistan with the support of the Taliban regime and Pakistan's army to unleash a wave of terrorist strikes around the world. Sovereign nations still continue this dangerous practice, as the examples from Iran, Syria, and Sudan's support to Palestinian and Lebanese terrorists operating against Israel suggest. Chechnyan terrorists causing mayhem at many centers in Russia also get their support from several Islamic nations. Terrorism will not stop unless sovereign nations do not stop raising such Frankensteinian monsters.

What is not seen immediately is that almost all these groups then go beyond their mandate and begin selecting their own targets. As the Pakistani authorities are realizing, their mujahideens are now targeting their own president. The Islamic militant groups nurtured by Pakistan have made two attempts against Pervez Musharraf in recent years. The recent suicide attack on Pakistani army recruits in Dargai, which killed forty army men (Khan 2006), suggests that these armed militias are now turning back on their benefactors. However, the states are unable to stop the association as their own military/police are engaged with these terrorist outfits. As Pakistan is discovering to its dismay, the attempts to nurture terrorists for carrying out attacks in India have created a system where a fair proportion of its own military personnel are so deeply entrenched with these groups that they are one with them. Gall (2006) reports intelligence gathered from a captured suicide bomber in which "after a bombing cell of 12 people was picked up in Kabul recently, two of the men continued to receive cell-phone calls while in custody, urging them to explode their bombs, the intelligence official said. The calls came from an Afghan commander called Pir Farouq, who lives in the Shamshatoo Afghan refugee camp in Peshawar, a frontier town, and is closely allied with Mr. Hekmatyar. When Afghan intelligence, at NATO's behest, passed on the cell-phone number of Pir Farouq to Pakistani intelligence officers, their informer, a member of the commander's inner circle, was swiftly killed, his body cut into eight pieces and dumped in the camp. NATO officials described the killing to journalists."

Consequently, even though the army leaders may want some of these outfits to be dismantled, like Jaish-e-Mohammad, they are unable to carry out the policy since many of their own personnel are involved. They either do not take action or inform the terrorists about impending raids so that they can escape. The inability of the Pakistanis to arrest major figures of Taliban and al-Qaeda should be seen in this light. Despite the fact that it is known that bin Laden, Mullah Omar, Ayman al-Zawahiri, and such leaders are hiding in northwest parts of the country, Pervez Musharraf has not been able to take action against them. Indeed, when he did attack at the behest of the Americans a madrassa in Bajaur, killing eighty-two people, it led to retaliation at Dargai, mentioned above. Pakistan has been forced to abandon pursuit of terrorists and withdraw its army from certain regions where a virtual civil war is ensuing. Now Pakistan has signed a treaty which literally permits the Taliban to operate in many of these regions (BBC 2006a).

What is also well established is that terrorism flourishes as it operates through organized crime cartels/smugglers (Shelley and Picarelli 2002). Afghanistan is at the center of Golden Crescent and produces almost 80 percent of the world's poppy supplies. Pakistani and Afghan nationals have been indulging in drug trafficking for years, and a good part of arms smuggling, financing of terrorism, and training of Muslim children in madrassas has been financed through these drug trades. The groups that indulge in drug trade then become associated with arms smugglers and ultimately with terrorists, who use their services to travel across boundaries and channel their funds, communications, and arms through such conduits. In India, hawala operators have been engaged in illegal financial transactions for several years. They have links in foreign countries where they channel foreign currency into India through illegal conduits. These operators have emerged as big players in the underworld and invariably have become associated with smugglers and organized syndicates. Many such gangsters have assisted terrorists or actually become terrorists. The case of Dawood Ibrahim is well known in this respect. Starting as a petty smuggler, he rose to be the biggest operator of gold smuggling from Dubai to India. Forced to flee from Indian police he set his operations in the Middle East and spawned a large network of criminal syndicates. His group, known as the D company, financed films and cricket matches while remaining outside the law. Dawood Ibrahim carried out large-scale terrorist attacks in Mumbai in 1993 and fled to Pakistan after it became impossible to stay in Dubai. He still operates from Pakistan, where his daughter married the son of a well-known Pakistani cricketer (Sen 2005). Again, Pakistan has been using him to attack India and has refused to take action despite demands made by India.

There is growing alarm at Pakistani involvement and questions are being raised about the commitment of General Musharraf to dealing with the terrorists. Many authors have begun to state clearly that "Pakistan has traditionally relied on violent extremists to accomplish its strategic objectives in both Afghanistan and India" (Curtis 2006: 1). The links between Pakistani-supported Kashmiri militants and international terrorists are being increasingly commented on by several researchers (Watson and Zaidi 2006). The Jaish-e-Mohammad (JEM) terrorist group, whose leader Maulana Masood Azhar was released by India to end the hijacking of Indian Airlines in 1999, has been involved in several attacks against Westerners. This group and its British-born accomplice Omar Sheikh have been found to be involved in the kidnapping and murder of Daniel Pearl, the *Wall Street Journal* correspondent. Ironically, JEM has its roots in the Afghan war, and many of its cadres were trained by the Americans. It is well known that Bill Clinton seriously considered labeling Pakistan as a state sponsor of terrorism for its support to Kashmiri militants. Curtis (2006: 7) adds that "President Musharraf is clearly hedging in talks with India by allowing Kashmiri militant groups to continue to operate." Curtis further states that "Washington should privately acknowledge the links between the Taliban, Al Qaeda and Pakistan based groups that target India and should convey U.S. expectations that Islamabad develop an equally uncompromising policy toward all three groups" (9). Terrorism in this part of the world and through the growth of al-Qaeda–type organizations emerging from these state-sponsored units is likely to continue until Pakistan establishes a system of civilian rule which in turn controls the activities of its army. This seems an impossibility today as the Pakistani army is fully supported by the United States. Until the period of time when American policymakers decide to pursue another course of action that does not create Frankensteinian monsters and turn a blind eye towards violence perpetuated in India, terrorism will be difficult to control for Indian authorities.

## POLICE/ JUSTICE RESPONSES

After 9/11, India was one of the first countries to offer cooperation to the U.S. in dealing with al-Qaeda, which was known to be operating at the outskirts of J and K. However, in a turnaround, Pervez Musharraf joined the U.S., ditching the Taliban, its own creation, and the Afghan militants who were operating under the directions of the ISI. Pakistan's strategic location and the long border with Afghanistan offered better avenues to the U.S. for pursuing al-Qaeda and removing the Taliban from the seat of power in Kabul. As described above, the U.S. has ignored Pakistan's involvement in terrorist attacks on India and has even destroyed material evidence of Pakistani complicity provided to them by India. Raman states that a timer used in Mumbai blasts of 1993 perpetuated by Dawood Ibrahim at the behest of the ISI was identified by U.S. forensic experts "as part of consignment supplied to Pakistan during the Afghan war of the 1980s." However, "they did not return the timer, which they had taken to the United States for forensic examination. U.S. officials later claimed it had been destroyed by mistake" (2006: 158). India has therefore largely been combating terrorism on its own although the U.S. has attempted to rein in Pakistan at times when the conflict between the two nations has assumed serious proportions. For instance, the terrorist attack on the Parliament of India in 2003 led to an escalation of tensions between the two countries, and both mobilized troops on the border. A situation of direct conflict between the two nuclear-armed nations alarmed the world, and the U.S. prevailed to defuse the tension. Pervez Musharraf promised not to let Pakistani soil be used for terrorism and, further, he temporarily banned several groups like Jaish-e-Muhammad that were involved in terrorism against India. For some time, the U.S. pressure curbed the direct support that Pakistan was extending to the Islamic militant groups operating against India. However, Pervez Musharraf has not given up the option of using terrorism as a means for tying India and hurting its economic growth. The recent attacks on local trains at Mumbai that killed almost 280 people were traced back to Lashkar-e-Toiba and training provided by Pakistan's ISI (BBC 2006b).

In combating terrorism, India has found a more reliable ally in Israel, which is also a victim of terrorism. India and Israel have collaborated in training, exchange of technology, and transfer of arms (Sharma 2003). India has also attempted to seek the assistance of INTERPOL in pursuing wanted terrorists hiding in Pakistan. After the change of government of Afghanistan and the advent of Karzai as the president, India and Afghanistan have also been collaborating extensively. Considering that both nations are the victims of Pakistani-sponsored terrorism it is natural that this cooperation is expanding. The economic growth in India has also attracted a lot of attention of U.S. companies that are flocking there to expand their businesses. This is also forcing some change in the U.S. policies, which are beginning to show more understanding of India's fight against terrorism. There have been reports (U.S. Embassy 2005) of cooperation between the Indian and U.S. armies, navies, and air forces. John Gill (2006: 125) informs us, "The Malabar naval exercises, air force combat training in India and in the United States, the array of special forces, counterterrorism exchanges, and army exercises in small-unit tactics and peacekeeping scenarios represent only a small sample of the growing list of substantive, sophisticated U.S.-India interactions." These developing joint training sessions and exchanges of personnel are leading the countries to greater understanding of each other's positions. India is a signatory to the UN treaties governing drug and human trafficking and has played a major role in combating these menaces. The director of the Central Bureau of Investigation has been designated as the nodal officer to work with INTERPOL, and Indian intelligence agencies also support investigative efforts in pursuing traffickers. Unfortunately, there is little cooperation with Pakistan and even other neighbors and no treaties exist to deal with jurisdictional problems. Consequently, there is no agreement about hot pursuits. Indian plans to pursue terrorists in Pakistani-occupied Kashmir are vehemently opposed by Pakistan.

Within the country, the cooperation amongst the police agencies is facilitated by the fact that leadership of the police is in the hands of officers of the Indian Police Service (IPS). All ranks of superintendent and above are held by members of this service, who can move from one unit to another. Thus, even though police is state-subject, cooperation is possible through the intervention of IPS officers. Further, the intelligence agencies also cooperate fully with the state forces and joint operations are frequently launched to deal with intrastate offenders. Moreover, laws are uniform across the country and the Supreme Court of India has national jurisdiction that ensures uniformity of action and cooperation amongst the enforcement agencies.

## FUTURE DEVELOPMENTS

As a victim of terrorism and transnational criminal activities, India has not only recognized the seriousness of this threat but also made considerable efforts in combating it. The Parliament of India has time and again unanimously adopted resolutions to combat terrorism. Although there have been differences about the enactment and application of preventive detention laws, both the Congress Party and the Bharatiya Janata Party, which have ruled at the center, have legislated such laws. The parliament has spoken with one voice about terrorism in Punjab and J and K and has supported the government's efforts in dealing with extremist groups. India is also a signatory to UN declarations on transnational crimes and has fully supported international efforts in dealing with these offenders. India has also provided considerable material, economic, and personnel assistance to the UN agencies engaged in these tasks. Indian army and police personnel have served in large numbers in almost all hot spots of the world. Indian contingents continue to serve at Kosovo, Bosnia, Cyprus, Angola, Sierra Leone, and East Timor. India's famous female police officer, Kiran Bedi, served as the chief of the United Nations' civilian police force, and even today a large number of Indian officers are actively engaged in UN peacekeeping and investigative efforts.

However, terrorism in this part of the world cannot be understood from regional perspectives alone. National conflicts, transnational crimes, and terrorism in particular have their roots in the Cold War between the U.S. and the erstwhile Soviet Union. The attempts by the two blocs to extend their spheres of influence played havoc with many nations and laid the basis of the present-day scourge of extremism. The policies of the U.S. have laid the basis of terrorism that is threatening the world. Even today, the U.S. has not been able to stop the Pakistani army from covertly supporting many such extremist groups. Pakistan has taken efforts to ensure that these groups do not pose further threats to the U.S., but in return, again, there is considerable duplicity where India is concerned. Pakistan continues to train, equip, and control all the major groups operating in J and K, and most of these are associated with al-Qaeda. Unless a complete break is made and the U.S. sees the threat to India as one to itself and the world, the problem will remain.

It is also well understood that liberal democracies find it difficult to operate against clandestine groups and legal restrictions hamper operations. India and the U.S. remain open societies governed by a rule of law. The emphasis on due process creates a situation where the police have to operate slowly and carefully with proper procedures. This creates opportunities for the terrorist groups to slip in the country and find means to inflict considerable damage. Furthermore, national sovereignty and lack of treaties ensure that international cooperation is slow. Extradition of wanted terrorists takes time and thus enables terrorists to escape arrest. Unsettled nations such as Iraq and Afghanistan provide safe sanctuaries to these wanted terrorists. It is also not surprising that these regions also become conduits for drugs and human trafficking. Afghanistan is the largest producer of opium and a major supplier of illegal drugs. The boundaries of terrorism and drug and human trafficking blur and assume serious dimensions, as the world is beginning to understand.

In such unsettled conditions the Internet is further becoming a strong tool for terrorism and drug and human traffickers. The ability to communicate effectively and quickly without interference is the backbone of traffickers and transnational criminals (Weimann 2004). The easy availability of computers and communication equipment has spawned Internet sites where messages are easily exchanged and orders passed to sleeping cells to operate clandestinely. New laws that could control misuse of modern computers are needed, and police need modern training to deal with electronic communications if any breakthrough is needed. This takes time and organizational change that is usually slow to come. Hence the police are generally playing catch-up while the criminals and terrorists are committing their deadly acts. Moreover, "India has reasons to be concerned over what is perceived by many in India as the U.S. tolerance of the double game being played by Musharraf. While acting vigorously against the terrorist infrastructure of Al Qaeda in Pakistani territory, particularly in south Waziristan, which poses a threat to American lives, he has refrained from similar action against the terrorist infrastructure in Pakistani territory directed against India" (Raman 2006: 167). Liberal democracies like India and the U.S. have to find new means and cooperate with each other in order to deal effectively with transnational criminals and terrorists.

# REFERENCES

Bakhry, Savita. 2005. "Designing and implementing an action research project on trafficking: A perspective from NHRC India." Paper presented at the Regional Workshop on Trafficking and National Human Rights Institutions: Cooperating to End Impunity for Traffickers and Secure Justice for Victims, Sydney, Australia, November 20–23.

BBC. 2006a. "Pakistan 'Taleban' in peace deal," September 5, http://news.bbc.co.uk/2/hi/south_asia/5315564.stm.

BBC. 2006b. "Pakistan 'role in Mumbai attacks,'" September 30, http://news.bbc.co.uk/2/hi/south_asia/5394686.stm.

Bedi, Rahul. 1996. "Bid to protect children as sex tourism spreads," *News-Scan International*, March 19.

Bhelari, Kanhaiah. 1997. "Waking up to death," *The Week*, December 14.

Central Bureau of Narcotics. 2006. Licit cultivation, http://cbn.nic.in/html/operations cbn.htm.

Charles, Molly. 2001. "The drug scene in India," *Seminar* 501, August.

Chopra, R. N. and Chopra, I. C. 1990. *Drug addiction with special reference to India.* New Delhi: Council of Scientific and Industrial Research.

Coalition against Trafficking in Women (CATW). 2006. *Trafficking in women and prostitution in the Asia Pacific*, http://www.catwinternational.org/factbook/india.php, viewed November 2006.

Coomaraswamy, Radhika. 1997. "UN special report on violence against women," Gustavo Capdevila, *IPS*, April 2.

Curtis, Lisa. 2006. "Denying terrorists safe haven in Pakistan," *Backgrounder* 1981, October 26, pp. 1–9.

Dasgupta, Biplab. 1974. *The Naxalite movement*, Centre for the Study of Developing Societies, Monograph 1. Bombay: Allied Publishers.

Friedman, Robert I. 1996. "India's shame: Sexual slavery and political corruption are leading to an AIDS catastrophe," *Nation*, April 8.

Gall, Carlotta. 2006. "Pakistan link seen in Afghan suicide attacks," *New York Times*, November 14, http://www.nytimes.com/2006/11/14/world/asia/14afghan.html.

Gill, John. 2006. "US-India military-to-military interaction: In the context of the larger relationship." In Sumit Ganguly, Andrew Scobell, and Brian Shoup (eds.). *US-India strategic cooperation into the 21st century: More than words.* London: Routledge, pp. 113–30.

Gill, K. P. S. 1997. *Punjab: The knights of falsehood.* New Delhi: Har-Anand Publications Pvt. Ltd.

Goswami, Sabita. 1997. "Tata Buy-Buy," *Week*, October 26.

Haqqani, Husain. 2005. *Pakistan: Between the mosque and military.* New York: Carnegie Endowment for International Peace.

*Hindu.* 2006. "Charges framed in transistor bomb blasts case," May 8.

*Hindu.* 2004. "NGO seeks corporates help to check human trafficking," April 4.

*Hindu.* 1998. "NHRC for amendments to Child Marriage Act," August 17.

Human Rights Watch. 1995. "Rape for profit: Trafficking of Nepali girls and women to India's brothels," *Human Rights Watch* 12 (5A), http://www.hrw.org/reports/1995/India.htm.

*Indian Express*. 1997. "Global laws to punish sex tourists sought by Britain and EU," November 21.

The Information Technology (IT) Act. 2000. Ministry of Law, Justice and Company Affairs, Legislative Department, New Delhi, June 9.

Joshi, Manoj. 1999. *The lost rebellion*. New Delhi: Penguin.

Joshi, Manoj. 1993. "Combating terrorism in Punjab: Indian democracy in crisis," *Conflict Studies* 261, May.

Kashmir Information Network. 2001. The invisible refugees, http://www.kashmir-information.com/Refugees/index.html.

Khan, Ismail. 2006. "Suicide attack on army base: 40 troops dead; search on for bomber's aide," *Dawn* (Pakistan), November 9.

Lambey, Farida. 1997. "Devadasi system continues to legitimise prostitution: The devadasi tradition and prostitution," *Times of India*, December 4.

Linzer, Dafna. 2005. "U.S. misled Allies about nuclear export: North Korea sent material to Pakistan, not to Libya," *Washington Post*, March 20.

Menon, Meena. 1998. "Tourism and prostitution," *Hindu*, February 14.

Narcotics Control Bureau. 2006. Narcotics Control Bureau home page, http://narcotics india.nic.in/.

National AIDS Control Organization. 2004. An overview of the spread and prevalence of HIV/AIDS in India, http://www.nacoonline.org/facts_overview.htm.

National Crime Records Bureau. 2006. *Crime in India—2005*. Faridabad: Government of India Press.

Norris, Robert S. and Kristensen, Hans M. 2005. "North Korea's nuclear program, 2005," *Bulletin of Atomic Scientists* 61 (3), pp. 64–67.

*Oriental Times*. 1999. "Peace process receives a major boost," *Headlines* 2 (3–4), May 22–June 6, http://www.nenews.com/.

Punjabilok. 2000. "Clinton visit to India overshadowed by the massacre of Sikhs in Kashmir," March 21, http://www.punjabilok.com/news_files/sikhs_kashmir/clinton _visit.htm.

Raman, B. 2006. "Indo-U.S. counter-terrorism cooperation: Past, present and future." In Sumit Ganguly, Andrew Scobell, and Brian Shoup (eds.). *US-India strategic cooperation into the 21st century: More than words*. London: Routledge, pp. 154–72.

Raman, B. 2003. "Terrorism: India's unending war," *Rediff Special*, April 4, http://www.rediff.com/news/2003/apr/03spec.htm.

Raman, B. 1999. *Pakistani sponsorship of terrorism*, South Asia Analysis Group Paper 106.

Ramanujan, Anand. 1997. "No sign of political settlement with PWG," *Times of India*, January 13.

Sahni, Ajay. 2006. India assessment 2006. South Asia Terrorism Portal, http://www .satp.org.

SAPRA. 1996. World terrorism: An introduction, http://www.subcontinent.com/sapra/ research/terrorism/tr_1996_01_001_s.html.

Sen, Somit. 2005. "Dawood skips daughter's wedding," *Times of India*, July 9.

Sharma, Rajeev. 2003. "India, Israel vow to end terror," *Tribune*, September 10, http://www.tribuneindia.com/2003/20030911/main1.htm.

Shelley, Louise I. and Picarelli, John T. 2002. "Methods not motives: Implications of the convergence of international organized crime and terrorism," *Police Practice and Research: An International Journal* 3(4): 305–18.

Singh, K. K. 1999. "The killing fields of Jehanabad," *Times of India*, March 19.

Sleightholme, Carolyn and Sinha, Indrani. 1997. *Guilty without trial: Women in the sex trade in Calcutta*. New York: Rutgers University Press.

South Asian Association for Regional Cooperation. 2002. SAARC Convention on Preventing and Combating Trafficking in Women and Children for Prostitution.

UNAIDS. 2006. AIDS epidemic update—Asia, December 2005, http://www.unaids.org/epi/2005/doc/EPIupdate2005_pdf_en/Epi05_06_en.pdf.

U.S. Embassy. 2005. "Indo-US aircraft carriers to conduct joint exercise in Arabian Sea, press release, September 26.

Verma, Arvind. 2001. "Terrorist victimization: Case study from India," *International Journal of Comparative and Applied Criminal Justice* 25(1–2): 183–97.

Wadhwa, Soma. 1998. "For sale: Childhood," *Outlook*, http://www.outlookindia.com.

Watson, Paul and Zaidi, Mubashir. 2006. "British case renews focus on Pakistan," *LA Times*, August 13, p. A9.

Weimann, Gabriel. 2004. "www.terror.net: How modern terrorism uses the Internet," *United States Institute of Peace*, Special Report 116, March.

*Chapter Three*

# Policing in China

*Terrorism and the Mandate of Heaven*

Kam C. Wong

"That is to say when we look at terrorism as a problem we should be looking at it historically, dialectically and not be satisfied with 'general concept' (*fanhau gainian*) based on formal logic (*xingshi luoji*)."

—Rong Hanxsong (翁寒松) (2004)[1]

"China scholars should have their own definition for terrorism"

—Wang Yizhou (王逸舟 2002/01/23)[2]

Terrorism is an age-old social problem and a perennial political phenomenon.
Some have observed that the practice of terror is as old as civilization itself.[3]
In the West, Greek historian Xenophon (circa 431–350 BC) espoused the use
of psychological warfare and employment of terror tactics to intimidate the
enemy populations, and Roman emperors, such as Tiberius and Caligula, used
terror measures, such as banishment and execution, to discourage opposition
to their rule.[4] In the East, Chin Shih Huang (259–210 BC), first emperor of
China, used draconian measures and collective punishment to instill discipline and secure his rule (Shaohoul 1994:93).

Terrorism has become a global phenomenon, an international problem, and
a public concern only recently in the twentieth century, around 1960 with the
rise of the Irish Republican Army (IRA) and Palestinian Liberation Organization (PLO). The 9/11 terrorist attack on the United States was successful in
making terrorism a global problem and a public menace to be eradicated at all
costs.[5]

Thus far the effort to rein in terrorism has suffered from a lack of common
understanding of its nature and characteristics, causes, and remedies (Trimble

71

1998). If we were to consult terrorism literature, we would find many definitions of terrorism.[6] There are as many terrorist groups as there are explanations for their causes and justifications for their actions in achieving statehood (Morgan 2004). For example, Schmidt and Jongman (1988) once cited 109 different academic definitions of terrorism, in their book *Political Terrorism*.[7]

It appears that thus far all we can agree on is that the definition of terrorism shares some common features. According to Schmidt and Jongman, the list of 109 definitions contained many recurring elements and repeated keywords/phrases: violence, force (in 83.5% of the definitions); political (65%); fear, terror (51%); threats (47%); psychological effects, anticipated reactions (41.5%); victims not target of violence (37.5%); intentional, planned, systematic, organized (32%); and methods, strategy, tactics (30.5%) (Boaz, n.d.).

A review of occidental literature showed that there was very little research into and discussion of the historical roots or indigenous conceptualization of terrorism in China. This chapter investigates the idea of terrorism in China, past and present. This chapter is divided into six sections. The first two sections are the introduction followed by "Research Focus and Literature Review." After this brief introduction, I state the key questions posed by this research followed by a literature review that shows that while China of late and especially after 9/11 is very much interested in terrorism study, the corpus of research findings has focused mostly on how to deal with (international) terrorism, especially the separatist movement in Xinjiang. There is very little research into the conceptual roots and intellectual history of terrorism in China. This unexpected finding provides justification for this research. The third section, "Terrorism in Imperial China," offers a first-of-its-kind historical look at how terrorism was conceived and received in China. It observes that while the idea "terrorism" (as understood in the West today) has no counterpart in China's past, China has treated terrorist-like activities and criminality (with political overtones) most severely, as challenging the heavenly mandate (*tianming*) and disrupting the cosmic order (*dao*).

The next section, "Terrorism in Communist China," explores the People's Republic of China's (PRC) thinking about terrorism since 1949. It finds that the PRC's understanding has exhibited a remarkable continuity with the past, that is, until very recently there was no terrorism law but counterrevolutionary crimes, suggesting China, old and new, preferred to think about terrorism in more generic terms of political criminality, that is, violent challenges to dominant ideology such as the "mandate from heaven" of old and the Marxism/Leninism/Maoism/Dengism of new (Lindsay 1969). The following section uses a case study of the suppression of Falun Gong in China to make the point that political leadership in China treated all political dissent and social unrest as "terrorist" in nature. The last section offers a reflection on what has been learned and achieved with this investigation into China's conception, perception, and reception of terrorism. It affirms the fact that a people's reception of and reaction to crime is very much determined by past history and influenced by current ideology. Terrorism as an antistate political offense has long existed in China, but it has been looked upon and dealt with differently.

## RESEARCH FOCUS AND LITERATURE REVIEW

This research poses two interrelated research questions in searching for understanding terrorism on Chinese soil: how did China conceive of terrorism in the past and what is China's idea of terrorism in the present? More simply, is it possible to develop an indigenous notion of terrorism in China (Tao, n.d.) or terrorism with Chinese characteristics?

There is very little published research—in criminal justice, Asian studies, political science, and law—on the subject matter of terrorism in China, and virtually none on conceptual definition and historical development. A keyword search (China, terrorism) of criminal justice electronic search engines turned up three relevant items: Mabrey 2005; Wang 2003; and Anonymous 2002.[8]

In 2002, an anonymous author wrote about the upsurge of terrorism and related arrests in Xinjiang, China, after 9/11: "Chinese police in the capital of the far western region of Xinjiang arrested 166 violent terrorists and other criminals in a crackdown on crime. The arrests were made between Sep 20 and Nov 30 in a three-month push to crack cases in the predominantly Muslim region" (Anonymous 2002).

The next year, John Z. Wang (2003) published an article describing terrorism in Xinjiang China with more detail:

> The Eastern Turkistan Islamic Movement (ETIM) was designated a terrorist organization by Afghanistan, Kyrgyzstan, China, the United States, and the United Nations in 2002. However, no systematic studies have been published on the new terrorist organization in Xinjiang, China. Using a case-study approach and interviews, this article attempts to provide information in terms of its historical evolution, related religious and ethnic issues, organizational agenda, activities, and role in the current international terrorist network. This article argues that better international cooperation and the improvement of social and religious policies will help curtail activities of the ETIM.

Finally, in 2005, Mabrey confirmed the obvious—China was no longer insulated from terrorism, especially from separatists' attacks at high-profile international events: "The People's Republic of China has been well-insulated from the threat of terrorism, with less than 300 official terrorism-related casualties recorded in the last 10 years. However, the rise of religious separatist extremism in western China and China's role as host of the 2008 Summer Olympics in Beijing are making counterterrorism a new priority for the Chinese security forces."[9]

A keyword electronic search (China, terrorism) of political science/Asian studies journals turned up 566 articles.[10] Very few of them are directly related to terrorism in China. A detailed examination of this literature shows that the term "terrorism" started to appear with some frequency at the end of the nineteenth century and beginning of the twentieth century, a time of great social turmoil (Perry 1984) and political upheaval for China (Perkins 1939). The subject matter of terrorism was brought up in relation to dynastic rebellion, for example, the 1911 revolution (Wong 1977); domestic strife, for example, banditry (Tiedemann 1982) and warlords (Lary 1980); civil wars, for example, Kuomintang (KMT) vs. the Chinese Communist Party (CCP) (Boorman and Boorman 1966); anti-foreignism struggles, for example, the Boxer rebellion (Perry 1984); and external wars, for example, the war of resistance against Japan (Thaxton 1977).

More recently, research in terrorism has shifted to exploring internal unrest, for example, the Xinjiang separatist movement (Tanner 2004); international terrorism, that is, the multilateral approach (including China) in fighting terrorism (Lampton and Ewing 2003);[11] and global human rights issues, that is, how the terrorism fight raised human rights concerns (Hoffman 2004).[12]

Finally, a keyword (China, terrorism) search of legal journals[13] turned up 256 articles of interest.[14] A careful examination of this corpus of legal writings turned up two articles that discussed in some length recent development of terrorism in China. Both articles were written by Matthew D. Moneyhon, a law student then (2002–2003). Both of them were devoted to the reporting of political developments in Xinjiang, and with it the necessity to touch upon separatists' terrorist activities.

With "Recent Development: Controlling Xinjiang: Autonomy on China's 'NEW Frontier,'" Moneyhon discussed terrorism in the context of the independence and succession movement in Xinjiang. He observed that notwithstanding violence acts and terrorism activities by Xinjiang separatists/terrorists, the only political settlement that was acceptable to China would be constitutional "autonomy," not separate statehood, for the Uighurs, which will eventually mean "modernization, sinification, and ultimately, integration into the greater Han framework" (Moneyhon 2002).

In "China's Great Western Development Project in Xinjiang: Economic Palliative, or Political Trojan Horse?" Moneyhon (2003) set out to show that the PRC has been using economic development as a means to incorporate Xinjiang within its political fold: "Viewed within the context of China's evolving minority policy, Go West looks more like the latest incarnation of Beijing's strategy to integrate and assimilate ethnic minorities into the fabric of greater China, than it does a serious economic development and poverty alleviation plan" (Moneyhon 2003).

All the above studies adopted a conventional (Western) definition of terrorism in investigating terrorism in China. If we are to take up the added challenge of investigating China terrorism indigenously, that is, infusing the terrorism idea with local content and engaging in terrorism discourse within local context, we need to broaden the scope and deepen the reach of the literature search. Instead of basing the search for terrorism predominantly on preconceived conceptual categories and commonly accepted experiential labels, we need to branch out and dig deeper to look at terrorism from a Chinese indigenous perspective and as revealed by local grounded empirical data (Price 1977). For example, how did the state, government officials, and public react to armed group challenges (bandits) and secretly organized criminality (secret societies) in Imperial China?[15] This search strategy turned out to be much more fruitful and far more interesting.

Banditry was a serious social qua political problem in China.[16] Banditry took on political character when bandits directly challenged state authority in seeking political concession or indirectly questioned government legitimacy in seeking to restore cosmic order (Crenshaw 1981).[17] For example, in a May 1468 edict, the emperor wrote indignantly about the open challenge to his rule.

Recently banditry in and around the capital has become rampant. Openly riding their horses in gangs of several dozen, at night they set fires, brandish their weapons, and plunder residents' goods. During the day, [they] intercept the carts of those people who pass by, seizing their donkeys and mules. They even go so far as to take people's lives. Even though there are intendants charged with apprehending bandits, imperial soldiers from the warden's offices of the five wards, and patrolmen, they do not really try to capture the bandits; so that now they are totally unrestrained by fear and act outrageously. (Robinson 2000)

Bandits (of all ages) in China were akin—in purpose, constitution, organization, and methods—to modern-day terrorism: they were oppressed by the government; they were antiestablishment (e.g., local gentry) and against government (e.g., local magistrate or emperor); they sought political change by violent means, for example, redistributing wealth or returning to a Confucian state; they used terror tactics to induce fear, for example, making traveling unsafe;[18] they were well organized, for example, having charismatic leadership with loyal followings.

In Imperial China, secret societies were conspiring and organized groups that openly contested political legitimacy and secretly undermined government authority, with the use of violence and terror at the turn of the twentieth century.[19] The most famous one was the Triad Society (or "Triads"), which was formed to "resist Qing, and return to Ming" (*fan Qing, fu Ming*). By conventional standards, secret societies were consummate terrorist groups. Indeed, they were enlisted by both Sun to sabotage the Qing dynasty and by Chairman Mao to subvert the Nationalist government (DeKorne 1934 and Schram 1966).

What have we learned from this literature search about the conception of terrorism in China? There was very little serious research into terrorism in China as a domestic problem and domesticated concept.

To look at terrorism as a *domestic* problem is to recognize terrorism as a socially constructed experience (Berger and Luckmann 1996). It cautions against taking for granted how (Chinese) people think, feel, believe, and act towards terrorism, still less its history, culture, and conditions. To investigate terrorism as a domestic issue is to research how terrorism, as an imported idea, is given meaning anew in contemporary China. China "terrorism" research to date has not seen fit to question the appropriateness and utility of applying the conventional (Western) idea of terrorism to understanding associative terrorism experience in China.


## TERRORISM IN IMPERIAL CHINA

Until very recently, the term terrorism did not exist in China. Currently, the investigation, analysis, discussion, and debate over terrorism is preoccupied with contemporary and international terms of reference.[20]

In order to understand terrorism in China, we must first understand China's views on (gratuitous) violence and the idea of (cosmic) order (or *dao*). In Imperial China, all forms of gratuitous violence were frowned upon as immoral and destructive, that is, unnatural and dysfunctional (Puett 1998). Violence was considered contrary to human nature and disruptive of the cosmic order (*luan*) (Turner 1993).[21] Furthermore, the use of violence to challenge the emperor's regime, destabilize the state, harm the citizens, and disrupt social order was punished in the most serious manner. The emperor had an affirmative duty to restore the cosmic order (*tianming*) in accordance with rule of nature (*dao*) (Van der Valk 1938). Conduct seeking to undermine the legitimacy or authority of the emperor, for example, individual assassination; or disrupt the stability of the state, for example, collective violence, was strictly prohibited, resolutely deterred, and severely punished (Puett 1998). This is particularly the case with alien governance and under barbarian rulers, for example, the Northern Wei, Northern Zhou, Liao, Jurchen Chin (1115–1231),[22] Yuan, and Qing dynasties.

Terrorism was considered a crime against the state. As political violence, terrorism took on a radically different meaning in Imperial China. In Imperial China, political criminality (*zhengzhi fenzui*) was violence directed against the emperor, inducing fear and causing "chaos" (*luan*). Such kinds of violence were much feared by the emperors as being secretive and unpredictable. Emperor Sung Taizhong was reported to have said: "If there is no external threat [*waiyou*], the state must have internal trouble [*neihuan*]. External threats are only at the border and can be protected against. However those who are treacherous [*jianxie*] have no form, as internal threats, they are much to be feared! The emperor should always pay attention and be aware of this possibility."[23]

State historian Au Yangxiu, who has written an authoritative historical account of China—*Shiji*—after traveling cross the country twice, has equated external threats by barbarians as those afflicting the skins and internal attacks by hoodlums and traitors (terrorists) as those corrupting the internal organs (*fuxin zhi huan*[24]).[25]

Throughout the centuries, Chinese emperors have spared no effort to prevent such fear.

During the *Qin* dynasty, those who committed political crimes (*zhengzi fanzui*) against the emperor were punished at the minimum with death, most of them were punished with purging the clan. According to historical account, those who engaged in "wei luan"[26] (creating disorder) and "wei ni" (creating dissent)[27] are often torn apart by vehicles, before death they are subjected to "five punishment,"[28] then "yi san zu" (termination of three clan),[29] "mei qizong" (extermination of the ancestor), this often implicates thousands of households and tens of thousands of people. People who engaged in crimes of slandering (*feibang*) and heresy (*yaoyan*) against the emperor, must be punished with the most heavy penalty. Even those who disclosed the whereabouts of the emperor must be severely punished with death.[30]

Through the centuries and dynasties, political violence against the emperor took many forms, for example, from regal assassination to civil uprising to destruction of royal temples, and comes from many quarters, for example, from deprived citizens to the disaffected public to disillusioned intellectuals.[31]

However, the use of political violence against the emperor and officials, while considered illegal and generating apprehension in the ruled, might be undertaken for justifiable reasons and under the most exceptional circumstances, for example, *guan bi min fan* (people rebel as a result of oppressive officials) (Wakeman 1977). Thus, while official history might condemn individual assassins and collective violence, contemporary unofficial history and later historical records often lauded such acts as heroics and necessary in disposing a tyrant, in venting anger of the people, or in doing heaven's justice.[32] The issue of the benevolence vs. malevolence of "terror" was ever present but rarely discussed in official history of the time.[33]

As for response to political violence, as early as the Spring and Autumn (*Chunqiu* 770–475 BC) and Warring States (*Zhan guo* 475–221 BC) periods, historical records described early forms of specialized violence suppression officials called *jin bu shi* (violence suppression officials) whose functions are much like our antiterrorist units today: that is, control of violence, broadly defined.[34] Emperors took extensive precautions against assassinations and adopted draconian measures against collective violence. The imperial security system at the capital, much like that of the secret service today, made sure the emperor was well protected (Dray-Novey 1993). The comprehensive *bao-jia* system of the Qin dynasty and the elaborate spy system during the Sung era made sure that the emperor was well informed of every plot against him.[35] The spy system in the Nationalist government and the national security office in PRC helped to keep the nation harmless by perpetrating their own brands of state terrorism (Wakeman 1992).

After this brief discussion of terrorism-like political violence in Imperial China, three challenging intellectual issues present themselves. First, can terrorism as we come to know it be perpetrated by the state in China?[36] In China, "punishment" and "terror" were extended beyond the individual body to the corporate body, the blood family. This state-sponsored terror was openly conducted and explicitly endorsed, and was most rational in design and functional in operations. The emperor wanted to punish and terrorize the family because, first, geographically (isolated villages separated by great distance), organizationally (agriculture society), socially (insularity of self-sufficiency), and morally (Confucianism), China practiced collective responsibility, with family, clan, community, and nation as the respective units of accountability. Second, functionally, the family was the site of de jure and de facto education, supervision, and control. Third, both moral and practical reasons suggested that clan and family "deserve" to be punished for collective guilt; treacherous acts seldom went unnoticed and without support from intimate others living in close quarters with social and moral obligations to support each other. Fourth, revenge was expected and demanded of family members whose family members were aggrieved. Total annihilation of the blood family was considered prudent and necessary to lay to rest future threats to the emperor.

Second, can terrorism be perpetrated by "pure" speech alone? This line of inquiry suggests itself when we consider that in the learned society that was Imperial China, the power of the pen and the impact of words on the people was enormous. Speech was strictly controlled and words were meticulously vetted. Qin burned all the books, while Qing prosecuted people for speech crime. Intellectuals were viewed with much suspicion. To the emperors, dissenting intellectuals with pens were as dangerous as terrorists with guns, and were treated no less resolutely and severely, as annals of history clearly document and research of today amply suggests (Kessler 1971).[37]

> The court, ever so sensitive to slights and expression of hostility to Manchu rule, decided to deal harshly with offenders. The purported author, Chuang T'ing-lung, was dead, and so his father was arrested and thrown into a Peking jail, where he later died. When the case was closed in 1663, the father's and son's bodies were disinterred and mutilated, their families were bound over to Manchus as slaves, and their possessions were confiscated. A similar fate lay in store for all the scholars involved in preparing the history, the printer, and even some of the purchasers. Altogether seventy men were executed.[38]

Third, the remaining theoretical-conceptual issue to discuss is whether all forms of violent challenge to state authority, directly or by proxy, were deemed to be terrorist in nature. Inasmuch as the China emperor ruled his empire and governed his citizens by proxy and through the family, the family head assumes the honorific role and real functions of state. Any challenge to the family head is a challenge to the emperor, symbolically and indirectly. Philip Kuhn has called this the third realm (Huang 1993). Another scholar has described it as "more or less government" (Wong 1998). They amount to the same thing: government has coopted local communities to rule themselves. Assault on or threat to the family power structure is treated every bit as seriously as challenging the authority of the state, that is, considered one of the ten most serious crimes.[39] By this logic, terrorist acts are not only those that threatened the state/emperor but also those that intimidated the clan/family heads. Any disobedience to parents was severely dealt with by state law, family rules, and social norms.

## TERRORISM IN COMMUNIST CHINA

As observed, the concept of terrorism is new to China, but the experience of "terror" is not. Terrorism as we have come to know it in the West, as a discrete intellectual idea, scholarly concept, legal classification, cultural label, or conventional referent, was alien to China. However, the use of terror as a political instrumentality was well established and current experiences with "terror" are never too far from Chinese consciousness both as a nation and through personal experiences. Ever since the formation of the Communist Party in the 1920s, CCP members have been perpetrators and recipients of political terrors. KMT used terror tactics to purge the ranks of the CCP. The CCP resorted to terrorism—assassination and bombing—to intimidate KMT officials and destabilize the KMT government. More recently, the Cultural Revolution recalled French terror and the "Strike Hard" campaign qualified as state-sponsored terrorism in both theory and practice.

According to the official and authoritative PRC "police encyclopedia," the *Gongan baike quanshu*,[40] counterrevolutionary crime (*fan geming zui*)[41] is defined as "conduct which harmed the People's Republic of China with the purpose of over-throwing people's proletarian dictatorship and socialist system."[42]

The PRC Criminal Law (1979) provides in Article 90 that "conduct which is harmful to the People's Republic of China and done with the purpose of over-throwing the proletarian dictatorship and socialist system are all counter-revolutionary crimes." Counterrevolutionary crimes include such acts as (1) inciting people to resist and harm the implementation of state law and order and (2) use of counterrevolutionary slogans, pamphlets, and other means to incite others to overthrow the proletarian dictatorship and socialist system (The PRC Criminal Law [1979] Article 102). (Amendment III to the Criminal Law of the People's Republic of China, adopted at the 25th meeting of the Standing Committee of the Ninth National People's Congress on December 29, 2001, now provides specifically for terrorism and related offenses.) An exhaustive review of prior and existing counterrevolutionary laws, regulations, and directives is not informative on what constitutes counterrevolutionary conduct, beyond the fact that it refers to speech or conduct which is *intended* to or *in effect* was harmful to the state's political order or challenges the established government.[43]

As the police definition intimates, legal literature confirms, and case studies reveal,[44] counterrevolutionary crimes are an "intent" (in China "purpose")[45] more than a "conduct"[46] and "result" crime.[47] Thus, for the same harmful conduct, for example, personal or property damage, the existence of counterrevolutionary purpose (*mudi*)[48] separates the crime versus noncrime (*zui yu fei zui*[49]).[50] Collaterally, harmful conduct is used to demonstrate and prove the existence of counterrevolutionary motive (*dongji*) and purpose (*mudi*).[51]

In this analysis counterrevolutionary crime covers *more* than conventional terrorist conduct. *All* criminal activities, not just violent ones, that pursue a counterrevolutionary purpose, for example, distribution of antirevolutionary propaganda materials, are covered. This literal and analytical "over-coverage" should not detain us for long. It is likely that as applied, most, if not all, counterrevolutionary crimes in China are covered as terrorist conduct. First, by law, in order for a prosecution under counterrevolutionary law to be successful, it must be proven that the impact of such conduct on the social (e.g., socialist economy) and political (e.g., proletarian dictatorship) order is other than de minimis, that is, there must be substantial harm. In such cases, the conduct being prosecuted is more likely to be disruptive and threatening, if not violent or damaging.[52] Second, proving a counterrevolutionary crime requires the demonstration of "harmful" purpose and intent. In most cases only violent conduct is likely to be prosecuted and convicted.[53] In fact, a comprehensive review of pertinent PRC Criminal Law provisions covering counterrevolutionary crimes shows that most of them required the use of force to bring about damage to property, disruption to services, and harm to people.

Nevertheless, in the written law (not in practice), counterrevolutionary crime is covering *less* than conventional terrorist conduct since *only* conduct with a counterrevolutionary purpose, not all political crimes, are covered. Take the case of holding a hostage to make a demand on the PRC government to purge corruption. This falls squarely within the ambit of contemporary definitions of terrorist acts, that is, using violence to change government policy and not topple the government. Thus, only some but not all violent acts are deemed to be carried out against the state based on the written law.[54]

Doctrinally, the most authoritative statement of the nature and treatment of political violence—from revolution to terrorism—can be found in an essay written by Mao,[55] "On the Correct Handling of Contradictions among the People."[56] The intellectual foundation of the "on contradiction" doctrine was Hegel's dialectics.[57] The doctrine has been applied to justify governmental draconian anticrime measures at the expense of human rights concerns (Clarke and Feinerman 1995). In "On Contradiction" Mao taught that there are two kinds of contradictions (conflicts), one within the ranks of the people and the other between the people and the class enemy. The former can be resolved peacefully, that is, through education and punishment; the latter cannot be resolved amicably without resort to force, that is, war. Terrorism belongs to the second type of contradiction.

## DISCUSSION: POLITICAL AND SOCIAL DISSENT AS TERRORISM

How might historical Imperial conception and contemporary Communist understanding of terrorism help to shape the PRC's counterterrorism policy and practices at home? A case study of the treatment of Falun Gong (FLG) by the PRC political leadership should make clear that all challenges to China's political security and social order are considered to be terrorism, to be condemned unrelentingly and suppressed at all costs.

On April 25, 1999, FLG caught the Chinese government by surprise[58] when ten thousand of its members staged a peaceful demonstration outside the Communist party headquarters at Zhongnanhai in Beijing to demand official recognition of FLG.[59] The battle line was drawn.[60] All issues—social,[61] political,[62] economic[63]—were merged with China's past,[64] present,[65] and future,[66] sublimated into a life-and-death struggle between PRC and FLG.[67] A "perfect storm" was in the offing.[68] To the PRC authorities, FLG must be banned in China. Li Hongzhi must be purged of all influences. FLG and LHZ's followers must be reformed, at all costs and with full speed.[69]

The future of the party, if not China, hung in the balance. FLG forced the hand of the PRC government. If successful, FLG could define the PRC's political landscape and with it usher in a whole new political ideology and social relations, that is, a new relationship between party, state, and people, as well as the place of religion and society. On the eve of banning FLG, the *People's Daily* online issued an editorial rallying the party and the people to a "call to arms" in the most apocalyptic terms: "The editorial says that Party members, government officials, and the people as a whole should understand that *this is a serious ideological and political struggle* which has bearing on the fundamental beliefs of Party members, on the basic ideological foundation for the Chinese people's cause and unity, and on the future of the Party and state" (emphasis added).

On July 22, 1999, the PRC authorities, feeling the threat and fearing the worst,[70] decided to outlaw FLG and other *qigong* groups[71] as cults.[72] The government accused FLG of "spreading fallacies, hoodwinking people, inciting and creating disturbances and jeopardizing social stability."[73] Li Hongzhi (LHZ) responded by calling upon people all over the world for support and help, requesting "all governments, international organizations, and people of goodwill worldwide to extend their support and assistance to us in order to resolve the current crisis in China."[74]

On July 29, 1999, the Chinese government wanted LHZ, its putative leader, to be arrested for organizing demonstrations without first applying for permits and spreading "superstition and malicious fallacies to deceive people, resulting in the deaths of many practitioners."[75] Specifically, LHZ was blamed for spreading "superstition" and "witchery," which caused the death of 743 followers who refused medication or committed suicide.[76] China offered a reward of six thousand dollars (converted into United States dollars by the author) for the capture of LHZ.[77] China has asked various countries to bar the entry of members of LHZ, for example, the United Kingdom.[78] Since then, the PRC authorities have launched one of the most suppressive campaigns since the cultural revolution of the 1950s to purge FLG of its increasing political-subversive power and deepening social-divisive tendencies.[79]

The above case study of Falun Gong is introduced here to show that for the Chinese government of today, just as in the past, "terrorism" includes any reactionary activities that are intended to, or have the effect of, challenging the "mandate of heaven" and disrupting the "cosmic order."

## CONCLUSIONS

This chapter began with an observation that the effort to treat terrorism as a uniform set of human experiences and a universal conceptual category ill serves the purpose of academics and practitioners in the quest to understand and fight terrorism. Rather, it is suggested that a true understanding of terrorism must necessarily develop insights into cultural origin and development, law, causation and remedy, impact, and implications. This is especially true in the cases of China and other non-Western countries where people do not share the same history and values.[80] In order to understand terrorism in China on its own terms there is a need to investigate terrorism-like activities in local context and with local perspective; in practical terms, how "terrorism" originated indigenously and developed historically in (Imperial) China. This entails the study of history, culture, and above all else philosophy. In the case of China, the ideas and the ideal of Confucius are critical; specifically, how China and the Chinese view order, violence, and control.

This chapter shows that the concept of terrorism, as conventionally understood in the West, did not exist in Imperial China. The Western concept of terrorism is not able to adequately capture the essence and characteristics of what terrorism is in the Eastern or Chinese sense. Western ideas and philosophies are alien to the East and, therefore, cannot fully account for the experience and discourse to accurately communicate the specificity and nuance of terrorism-like "political violence" in historical China. On the one hand, the idea of terrorism includes much more, for example, state terrorism; on the other, much less, for example, clan violence. Additionally, it accentuates some aspects, for example, terror on innocence, at the expense of others, for example, terror on parents. Finally, it is understood analytically and logically, that is, the constitution of the violent act, more than being appreciated intuitively and emotively, that is, the total effect of the phenomenon on people, society, and cosmos.[81] Some of the inadequacies of the conventional terrorism label in capturing the Chinese experience are summarized below.

First, as an agriculture society China sought order, stability, continuity, and above all else, harmony (Wright 1953). Thus, Confucian ethics taught that conflicts are to be avoided and violence condemned (Wall and Blum 1999).[82] The former is a precursor of the second. The second is a consequence, a reinforcer, and a regenerator of the first. Both have a tendency to disturb established social relationships (*wunlun*)[83] and if left unchecked rupture (*luan*) the preordained cosmic order (*dao*), which take years to establish and still more time to rehabilitate. Thousands of years of Confucian education were successful in fostering a culture, creating a custom, and developing a personality that equates conflicts with "bad" and violence with "evil" at a cognitive and emotive level. Thus, people were taught to avoid conflicts at all cost, even if they were in the right. Violence was found to be objectionable. It was prosecuted (violence versus threat versus terror) regardless of who it was directed against (emperor, officials, parents, peers) and whatever the impact (physical injury versus psychological harm). There were few attempts to discriminate one type of conflict and violence from another. Every effort was made to avoid conflict and suppress violence individually, collectively, and nationally. The focus is on maintaining peace and order, not discriminating causes, for example, judging the state of "cosmic order" (Hsu 1970) and entitlement to the "mandate of heaven." Thus, emperor and officials were equally to be blamed for natural disasters and human upheaval.

Second, like other countries, old and new, East and West, political violence, of which "terrorism" is a species, did exist in China in abundance (Perry 1984), for example, assassination, banditry (Tiedemann 1982; Billingsley 1981), secret society activities,[84] and peasant rebellion (Harrison 1965). These violent acts were found to be particularly odious because they were secretly organized and openly challenged the emperor's authority and legitimacy. To a Confucius scholar and by extension the sage ruler, they were acts of disloyalty and signs of chaos (*luan*), both affronts to the emperor's mandate to rule. Here again it matters not how political violence was perpetrated, for example, slandering versus assassinating versus rebellion. What matters is that the emperor's authority must be reestablished, *luan* quelled, and the mandate from heaven restored.

Third, terrorism is the instrumental use and strategic employment of threat, violence, or terror to achieve political—regime change or policy reform—objectives. Terrorism, as an instrumental use of violence, has no place in Chinese ethical and jurisprudential thought. The instrumental use of violence is frowned upon and thus treated as barbaric and animalistic, that is, Chinese ethics have no principles of the end justifying the means.[85] The use of violence as a means to achieve political ends makes the perpetrator as morally apprehensible as the oppressive government he or she attempts to remove.

The strategy of using violence will likely fail, in principle if not in practice. The way to reform government and change policy is through adherence to Confucian ethics and the use of moral reasoning, starting with appealing to higher moral principles and setting a good personal example. Fighting violence with violence is not recommended,[86] and not likely to succeed or prevail. People were taught not to bend to raw power but to succumb to sound reason.

Fourth, one of the characteristics of terrorism is the indiscriminate killing of innocent people to promote fear and terror. This would not happen in Imperial China for two reasons, one philosophical, the other practical. First, philosophically, killing indiscriminately or terrorizing innocent people was ipso facto not reasonable, however noble the cause, that is, it was against *qing* and *li* in China.[87] Second, practically, China was a nondemocratic (autocratic) country,[88] and there was no point in attacking civilians, since they have no say over the conduct of the emperor. Nor would the emperor yield in the face of the slaughtering or terrorizing of his civilians for three reasons. It is morally wrong to negotiate on matters of governance principle. It is also morally wrong for the learned and educated (*zhunzi*) to defer to and make concession to the uncultivated and uneducated (*xiaoren*).[89] It is also unimaginable for the emperor/parent to negotiate with citizens/subordinates.

Fifth, there was no state terrorism in paternalistic China (Ling 1994). In accordance with Confucian teachings the state is built upon a family model.[90] The relationship between emperor/office and citizens/charges was, and still is, that that exists between father and sons. Sons have to show respect and demonstrate loyalty to familial authority figures, from parents to officials to emperor. The family authority figures have a moral duty to ensure the best interests of the children, for example, food, shelter, and education. Thus when citizens challenge the state—from dissenting to resisting to rebelling—the state has the authority and duty to react in a most violent manner. This is not considered state terrorism. This is viewed as the state performing its moral duty. If the citizens misbehave they can hardly blame the state for acting "violently" against their misconduct, seeking a return to the right path or *dao*.

Sixth, the Western concept of terrorism is also not able to make allowance for good "political violence" (Reid 1923).[91] The only proper course and effective measure by the oppressed people against the abusive state (or a nonbenevolent [*buren*] emperor) was to engage in *righteous* political resistance, from assassination to rebellion, in a *last-ditch effort* to return the country to the prescribed and preordained heavenly way. The aim was never to overthrow the emperor but to return the throne to proper "heavenly" authority. Viewed in this light, they are righteous acts of violence to correct violations of the heavenly mandate and not illegal, still less immoral, terrorism acts to disturb the cosmic order.[92] The "terrorist" act that challenges the emperor resulting in cosmic disorder is brought on by the emperor, manifesting heavenly displeasure and a sure sign of the emperor having lost his mandate from heaven: in modern terms, a denial of political legitimacy. In order for such resistance to be recognized as legitimate, the resisters must be righteous in their cause and proper with means. Conversely, violence used to press the rulers to conform to the cosmic order and return to heavenly (benevolent) rule is deemed as understandable, if not indeed justifiable (Crowell 1983)[93] and necessary (Thaxton 1977).[94] Years later, Mao has justified such grassroots peasant rebellions as examples of class wars, considering them present-day freedom fighters rather than terrorists. In the ultimate analysis, the use of violence for or against the emperor in China must be evaluated against a fixed moral universe and universal ethical precepts espoused by Confucius and enshrined within Confucian teachings.

To conclude and reiterate, since the beginning of the Republic (1949 to 1959) and up through the economic reform period (1979 to now), the preoccupation of the Communist leadership has been with ensuring security (to defend the "mandate from heaven") and achieving stability (to maintain "cosmic order"). Conceptually, terrorism, as we come to know it in the West, did not gain a foothold in the leadership's thinking. "Terrorism," as threat to political security and social stability, was treated just like any other destabilizing acts, that is, treated as contradictions between the people and an enemy of the state. Conversely, all political dissent and social unrest having the potential to disrupt party rule is considered terrorist-like. As observed, this indiscriminate way of thinking about political-social "violence" is traceable to China's past, where the emperor ruled absolutely and resolutely with a mandate from heaven in maintaining a cosmic order against all challenges.

## NOTES

1. "Anti-terrorism should be vigilant over nuclear and bio-chemical attacks"—dis-
..us ion with expert on third anniversary of 9/11 [Fankong xuyaogaodu jingti he xiji he zhenghua xij—911 sannian zhuanjia tan,反恐需要高度警惕核袭击和生化袭击—"911" 三周年专家访谈], September 9, 2004, http://www.people.com.cn/GB/junshi/1078/2773574.html. (In support of his analysis and assertion that the concept of terrorism is both porous and relative, Rong, a respected military expert and sought-after media commentator, observed that in World War II, the indiscriminate bombing of London by Germany was considered an act of terrorism, whereas the carpet bombing of major cities in Germany was justified as self-defense.)
2. Wang (王逸舟), "China scholars should have their own definition for terrorism" [Zhongguo xuezhe yingdong you zhiji de kongbu zhuyi ding yi—

中国学者应当有自己的恐怖主义定义], January 23, 2002. The author argued against a Western approach to the conceptualization of terrorism in favor of an indigenous one. There are two opposing schools of thought on defining terrorism in China. The first school was represented by Li Xiaojun of Chinese Social Science Academy. He has defined terrorism as the use of organized violence or a threat of violence to harm or intimidate unarmed people for political purposes. See *Revelations of International Safety* [Guoji anquan shilu] (Jincheng chubanseh, 1997), 246. The second school was represented by Li Dongyin of the Global Economic Research Institute. See *Confrontation between good and evil* [Zhengyi yu xir e de jioaliang] (Beijing: Zhongguo shehui kexue Chubanshe, 1997), 71, 91. He observed that terrorism is not determined by legal principles but ideology (yishi xingtai), values (jiashi), and feelings (genqing). Available at "Introduction to international politics," reading materials (Guoji zhengzhi gailun, Yuedu cailiao; 国际政治概论 阅读材料), http://www.sis.pku.edu.cn/wanglian/reading/reading.htm.

3. "History of Terrorism," Terrorism Files, http://www.terrorismfiles.org/encyclopaedia/history_of_terrorism.html.

4. Ibid.

5. "The Global War on Terrorism: The First 100 Days," White House, http://www.whitehouse.gov/news/releases/2001/12/100dayreport.html.

6. For an excellent discussion of the difficulties of and issues with defining terrorism from a Western perspective, see Best and Nocella (2004). For a discussion of definition issues from an Islamic perspective, see Ayatullah Shaykh Muhammad 'Ali Taskhiri (1987). For a UN approach, see "Definitions of Terrorism," United Nations Office for Drug Control and Crime Prevention. For a discussion of the problems and impact of defining terrorism in the international arena, see Peter Weise (2002).

7. A 1988 army report came up with 100 definitions for terrorism.

8. ProQuest (August 25, 2005), criminal justice data set. A confirmation with a web search of Wilson Web with the keywords China and terrorism yield 130 items. Only one is a peer-reviewed article related to China terrorism (Wang [2003]).

9. Ibid., abstract.

10. Project Muse Political Science Journals (October 5, 2005).

11. http://www.nixoncenter.org/publications/monographs/US-ChinaRelations 2003Intro.pdf (accessed July 12, 2004), cited at note 6, Xinbo Wu, "The Promise and Limitations of a Sino-U.S. Partnership," *The Washington Quarterly* 27(4), Autumn 2004, 115–26.

12. 9/11 allowed the PRC to suppress Xinjiang separatist aspirations of the Xinjiang-Uighur Autonomous Region (XUAR) and independence claims of the ethnic Uighur community in the name of fighting terrorism.

13. Lexis Nexis Academic Universe (October 7, 2005).

14. Search function adjusted to China and terrorism appearing within same paragraph.

15. Bandits were variously called *dao* and *zei*, see *Hanyu dacidian*, vol. 7, 1431–32, and vol. 10, 183, respectively.

16. James W. Tong, *Disorder under Heaven: Collective Violence in the Ming Dynasty* (Stanford, CA: Stanford University Press, 1991); Elizabeth Perry, *Rebellion and*

*Revolution in North China, 1845–1945* (Stanford, CA: Stanford University Press, 1980) and Esherick, *The Origins of the Boxer Uprising* (Berkeley: University of California Press, 1987), chapter 2.

17. Terrorism is the premeditated use of threat of symbolic and low-level violence by a conspiratorial group for political purpose against the state [379].

18. The pirates in the seventeenth century used flags to announce their presence and induce fear in their victim, so that they could achieve their piracy without a fight (http://www.kipar.org/piratical-resources/pirate-flags.html). In the 400s the bandits in China build up a reputation of ruthlessness to effect their exploits. For example, the "whistling arrow bandits" (*xiangmazei*, commonly abbreviated to *xiangma*) attached bells to their mounts or used whistling arrows when they raided. Ibid., 529.

19. David Ownby, "Recent Chinese Scholarship on the History of Chinese Secret Societies," *Late Imperial China* 22(1) (2001), 139–58. David Ownby, *Brotherhoods and Secret Societies in Early Qing China: The Formation of a Tradition* (Stanford, CA: Stanford University Press, 1996). Jean Chesneaux, *Secret Societies in China in the Nineteenth and Twentieth Centuries*, tr. Gillian Nettle (Ann Arbor: University of Michigan Press, 1971) and Jean Chesneaux, ed., *Popular Movements and Secret Societies in China, 1840–1950* (Stanford, CA: Stanford University Press, 1972).

20. "Literature review," in *Contemporary terrorism and response* [Dangdai shijia kongbu zhuyi yu duice], ed. Hu Lianhe (Beijing: Dongfang Chubanshe, 2001), 2–11.

21. This is contra distinctive from Hobbes who assumed that the nature of man is self-interested and barbaric and that nature is chaotic and disorderly, where man eats man. Hobbes, *Leviathan* (1660), especially chapters 13 to 24, http://www.orst.edu/instruct/phl302/texts/hobbes/leviathan-contents.html. In "Luxing," it was said that people are born to peace only to have disorder imposed on them by evildoers. As a result the five punishments were established. *Book of History* (Shangshu' Henan Chubanshe, 1996), 264–80 ("Minister Lu on Punishment"). See also Puett (1998).

22. Tao (1970) notes that as an alien ruler from a lesser (barbaric) culture, the Chin emperor has to walk on thin ice to come to terms with China's high culture and Confucian officialdoms. The Juren emperors resorted to violence and terror to bring Chinese (Han) officials to their knees, for example, in one case eight officials were executed and thirty-four were banished for engaging in factional activities.

23. Zhu Shaohou, *Zhongguo gudai zhian zhidu shi* [A history of ancient China public security system] (Henan: Henan daxue chubanshe, 1994), 446.

24. Literally, "disease in one's vital organ," that is, serious hidden trouble. *The Pinyin Chinese-English Dictionary* (Hong Kong: Commercial Press, 1979), 766L.

25. Zhu Shaohou, *Zhongguo gudai zhian zhidu shi* [A history of ancient China public security system] (Henan: Henan daxue chubanshe, 1994), 447.

26. *Luan* literally means public disorder or loss of control as a state of affair, both of which implicate the emperor's capacity and legitimacy to rule. *Hangyu Dacidian* (Shanghai: Hangyu Dacidian, 1994), vol. 1, 797R.

27. *Ni* liberally means contrary, here being contrary to order and regulation. *Hangyu Dacidian* (Shanghai: Hangyu Dacidian, 1994), vol. 10, 823R.

28. *Wun xing* are the five chief forms of punishment, torture really, in ancient China, being tattooing the face, cutting off the nose, cutting off the feet, castration,

and decapitation. *The Pinyin Chinese-English Dictionary* (Hong Kong: Commercial Press, 1979), 731R. *Wuxing* is a serious punishment not only because it is painful but also because it is humiliating to the person and a loss of face to the family. In the text of *Xiaojing. Kaizhong Mingyi* [Filial piety. Making clear the principle in the beginning] it is said: "Shenti fafu, shou zhi fulwu, bugan huishang, yao zhi shi ya" ("The body and its associate parts [hair and skin] are given by the parents, dare not harm. This is the beginning of filial piety.") In essence the body is a family trust. This conception of "body politics" is to have grave implications on Chinese social control strategy and policy.

29. The three clans being the offender's family, his mother, and his wife.

30. Zhu Shaohou, *Zhongguo gudai zhian zhidu shi* [A history of ancient China public security system] (Henan: Henan daxue chubanshe, 1994), 93.

31. Joseph W. Esherick, "Symposium on Peasant Rebellions: Some Introductory Comments," *Modern China* 9(3) (1983), 275–84. (Throughout history, e.g., six dynasties, oppressed peasants, social bandits, and powerful warlords with legitimate grievances challenged the central authority with all the means at their disposal.)

32. Ching-Yueh Yen, "Crime in Relation to Social Change in China," *The American Journal of Sociology* 40(3) (1934), 298–308. (Bandits organized themselves to "execute the will of God by killing the wicked rich and saving the honest poor." They were fighting the soldiers as "official bandits.")

33. R. G. Tiedemann, "The Persistence of Banditry: Incidents in Border Districts of the North China Plain," *Modern China* 8(4), 395–433. (Banditry lived on the fringe of Chinese rural society and "exists at the fringe of history" [395]. Local officials had little incentive to report such incidences, which reflected poorly on their administration [396].)

34. *Zhongguo jincha zhidu jianlun* (Bejing: Qunzhong chubanhe, 1985).

35. The *baojia* system was used by Japan during its colonization of Japan to spy on residents (see Chen 1975).

36. From antiquity, the utility and legitimacy of the state to use violence to suppress violence—from punishment to warfare—has never been questioned, and in fact was considered a duty of a sage emperor. The issue was on its proper—purpose and degree—use. Puett (1998) states, "What is the purpose of making armor, shields, and the five weapons? It is done in order to restrain robbers, disorderly elements, bandits, and thieves" (citing Maozi). It is important to note that the Chinese considered state-sponsored violence (or organized violence) as a continuum to be deployed as appropriate in response to challenges to authority or disruption of order. Emperors and officials were cautioned against arbitrary, gratuitous, and excessive use of violence, but certain kinds or degrees were never objected to as "cruel and unusual." The idea of proportionality—an eye for an eye—was also missing. For example, Shangyang, putative father of legalist school, proposed the use of heavy punishment for minor offenses in order to hold off bigger harm to come. Cheng Liangshu, *Shangyang and his school of thought* [Shangyang ji qi Xuepei] (Taiwan: Taiwan Xuesheng shuju, 1988), 284. "Moreover, if you use war to get rid of war, even war is acceptable; if you use killing to get rid of war, even killing is acceptable; if you use punishment to get rid of (the need for) punishment, even punishing is acceptable" ("Shangjunshu, Huace").

37. In the Shun-chih period, the northern Chinese degree and office holder cooperated with the Qing emperor in purging the ranks of the southern intellectuals and scholars. For example, in 1661, Chuang T'ing-lung suffered the most egregious literary inquisition for having adding to existing Ming history.

38. Ibid.

39. Geoffrey MacCormack, "On the Pre-Tang Development of the Law of 'Treason': moufan, dani and pan," http://jalh.ku.edu/article/maccormack2005.pdf. The three most heinous crimes, called abominable, in the Han Code were plotting rebellion (*moufan*), sedition (*dani*), and rebellion (*pan*). *Buxiao* (不孝 'lack of filial piety') made the list of ten most abominable crimes, at eight.

40. The newest edition is: Editorial committee, *Zhongguo gongan da baike quanshu* [China police large encyclopedia], two volumes (Jinlin: Jilin Chubanshe, 2000).

41. The idea of counterrevolutionary crime originated in Russia in 1911.

42. Editorial committee, Zhongguo gongan baike quanshu [China police encyclopedia] (Jinlin: Jilin Chubanshe, 1989), 350R.

43. See, for example, "Zhongguo Renmin Zhengzhi Xieshang Huiyi Gongtong Ganlin" [The Chinese People's Political Consultative Conference Common Program], promulgated on September 29, 1949, article 7; PRC Constitution, promulgated on September 20, 1954, article 19; Zhengwuyuan, Zuigao Renmin Fayuan, "Guanyu Zhenya Fangeming Huodong de Zhishi" [Government Administrative Council and Supreme People's Court, "Directive on the suppression of counterrevolutionaries"], promulgated on July 23, 1950; Zhonghua Renmin Gongheguo Zhenzhi Fangemin Tiao Li [PRC punishment of counterrevolutionary regulations], promulgated on Feb. 20, 1951, article 2; Zhongyang Sifabu, "Guanyu Eba, Guanfei, Bufa Dizhu Ruhe Shiyong Zhenzhi Fangemin Tiaoli Pifu" [Party Central Judicial Department, "Reply regarding how to apply punishment of counterrevolutionary regulations to local tyrant, habitual criminals, and illegal landlord"], promulgated in 1951; Zhongyang Xiren Xiaozu, "Guanyu Fangeming-fenzi he Qita Huaifenzi de Jieshi ji Chuli de Zhengce Jiexian de Zanxing Guiding" [Party Central Party of Ten Committee, "Temporary regulations regarding policy and limits on explaining and handling of counterrevolutionary elements and other bad elements], promulgated March 3, 1956; Zhonggong Zhongyang Xiren Xiaozu Dui, "Guanyu Fangeming-fenzi he Qita Huaifenzi de Jieshi ji Chuli de Zhengce Jiexian de Zanxing Guiding" de Buchong [Communist Party Central Party of Ten Committee, "Supplement to temporary regulations regarding policy and limits on explaining and handling of counterrevolutionary elements and other bad elements], promulgated June 24, 1957 (counterrevolutionary damages mean causing damage with counterrevolutionary intent and purpose); Renmin Gongan Pianweihui Guanyu Zhongyang Xiren Xiaozu, "Guanyu Fangeming-fenzi he Qita Huaifenzi de Jieshi ji Chuli de Zhengce Jiexian de Zanxing Guiding" de Buchong Jieshi Zhong Yixie Wenti de Jieda [PRC Organizing Committee, "Answers to certain questions on supplementary explanation regarding temporary regulations regarding policy and limits on explaining and handling of counterrevolutionary elements and other bad elements"), promulgated 1957 (contemporary counterrevolutionary elements means people who spread reactionary pamphlets with counterrevolutionary in-

tent); Zhongyang Xiren Xiaozu, "Guanyu Putong Fangemin Fenzi ji Qita Fandong Fenzi de Jieshi" [Committee of Ten from Party Central, "Explanation regarding common counterrevolutionary elements and other reactionary elements"], November 1957 (counterrevolutionary elements are people who insist upon their reactionary class viewpoint); Zhongyang Zhengfa Xiaozu, "Guanyu Xinde Fangeming Fanzui Xingwei de Jiexian" [Party Central Political-legal Committee, "Regarding the classification of Counter-revolutionary Elements"] (1962) (people who are merely critical of the party or government policy or implementation are not counterrevolutionary); Zuigao Renmin Jianchayuan, *Xingshifanzui Anli Conshu (Fanfeminzui)* [Book on Criminal Cases (Counter-revolutionary Crimes)] (Beijing: Zhongguo Jiancha Chubanshe, 1990), 269–311.

44. Zui gao renmin jiancha yuan "xingshifanzui anli congshu" bianwei hui [Supreme People's Procuracy "Crime cases series" editorial committee], *Xingshifanzui anli congshu* [Crime cases series] (Beijing: Zhongguo jiancha chubanshe, 1990).

45. A "purpose" (*mudi*) crime is one that punishes people for motive and purpose. It is similar to the common law basic intent vs. ulterior intent distinction, for example, burglary—breaking and entering of others' premises at night with the intent of committing a felony therein.

46. A "conduct" (*xingwei*) crime is one which punishes certain conduct, irrespective of the result intended, for example, perjury.

47. A "result" (*youguo*) crime is one which punishes the result, for example, murder. However, the war separating "intent" and "result" crime is not as firm and insular as it might first appear. This is so for two reasons. First, because intention cannot be judged by one action and action is most evident with its impact and consequences. The "result" of the action speaks to the intent of the actor, both as direct and circumstantial evidence. Direct because one is charged with the natural consequence of one's act. Word is not more than action. Circumstantial because of how one's intent might be explained given a certain action. Actions speak louder than words. Second, even if one does not intend one's action, the result of the act is all the same. People are responsible for serious harm to society, a reckless type of attribution of responsibility.

48. The PRC criminal law jurisprudence does not draw a clear distinction between intent (*yitu* or *zuiyi*), purpose (*mudi*), and motive (*dongji*) in the finding of guilt and imposing of punishment. It is embraced by the term *fanzui zhuguan*, subjective mental condition (*xinli zhuangkuang*). Editorial Committee, *Faguan shouce* [Judges handbook] (Sangxi: Shangxi renmin chubanshe, 1995), 51. PRC legal scholars do draw an analytical distinction between *fanzui mudi* (criminal purpose) and *fanzui donji* in that *mudi* is precipitated by *dongji*. Ibid., 55. In common-law jurisdiction, only intent is the mental state (*mens rea*) that needs to be proven. Intent is usually defined as "knowingly" and "purposely." Motive is considered irrelevant as a legal principle or immaterial as evidentiary proof. However, increasingly and by statute, motive is being considered as important in the Anglo-American jurisprudence, for example, hate crime with racial animus.

49. The *zui yu fei zui* is an analytical, rhetorical, and instructional device to highlight the main differences between one crime and another, especially as interpreted

and applied. This is usually done by comparing two similar cases along critical dimensions (in counterrevolutionary crimes, the issue of intent).

50. Editorial committee, *Zhongguo gongan baike quanshu* [China police encyclopedia] (Jinlin: Jilin Chubanshe, 1989), 351L. *Fen ge ming mudi* (counterrevolutionary purpose or intent) is defined as "with the purpose of overthrowing people's proletarian dictatorship and socialist system, is an important element constituting counterrevolutionary crime, is a distinction between counter-revolutionary crime, counter-revolutionary and other crime."

51. Editorial committee, *Zhongguo gongan baike quanshu* [China police encyclopedia] (Jinlin: Jilin Chubanshe, 1989), 351L. *Fen ge ming mudi* (counterrevolutionary purpose or intent) is defined as "we can ascertain the purpose of perpetrator by looking at the counter-revolutionary conduct and effect in practice."

52. Editorial Committee, *Gaguan shouce* [Judges handbook] (Shangxi: Shangxi renmin chubanshe, 1995), 75.

53. Editorial committee, *Zhongguo gongan baike quanshu* [China police encyclopedia] (Jinlin: Jilin Chubanshe, 1989), 351L. *Fen ge ming mudi* (counterrevolutionary purpose or intent) is defined as "we can ascertain the purpose of perpetrator can by looking at the counterrevolutionary conduct and effect in practice."

54. In order for one to survive this argument, one can adopt a broader and more inclusive definition of counterrevolutionary crime in arguing that anytime *violence* is used *contrary to law* in order to change state policy and practices, even if legitimate and ill-advised, it is deemed to be ipso facto counterrevolution in effect. This argument stretches counterrevolutionary acts to include violent conduct seeking to change policy and practices that are themselves illegal, improper, and otherwise disapproved by the PRC.

55. As a consummate military strategist in guerrilla warfare, Mao was the quintessential terrorist par excellence, one who looked upon violence as a means not an end, in service of a larger cause.

56. From the *Selected Works of Mao Tse-tung* (Peking: Foreign Languages Press, 1977), vol. V, 384–421.

57. "On Contradiction," August 1937, http://www.marxists.org/reference/archive/mao/selected-works/volume-1/mswv1_17.htm.

58. On the one hand, the PRC leadership was taken by surprise by the ability of LHZ and capacity of FLG, and the audacity of both, to gather ten thousand FLG members in front of Zhongnanhai on such short order, and in such an organized and disciplined way ("Falun Gong Used Internet to Mobilize Demonstration," *Hong Kong Voice of Democracy*, May 14, 1999). On the other hand, the PRC leadership was much concerned and very disturbed by the inability of its security people to be forewarned about the April 25, 1999, incident. This is particularly annoying when PRC public security was known for its ability to keep abreast of the latest political challenges and dissentions in the nation. Francesco Sisci, "FALUNGONG Part 2: A rude awakening," *Asia Times Online*, http://www.atimes.com/china/CA30Ad01.html. (The fact that the security system was taken completely by surprise was a major blow to the leadership. This time it was a peaceful demonstration. Next time would it be re-

bellion against the government?) Otherwise, the PRC were fully aware of the ongoing struggle with FLG which has been going on for three years since the 1990s, when the PRC leadership orchestrated an attack on FLG and other less-than-wholesome *qigong* groups. Shiyu Zhou, PhD, "Why Persecute Falun Gong?" http://www.faluninfo .net/devstories/why/why_ persecute.asp. ("From the written attacks that begun during the Guangming Daily incident in June 1996 to the mobilization of police and use of violence in Tianjin in April 1999, the development and escalation of the Falun Gong persecution actually happened over a period of three or four years.")

59. "Falun Gong Followers Stage the Largest Protest in Beijing since 1989," *Hong Kong Voice of Democracy*, April 26, 1999, http://www.democracy.org.hk/EN/ apr1999/mainlnd_15.htm. ("About 10,000 followers of Falun Gong [Law Wheel Exercise], a Taoist-Buddhist Qi-gong sect, staged a demonstration at Zhongnanhai, the headquarters of the Chinese government, on April 25, 1999 to demand the right to practice qi-gong (a traditional Chinese meditation exercise). This is the largest demonstration in Beijing since the 1989 democratic movement, which began in the same month 10 years ago. Premier Zhu Rong-ji received the representatives of the demonstrators and discussed their demands for two hours. The demonstrators dispersed in the evening after 16 hours of silent protest.")

60. For a brief summary of actions taken by the PRC to ban FLG see "Zhonggong chuti Falun Gong" [Communists banned FLG], *Hong Kong Economic Journal*, July 28, 1999.

61. "Crackdown shows Communist Party cracks," *Asia Times Online*, July 24, 1999, http://www.atimes.com/china/AG24Ad01.html. ("The collapse of the ideological basis for communist rule in the rush towards a free-market economy has left a *spiritual void*. . . . Sect members incorporate healing techniques based on 'qi gong,' the traditional Chinese teaching of cultivating human energy. They do early morning exercises that aid meditation to improve physical and spiritual health and say the sect can help lead China to become a *more moral society*. . . . Most followers of Falun Gong come from the bottom rungs of society—retired women, workers, officials and many peasants." Emphasis added).

62. FLG raises a number of difficult political problems for the PRC government and CCP. The two most prominent ones are, first, whether FLG is being used by foreign governments to destabilized China. "China, Falun Gong and the politics of economic depression," STRATFOR's Global Intelligence Update, Weekly Analysis, July 26, 1999, *Asia Times Online*, http://www.atimes.com/asia-crisis/AG27Db01.html. ("The common denominator is that the United States is using issues like human rights to increase its control over the evolution of events in China. Falun Gong, whose leader Li Hongzhi lives in New York, is seen as part of this strategy.") Second, whether LHZ is using FLG to challenge the legal authority of the PRC government or political legitimacy of CCP. See "Party paper links Falun Gong politics to anti-China forces," BBC Monitoring, Jan. 7, 2001. Reprint in *Apologetics Research Resources*, http://www.gospelcom.net/apologeticsindex/news1/an010108.html#2.

63. "China, Falun Gong and the politics of economic depression," STRATFOR's Global Intelligence Update, Weekly Analysis, July 26, 1999, *Asia Times Online*,

http://www.atimes.com/asia-crisis/AG27Db01.html. ("The crackdown on Falun Gong expresses Beijing's deep-seated insecurity. If China's economy can't recover, can the regime survive?")

64. See David Ownby, "Falungong as a Cultural Revitalization Movement: An Historian Looks at Contemporary China," www.ruf.rice.edu/~tnchina/commentary/ownby1000.html. ("In my opinion, the Falungong, or the Qigong movement as a whole, are contemporary reincarnations, with numerous and important alterations of a popular religious tradition, or a number of related traditions, that date back in their organized form to the middle of the Ming Dynasty.") For an opposing view, see Michael Lestz, "Why Smash the Falun Gong?" *Religion in the News* 2(3) (Fall 1999), http://www.trincoll.edu/depts/csrpl/RINVol2No3/Falun%20Gong.htm. (China takes on FLG less for historical reasons—from political fear of White Lotus and Boxers to ideological objections to feudalism—than because of a lack of tolerance of antagonistic sects.)

65. Suppression of FLG was considered necessary and important to maintain stability in society to further economic development in the country. See "Senior CPC Official on Falun Gong Prohibition," *People's Daily Online*, July 24, 1999, http://english.peopledaily.com.cn/special/fagong/1999072400A104.html. ("This is an important decision of the CPC Central Committee, and it is of great significance for the building of the Party, the enhancement of the cohesive and combat strength of the Party, and the maintenance of China's reform, development and stability.")

66. See "People's Daily Editorial on Falun Gong Ban," *People's Daily*, July 23, 1999. ("The editorial says that Party members, government officials, and the people as a whole should understand that this is a serious ideological and political struggle which has bearing on the fundamental beliefs of Party members, on the basic ideological foundation for the Chinese people's cause and unity, and on the future of the Party and state."). See also Erick Eckholm, "China Says Its Future Depends on Routing Banned Spiritual Movement," *New York Times* online, November 6, 1999.

67. One of the more informed, reflective, and thoughtful analyses answering the question of why the PRC acted to suppress FLG can be found at "China, Falun Gong and the politics of economic depression," STRATFOR's Global Intelligence Update, Weekly Analysis, July 26, 1999, *Asia Times Online*, http://www.atimes.com/asia-crisis/AG27Db01.html.

68. In October of 1991 a storm stronger than any in recorded history hit the coast off of Gloucester, Massachusetts. This "perfect storm"—so called because it was three storms combined into one—created an almost apocalyptic situation in the Atlantic Ocean, where boats encountered waves of 100 feet (30 meters), the equivalent of a ten-story building. These storms are some of the strongest and most terrifying manifestations of nature's strength. Later the "perfect storm" was made into a movie and released by Warner Brothers in 2000 (http://perfectstorm.warnerbros.com/cmp/flash-thefilm-fr.html).

69. See "Senior CPC Official on Falun Gong Prohibition," *People's Daily Online*, July 24, 1999, http://english.peopledaily.com.cn/special/fagong/1999072400A104.html. (Party members and private citizens should absolutely and resolutely abide by the law and expose FLG for what it is.)

70. Reuters, "China Says Falun Gong Aims to Replace Governmen," *People's Daily*: ("Li Hongzhi deceives the people to deify himself and he deifies himself in a scheme to take the place of the government and rule the world," July 28, 1999. http://www.uygur.org/enorg/wunn99/990729e.htm [visited Aug. 10, 2001]).

71. FLG was banned under Regulations on Registering and Managing Mass Organizations, which provided that mass organizations have to be registered, must abide by China's constitution, laws, regulations, and policies, and should not violate the fundamental principles of the constitution or jeopardize the interests of the nation and people or of other organizations. It was the position of the PRC government that Falun Data Research Society and the FLG had not gotten the approval of government departments and were not registered and were, therefore, illegal. See "Chinese Official Says Falun Gong Ban Follows Chinese Law," *People's Daily Online*, July 24, 1999, http://english.peopledaily.com.cn/special/fagong/1999072400B101.html. FLG is not the only group being outlawed, for example, equally popular Zhong Gong was banned. See, on Zhong Gong, Charles Hutzler, "China Moves against Exercise Group," *Associated Press*, January 31, 2000, http://www.cesnur.org/testi/falun 032.htm#Anchor-14210 (visited June 1, 2001). (Both Falun Gong and Zhong Gong followers practice *qigong* to promote better health and attain supernatural powers. Falun Gong adds a spiritual dimension, that is, it claims to be able to improve morality. Zhong Gong, founded in 1988, has attracted 20 million followers. In 1992, on the advice of Hubei province's Communist Party secretary, Chinese president Jiang Zemin consulted senior Zhong Gong master Zhang Chongping to try to cure his arthritis and back problems. By the time it was banned, the group had more than one thousand propagation centers in China and more than 180,000 practice coaches.) Many other registered and unregistered *qigong* were operating in China during this period of *qigong* resurgence, that is, between 1987 and 1992. Purportedly, three thousand registered groups operated before 1998 under that aegis of the Qigong Science Research Society. The Chinese government encouraged the growth of qigong as a unique cultural asset and health promotion system, starting in the 1980s. Unregistered groups include Qing Yang and Tain Tang Baolian qigong groups operating in Liaoning Province between 1993 and 1998. Qing Yang and Tain Tang Baolian qigong groups are listed in the Amnesty International list of targeted groups (March 2000). Qigong groups listed in the report, besides Falun Gong and Zhong Gong, included Guo Gong [nation gong] and Cibei Gong [compassion gong]. Guo Gong emerged in reports in November 1999, with the arrest of alleged leaders in Sichuan Province, founder given as Liu Jineng. Cibei Gong was reported after the arrest of the alleged founder, Xiao Yun, in Wuhan city, Hunan Province, on September 8, 1999.

72. See "Full text of New Chinese Legislative Resolution Banning Cults," CESNUR, http://www.cesnur.org/testi/falun_005.htm. "Official Guidelines for Enforcement: "Judicial explanations on crimes by cults," *China Daily*, Nov. 1, 1999, http://www .cesnur.org/testi/falun_005.htm#Anchor-MI33.

73. For a comprehensive treatment of *People's Daily* news reports on PRC government's positions on and treatment of FLG, LHZ, see "China Bans Falun Gong," *People's Daily Online*, http://english.peopledaily.com.cn/special/fagong/all.html

(visited October 6, 2002). The series capture events from July 22, 1999, to December 29, 1999.

74. See "Statement by Master Li on Falun Gong and the situation in China," July 23, 1999, http://minghui.ca/eng/china/calldialogue.html. See also "Falun Gong and Falun Dafa: What it is, what it does, and why the Chinese government is so terrified of it," for wars of words between LHZ and PRC government. See http://www.religious tolerance.org/falungong.htm (visited May 1, 2001).

75. Many foreign governments refused to honor PRC's INTERPOL request for assistance to arrest LHZ. Particularly, INTERPOL has formally rejected China's request to member states for the arrest of LHZ, stating, "The General Secretariat has informed the National Central Bureau of Interpol in China it cannot use Interpol channels to ask member states to locate and arrest Li Hongzhi, in the absence of any information about ordinary law crime he would have committed." Associated Press, "Cult chief at top of police wanted list," August 4, 1999, 8. See also "Interpol will not arrest sect leader," *BBC Online Network*, August 3, 1999, http://news.bbc.co.uk/1/hi/world/asia -pacific/410779.stm.

76. Vivien Pik-kwan Chan, "Arrest order on cult leader," *South China Morning Post*, July 30, 1999, 1.

The PRC authorities claimed that FLG has led to the death of thousands. It was alleged that before the Chinese government banned the FLG organization on 22 July 1999, more than 136 practitioners had "given up the care for life" to "go to the heaven" and achieve "real completion." After the ban, another 103 persons committed suicide. This does not include those who refused medication and died. According to incomplete statistics, Falun Gong has killed 1660 practitioners or innocent people. Mr. Liu Jing, person in charge of the State Council Office for the Prevention and Handling of Cults, speech at the press conference of the State Council Information Office, February 27, 2001, Beijing, http://www.china-un.ch/eng/premade/13641/liujin.htm. Not to be outdone, the Falun Gong Information Center maintains a running list of all persons who have died in the hands of PRC authorities, for example, police, as a direct result of PRC action, for example, interrogation in custody. The list tops 487 as of October 2, 2002 (http://www.faluninfo.net/news_frame.asp?category=Killed _Practitioners&company_name=FaluninfoEnglish).

77. "China: Reward for Banned Sect Leader," *New York Times*, August 4, 1999, http://www.rickross.com/reference/fa_lun_gong/falun74.html?FACTNet.

78. "Focus: China asks UK to bar Falun Gong leader," *Reuters*, August 17, 1999. (China asked the UK not to admit LHZ to attend a conference. The UK declined, claiming that "as the Falun Gong is not an illegal organization in the United Kingdom, and also in view of Interpol declining a Chinese request to treat Li as an international criminal, there is no case for action on our part.") http://www.rickross.com/ reference/fa_lun_gong/falun90.html.

79. For a detailed account of PRC oppressive and abusive actions, see "Reports on Extensive and Severe Human Rights Violations in the Suppression of Falunn Gong in the People's Republic of China," http://hrreports.faluninfo.net/index.html (visited October 8, 2002).

80. See "3. How (and What) to Compare?" in Mathias Reimann, "The Progress and Failure of Comparative Law in the Second Half of the Twentieth Century," *Am. J. Comp. L.* 50 (2002), 671, 689–690. See also Ran Hirschl (2005).

81. The investigation of the idea of terrorism in China provided a rare opportunity to look into the comparability of philosophies and allowed us to look at how the two cultures think and act in processing information and articulating ideas. "Comparative Philosophy: Chinese and Western," *Stanford Encyclopedia of Philosophy*, http://plato .stanford.edu/entries/comparphil-chiwes/; "Philosophy of Language in Classical China," Hong Kong University, http://www.hku.hk/philodep/ch/lang.htm. (Chinese language is a pictorial, prescriptive, and action-oriented language. English language is a symbolic, instrumental, and analytical language. These linguistic properties separate, reflect, and reinforce how the two cultures think.) See Bloom (1979). Because of the structure of Chinese language, it moves away from speculative theory construction to actuate description of reality.

82. Confucian teachings and field research indicate that it was better to endure suffering than to cause disputes and destroy relationships with others. For a rejoinder, see Diamant (2000).

83. The five relationships (*wulun*) are ruler-subject, father-son, husband-wife, elder brother–younger brother, and friend-friend.

84. James Polachek, "Review: Secret Societies in China and the Republican Revolution: Reviewed Work(s): Secret Societies in China in the Nineteenth and Twentieth Centuries by Jean Chesneaux, Gillian Nettle and Popular Movements and Secret Societies in China, 1840–1950 by Jean Chesneaux," *The Journal of Asian Studies* 32(3), 483–87.

85. One possibility is to argue that Confucianism is not a set of ethic principles as much as it is a set of rules for practical reason to deal with life contingencies. Zhang Rulun, "Is an Ethics of Economic Activity Possible?" in *Economic Ethics and Chinese Culture*, Chinese Philosophical Studies 14, ed. Yu Xuanmeng, Lu Xiaohe, Liu Fangtong, Zhang Rulun, and Georges Enderle, http://www.crvp.org/book/Series03/III-14/contents.htm. ("For Confucius, *jen* is an all-encompassing ethical ideal. . . . It is an existential goal which one must attempt to achieve for oneself through one's own self-cultivation. All the "worldly goods" are totally subordinate to the higher goal of *jen*. But this does not mean that people can do anything to achieve this goal.")

86. This is not to deny the equally strong instinct and custom to seek revenge for one's family.

87. The propriety of actions, including the use of violence, must be judged by three independent but supplementary ideas and ideals, that is, "Qing" "Li" "Fa" (《情理法》) ("QLF") or "compassion," "reason," and "law." Thus one must not only act legally, but also morally and reasonable within a given context and in light of evolving circumstances. Fan Zhong Xin [ 范忠信 ], *Qing Li Fa Yu Zhong Guo Ren* [Compassion, reason, law and the Chinese people; 《情理法與中國人》 (Beijing: Zhongguo renmin daixue chubanshe, 1992).

88. Karl Wittfogel, *Oriental Despotism* (New Haven, CT: Yale University Press, 1957).

89. The gentleman and base people lived in two distinctive world, separated by a great divide. The gentleman is regulated by principles of *li* and *ren*. The base people are moved by consideration of *li* (utility) and compelled by punishment (*xing*).

90. Ch'u Tung-tsu, *Law and Society in Traditional China* (Paris and The Hague: Mouton, 1961).

91. As an establishment scholar, Confucius always called for showing respect and loyalty to the ruled. But in describing the roles and responsibilities of ruler vs. ruled, he made clear that bad rulers will naturally and inevitably be dethroned and replaced, intimating grassroots rebellions from below. For example: "The ruler is like a cup, and the people like water," 193.

92. The cosmic order having been broken by the emperor, the citizens have a right to rebel, just as the learned intellectuals have a duty to advise and correct the emperor when he misspeaks or misbehaves, as measured against the nature's *dao* as expressed in the Confucian classics. Ibid., 196.

93. During the six dynasties, popular resistance to government oppression—excessive taxation, conscription, and corruption—resulted in people escaping into the mountains to become bandits. Ibid., 323–25. Since then, bandits have earned a good reputation as representing the social conscience of the people and have been romanticized as heroes. See Perry (2001).

94. Peasants rebelled not because they wanted to but because they had to. Peasants rebelled as a last resort in the traditional patron-client paternalistic-protective relationship, not to overthrow the government or disrupt the heavenly rule.

## REFERENCES

Anonymous. (2002). 166 terrorists nabbed. *Crime and Justice International*, 18(59), 16.

Ayatullah Shaykh Muhammad 'Ali Taskhiri. (1987). Towards a definition of terrorism. *Al-Tawhid (A Quarterly Journal of Islamic Thought and Culture)*, 5(1) (Muharram, 1408 AH).

Berger, Peter, and Thomas Luckmann. (1996). *The social construction of reality: A treatise in the sociology of knowledge* (51–55, 59–61). Garden City, NY: Anchor Books.

Best, Steve, and Anthony J. Nocella II. (2004). Defining terrorism. *Animal Liberation Philosophy and Policy Journal*, 2(1).

Billingsley, Phil. (1981). Bandits, bosses, and bare sticks: Beneath the surface of local control in early republican China. *Modern China*, 7(3), 235–88.

Bloom, Harold. (1979). The impact of Chinese linguistic structure on cognitive style. *Current Anthropology*, 20(3), 585–86.

Boaz, Ganor. "Defining Terrorism: Is One Man's Terrorist Another Man's Freedom Fighter?" http://www.ict.org.il/articles/define.htm.

Boorman, Howard L., and Scott A. Boorman. (1966). Chinese communist insurgent warfare: 1935–1949. *Political Science Quarterly*, 81(2), 171–95.

Chalmers, Johnson. (1968). The third generation of guerrilla warfare. *Asian Survey*, 8(6), 435–47.

Chen, Ching-Chih. (1975). The Japanese adaptation of the Pao-Chia system in Taiwan: 1895–1945. *The Journal of Asian Studies*, 34(2), 391–416.

Clarke, Donald C., and James V. Feinerman. (1995). Antagonistic contradictions: Criminal law and human rights in china. *The China Quarterly*, 135–54.

Crenshaw, Martha. (1981). The causes of terrorism. *Comparative Politics*, 13(4), 379–99.

Crowell, William G. (1983). Social unrest and rebellion in Jiangnan during the six dynasties. *Modern China*, 9(3), 319–54.

DeKorne, John. (1934). Sun Yat-Sen and the secret societies. *Pacific Affairs*, 7(4), 425–33.

Diamant, Neil J. (2000). Conflict and conflict resolution in China: Beyond mediation-centered approaches. *The Journal of Conflict Resolution*, 44(4), 523–46.

Dray-Novey, Alison. (1993). Spatial order and police in imperial Beijing. *The Journal of Asian Studies*, 52(4), 885–922.

Harrison, James. (1965). Communist interpretations of the Chinese peasant wars. *The China Quarterly*, 24, 92–118.

Hirschl, Ran. (2005). The question of case selection in comparative constitutional law. *American Journal of Comparative Law*, 53(125).

Hoffman, Paul. (2004). Human rights and terrorism. *Human Rights Quarterly*, 26(4), 932–55.

Hsu, Dau-lin. (1970). Crime and cosmic order. *Harvard Journal of Asiatic Studies*, 30, 111–25.

Huang, Philip. (1993). Public sphere/civil society in China: The third realm between state and society. *Modern China*, 19(2), 216–40.

Kessler, Lawrence D. (1971). Chinese scholars and the early Manchu state. *Harvard Journal of Asiatic Studies*, 31, 179–200.

Lampton, David M., and Richard Daniel Ewing. (2003). *The U.S.-China relationship facing international security crises: Three case studies in post-9/11 bilateral relations*. Washington, DC: Nixon Center.

Lary, Diana. (1980). Warlord studies. *Modern China*, 6(4), 439–70.

Lindsay, Michael. (1969). Contradictions in a totalitarian society. *The China Quarterly*, 39, 30–40.

Ling, L. H. M. (1994). Rationalizations for state violence in Chinese politics: The hegemony of parental governance. *Journal of Peace Research*, 31(4), 393–405.

Mabrey, Daniel. (2005). Counterterrorism efforts in China. *Crime and Justice International*, 20(84), 29.

Moneyhon, Matthew. (2003). China's great western development project in Xinjiang: Economic palliative, or political Trojan horse? *Denver Journal of International Law and Policy*, 31(491).

Moneyhon, Matthew. (2002). Recent development: Controlling Xinjiang: Autonomy on China's "new frontier." *Asian-Pacific Law and Policy Journal*, 3(4).

Morgan, Matthew J. (2004). The origins of the new terrorism. *Parameters*, Spring, 29–43.

Perkins, Ward. (1939). The failure of civil control in occupied China. *Pacific Affairs*, 12(2), 149–56.

Perry, Elizabeth J. (2001). *Challenging the mandate of heaven: Social protest and state power in China*. Armonk, NY: ME Sharpe.

Perry, Elizabeth J. (1984). Collective violence in China: 1880–1980. *Theory and Society*, 13(3), 427–54.

Price, H. Edward, Jr. (1977). The strategy and tactics of revolutionary terrorism. *Comparative Studies in Society and History*, 19(1), 52–66.

Puett, Michael. (1998). Sages, ministers, and rebels: Narratives from early China concerning the initial creation of the state. *Harvard Journal of Asiatic Studies*, 58(2), 425–79.

Reid, Gilbert. (1923). Revolution as taught by Confucianism. *International Journal of Ethics*, 33(2), 188–201.

Robinson, David M. (2000). Banditry and the subversion of state authority in China: The capital region during the middle Ming period (1450–1525). *Journal of Social History*, 33(3), 527–63.

Schmidt, Alex P., and Albert I. Jongman et al. (1988). *Political terrorism*. Amsterdam: SWIDOC and Transaction Books.

Schram, Stuart. (1966). Mao Tse-tung and secret societies. *The China Quarterly*, 27, 1–13.

Shaohoul, Zhu. (1994). *Zhongguo gudai zhian zhidu shi* [A history of ancient China public security system]. Henan: Henan daxue chubanshe.

Tanner, Murray Scot. (2004). China rethinks unrest. *The Washington Quarterly,* 27(3), 137–56.

Tao, Ahilong ( 陶世龙 ). Need to clearly recognize terrorism with Chinese Characteristic. [Xuyao yingqing juyou Zhongguo tesi de gongbu zhuyi] ( 需要认清具有中国特色的恐怖主义 ). http://www3.nbnet.nb.ca/stao/sles143.htm.

Tao, Jing-shen. (1970). The influence of Jurchen Rule on Chinese political institutions. *The Journal of Asian Studies*, 30(1), 121–30.

Thaxton, Ralph. (1977). On peasant revolution and national resistance: Toward a theory of peasant mobilization and revolutionary war with special reference to modern China. *World Politics*, 30(1), 24–57.

Thaxton, Ralph. (1977). The world turned downside up: Three orders of meaning in the peasants' traditional political world. *Modern China*, 3(2), 185–228.

Tiedemann, R. G. (1982). The persistence of banditry: North China plain. *Modern China* 8(4), 395–433.

Trimble, David. (1998). Nobel lecture. Oslo, Norway, December 10, 1998. http://nobel prize.org/peace/laureates/1998/trimble-lecture.html.

Turner, Karen. (1993). War, punishment, and the law of nature in early Chinese concepts of the state. *Harvard Journal of Asiatic Studies*, 53(2), 285–324.

Van der Valk, M. H. (1938). The revolution in Chinese legal thought. *Pacific Affairs*, 11(1), 66–80.

Wakeman, Frederic. (1992). American police advisers and the nationalist Chinese secret service: 1930–1937. *Modern China*, 18(2), 107–37.

Wakeman, Frederic. (1977). Rebellion and revolution: The study of popular movements in Chinese history. *The Journal of Asian Studies*, 36(2), 201–37.

Wall, James, and Michael Blum. (1999). Community mediation in China. *The Journal of Conflict Resolution*, 35(1), 3–20.

Wang, John Z. (2003). Eastern Turkistan Islamic movement: A case study of a new terrorist organization in China. *International Journal of Offender Therapy and Comparative Criminology*, 47(5), 568.

Weise, Peter. (2002). Terrorism, counterterrorism and international law. *Arab Studies Quarterly*, Spring–Summer.

Wong, Kam C. (1998). Black's theory on the behavior of law revisited II: A restatement of Black's concept of law, 26(1).

Wong, Young-Tsu. (1977). Popular unrest and the 1911 revolution in Jiangsu. *Modern China*, 3(3), 321–44.

Wright, Arthur F. (1953). Struggle vs. harmony: Symbols of competing values in modern china. *World Politics*, 6(1), 31–44.

## Chapter Four

# Urbanization, the State, and Privatization of Policing

## Urban Militias in Rio de Janeiro, Brazil

### Emilio E. Dellasoppa

"They are . . . the post-modern equivalent of jungles and mountains—
citadels of the dispossessed and irreconcilable. A military unprepared for
urban operations across a broad spectrum is unprepared for tomorrow."

—Lt. Col. Ralph Peters[1]

"The chief and permanent cause of this fact was . . . the slow and constant
actions of institutions."

—Alexis de Tocqueville,
*The Old Regime and the French Revolution*, p. 181

In the last decade, Brazil's policymakers have been facing increasing problems of regulation in the public security area. Proposed regulation plans did
not perform adequately when confronted with the complexity of a reality that
defies traditional models of policing (Dellasoppa et al., 2004; Dellasoppa,
2008). In the last forty years, Brazil experienced industrialization and development processes and paid a great toll in common goods: public security was
one of them. The form of resolution of the public security problem is still
open and will have increasing effects on the future social, political, and economic outline of the Brazilian democratic process.

Accordingly, a number of Brazilian scholars have explored the problem,
following different approaches.[2] Confronting the facts, we observe that the
Brazilian public security area, by almost all indicators, has experienced a
noteworthy worsening in the last thirty years. This chapter proposes an explanation for those processes, emphasizing the relationship between macro
and micro sociological realms connected by long-term processes (collusion), which operate to stabilize the Brazilian structure of social relations,

determining a notable inertia to changes. The proposed scheme follows Bunge's Boudon-Coleman diagram (Bunge, 1999).[3] Macro and micro explanatory variables are related by processes that lead to the weakening of the state monopoly of coercive power, confirming the decline of the Weberian formula in the Brazilian case. At the macro level, demographic dynamics triggered changes that produced growing economic stratification, inequalities, and social fragmentation that still linger at present. At that level, political processes like the authoritarian regime and the transition to democracy were influenced by micro-level conditions and the collusion processes that were isomorphically in effect at all levels of the Brazilian society, providing a strong restrictive frame of reference for the construction of democracy. A new legal order was established with the 1988 constitution, also limited by the restricting mechanisms of collusion described in the model.

At the micro level, the model works with the concept of faction formation, an approach related to the sociology of organizations (Crozier and Friedberg, 1977; Lindblom, 1995, 1980) and to the Weberian theory of bureaucracies and their logics of operation (Weber, 1969). Later, these concepts allow us to analyze the case of militia formation and development in the Rio de Janeiro state as also a result of a complex set of mechanisms that operate, linking together macro and micro features of the Brazilian structure of social relations. Another process, which began in the 1970s at the macro level, is the privatization of policing, resulting in a complex stock of policing policies and practices, but also in the weakening of the presence of the state in the public security area, with the associated loss of the monopoly of legitimate power of coercion and social control. These variables and processes, which recently included the presence of the Brazilian Army as an important stakeholder in the area of law and order, are presently developing and may be thought of as having many possible futures open.

## LONG-TERM MACRO-LEVEL INFLUENCING FACTORS: RAPID URBANIZATION AND ITS PROBLEMS

Urbanization in South America is the most rapid and large-scale urbanization process of any region in the world. In 1900, only 10 percent of the population was urban. In 1950, about 25 percent was, and in 2000, 75 percent. The Brazilian urbanization process was even faster and developed during the second half of the twentieth century. In the decade of the 1960s, the Brazilian urban population surpassed the rural population, as was verified by the 1970 demographic census. As a result, in 2000, 82 percent of the Brazilian population was urban. This urbanization was based on intense internal migration and resulted in rapid population growth in the larger Brazilian cities and metropolitan areas. Due to lower fertility rates and a decreasing number of immigrants, in the last two decades the growth rates of the larger cities and metropolitan areas has declined, but in 2000, about 40 percent of the Brazilian population inhabited the metropolitan areas.

In the case of Brazil, the pace of the urbanization/development process is much faster than that of older urbanization processes, such as the ones that occurred in European countries. In 1960, the Brazilian urban population consisted of approximately 31 million people, and in 2000, this number increased to 138 million. Within this time period of forty years, the urban population increased at a rate of almost 2.7 million per year. In the 1990s, more than 34 million inhabitants migrated to the metropolitan regions, which resulted in extreme pressure being placed on services provided by the state and the private sector. This included assistance for housing, transportation, jobs, public security, education, health, and leisure. With some services, such as education, existing programs and funding either collapsed or were reduced to dismal levels (judging by the results of students). "Rapid population growth places additional demands on the availability of affordable shelter and other amenities. These problems are compounded by the even higher absolute and relative growth of poverty in the cities and towns of the South. Gender, age, class, ethnic, and religious identity often affect the severity with which these problems are experienced" (United Nations, 2005).

The housing situation remains unsolved: about 1 million people live in slums in the city of Rio de Janeiro (10 percent of the population of the metropolitan area). According to a report released by the United Nations in June 2006, 52.3 million residents were living in the slums of Brazil in 2005. This translates to 28 percent of the Brazilian population. If this trend continues, there will be 55 million in 2020.[4] This process implies higher costs in terms of common goods, such as public security.

## URBAN VIOLENCE AND GROWING HOMICIDE RATES PARALLELED URBANIZATION AND DEVELOPMENT: A CASE TO BE EXPLAINED

When public security is considered, we observe fear and insecurity. This is inseparable from the high levels of violence that accompanied the urbanization/development process. Such fear and insecurity are observed to have risen in all social sectors, from the extremely poor to the very rich. However, the types of violent incidents that Brazilian citizens are subject to vary enormously in their causes, nature, and probability. They depend a great deal on age and location. The noted extreme economic inequality is also present here. Solutions may be different, and the militia's case, which will be considered, can also ambiguously be seen as a short-term solution by the slum dwellers and, not unexpectedly, by some public officials.

Homicide ranks as the most important external cause of mortality in Brazil, which exhibits homicide rates that are among the highest in the world. Brazil in 2005 was the eighth country in the world, with a rate of 49.1 homicides per 100,000 inhabitants, but the fourth among eighty-two countries when considering the youth (the 15–24 age group), with a rate of homicides of 79.6 per 100,000.[5] For the youth of Brazil, the 15–24 age group, in the municipalities, accordingly to 2006 data, these rates increase dramatically for the most critical cases. The highest rate is registered in Foz do Iguaçu (state of Paraná, near the border with Argentina and Paraguay), with 234.8 homicides for 100,000 inhabitants. The municipality of Recife follows, with a rate of 213.4. In the Rio de Janeiro metropolitan area, the municipality of Duque de Caxias registers 176.8 and Rio de Janeiro 83.6 homicides per 100,000 inhabitants.[6]

These results are worse in the metropolitan areas. For example, if we observe the case of the municipality of São Paulo based on the Programa de Aprimoramento das Informações de Mortalidade no Município (PRO-AIM) data for the year 2000, the absolute and relative importance of homicide's death toll becomes evident. The concentration of deaths by homicide in the 15–24 and 25–29 age groups is also significant. To evaluate the importance of these figures, we note that the total number of homicides in the 15–24 age group in only the year 2000 in the municipality of São Paulo is *higher* (2,234) than all the Palestinians killed between September 2000 and March 5, 2003, in the Middle East conflict (2,100).[7] We must note that the situation in the São Paulo state changed much for the better from 1999 to 2007, as will be explained later.

Considering a longer time interval, we observe that the homicide rate in the municipality of São Paulo increased from a figure of 5 homicides for every 100,000 inhabitants to 57.5 homicides per 100,000 inhabitants between 1960 and 2000,[8] the period associated with the Brazilian urbanization/development processes previously discussed.

This rate of 5 homicides per 100,000 inhabitants was a historic level, and had been a demographic indicator of the Brazilian structure of social relations for at least two decades prior to 1960. In 1946, when Mortara (1946) analyzed the death rate due to external causes in 1940 for the municipalities of Rio de Janeiro and São Paulo, his research found those very same levels: 5.4 per 100,000 inhabitants in Rio de Janeiro and 4.0 per 100,000 for São Paulo. The figures in 2000 were ten to fifteen times greater. They are related to the transformations in Brazilian society over the last decades. As Donolo (2001) notes, all development processes consume a great amount of common goods, and in Brazil, this process affected not only the environment but also public security and certainty about law.

In the municipality of São Paulo, the homicide rate grew 158.6 percent. It was 17.4 per 100,000 in 1980 and 45 per 100,000 in 1991. This increase is higher than those of the two previous decades (91.2% and 75%). It reflects qualitatively different levels of violence than those that emerged in the 1980s. In the twenty-one years between the census of 1970 and 1991, the homicide rate in the municipality of São Paulo increased 395 percent. The explanation for these complex phenomena must be sought in the interplay of the social, economic, and cultural realms influencing the transformations of the structure of social relations during the period. It is enough to observe corresponding figures on a national level to understand the significance of the situation. There were 11.7 homicides for every 100,000 inhabitants in Brazil in 1979, a figure that increased to 21.0 in 1994[9] and 27.0 in 1996.[10] In addition, these figures are a conservative estimate in that they do not account for registered cases, intentional and unintentional.

The high inflation rate that characterized the 1980s (often referred to today as the "lost decade"), rising unemployment rates, and extreme economic inequalities—measured, for example, through the Gini index—are factors to be considered. All violence-related indicators, such as mortality due to external causes, violent crimes, and homicides, increased. The difference between genders also grew. For example, the male homicide rate in São Paulo City rose 173.1 percent between 1980 and 1985 and an additional 24.6 percent between 1985 and 1990. The percentages are always much higher for males compared to females.

Several sectors of society noticed and condemned the state's chronic lack of consistent strategic planning to control the violence and its causes. Democracy and civil rights were formally reestablished in Brazil after two decades of authoritarian regime. Nevertheless, this process was accompanied by a systematic increase in the indicators of violence, such as the violent deaths rate and the number of years lost due to external causes. This increase, though of a smaller percentage, today affects much higher total values. A 10 percent increase today is equal to the total value of the rate in the 1960s. These indicators have been significantly greater among the younger age groups, a fact that is consistent with corresponding international statistics.

However, in the last six years the state of São Paulo has experienced a noteworthy decrease in homicide figures. From a maximum of 12,818 in 1999, there has been a constant decline: 2007 registered 4,877 homicides against 6,057 in 2006. The reduction from 1999 is an outstanding 62 percent. Several hypotheses were raised to explain this result, unfortunately not paralleled by the state of Rio de Janeiro. The most reliable candidate to explain this effect is demographic: the "end of the young wave." This means that fewer young men—the main victims—are ascending in the demographic pyramid, and the universe of potential victims is reduced. These hypotheses, as related to the improvements in policing and changes in the drug markets, must yet be tested against empirical evidence.


## BREAKDOWN IN THE MONOPOLY OF LEGITIMATE POWER

Analysis of police and policing in Brazil must account for the characteristics and limitations of the Brazilian construction of democracy. This also applies to the militia phenomenon. An inverse relationship was observed between the democratization process in Brazil and the increase in the levels of violence in Brazilian society (measured by mortality statistics). This result was exactly the opposite of what social scientists could expect.

For the last twenty years, Brazil has seen an increase in violence and crime. The global homicide rate for Brazil is now about 27 per 100,000 inhabitants. Urgent actions from the state for crime control are needed, as are public policies and changes in the regulation of political, judiciary, and social control systems, including the private sectors. *One major issue is that the government does not have a monopoly on legitimate violence.* This is a problem shared by many nation-states in the peripheries of capitalism. (Pinheiro, 2001:297; Adorno, 2002). In 1985, Anthony Giddens raised similar questions for the "European nation-state" (Giddens, 2001), as did Norbert Elias (Elias, 1988, 1995, 1997). Wieviorka (1997:19) calls attention to the decay of the efficiency of the traditional Weberian concept of legitimate violence in developed countries. But, accepting this argument, we must think what happens to the Weberian formula in countries where there was *never* a monopoly of legitimate force by the state. And for nation-states now under the influence of those complex processes of globalization, multiculturalism, marginalization, and increasing income differences, this ideal will be farther away than ever. This question is related to the complexities and problems of the democracies that emerged in South America after military governments failed (AA.VV., 2000; Debrun, 1983; Dellasoppa 2005, 2003, 2002a, 2002b, 2000; Méndez et al., 2000; and O'Donnell 1994, 1997, 1999). We can raise another question: how is it possible to regulate actions in the public security area and related areas in societies where the state never obtained the monopoly on legitimate violence within the rule of law?[11] And, finally, how do we control militia operations that, at least in the short term, provide public security by private means and are mostly approved by impoverished residents of the most violent and drug-riddled shantytowns in the city of Rio de Janeiro?

## SOCIOECONOMIC INFLUENCING FACTORS AT THE MACRO LEVEL: CHARACTERISTICS OF THE BRAZILIAN STRUCTURE OF SOCIAL RELATIONS

A previous paper (Dellasoppa, 2000) proposed an explanation of what were called "isomorphic structures of social relations in Brazilian society." There, the social fragmentation of Brazilian society was related to the emergence of broad and local consolidation networks based on collusive relations conceived as the structures that historically minimized transaction costs between social sectors. These structures could be observed in connection with drug traffic not only as challengers of the state in the monopoly on coercive resources but also as emerging as an alternative control of mediations in social transactions in a community. Presently, we consider militias to represent another important local consolidation network broadly based on collusion relations, and a theoretical explanation can be based on that previous model.

There are networks of collusive relations in the whole of Brazilian society at an intersubjective and intersectorial (of economic, political, and cultural groups, etc.) level that are a compelling part of daily life and simultaneously constitute an element that enables and operates in any political institution, from the municipality to the federal government. The result of the operation of these networks is a marked stability and great inertia in the structure of social relations in Brazil (Abranches, 1989).

This inertia occurs in the subsystems of the society and is more evident in those relations determined by clientelism and patronage. Typically, these events appear to be claiming some type of code of honor or ethical basis, which is linked to a clan structure or "collusion groups" based on relations of mutual trust and loyalty.

These networks of collusive transactions must be analyzed, considering that they are also powerful intersectorial forms of domination.[12] There is a tendency amidst the established system of mutual recognitions to maximize the incorporation of diverse autonomous sectors which "enter the game" in the consolidation network. There is also a tendency to marginalize sectors whose internal dynamics prevent or limit their participation in the game of mutual recognitions (Dobry, 1986:112).

Pragmatic principles of noninterference operate in the consolidation networks. The art of "take no notice of" is not limited to the routine of patrimonial use of public funds towards private political goals, but extends to juridical decisions as well as political decisions pertaining to the state's organization. This characteristic explains chronic instances of delegitimization of the political system, as well as the recurrent hands-off policy in dealing with the action of militias in Rio de Janeiro.

We must call attention to the "semi-clandestine articulation" of militias with members—both active and retired—of several government agencies, like the military police, the civil police, and the fire department. There is empirical evidence of the nontransparency of decision processes.[13] This, in turn, is related to decisions that are the product of independent intersectorial collusive relations. Also, changing government officials impose the specific logic of their political factions to bureaucratic and executive functions. This also reveals the peculiar logic to these bureaucracies, where the dependence of collusive intersectorial relations leads to an administration that does not take past experience into account if the outcomes are not useful or profitable for the political faction.

These collusive transactions can be found isomorphically at all levels and sectors of Brazilian society. There are exacerbated instances, such as in the case of the state of Rio de Janeiro during some periods (1988–1994), in which such relations constitute an almost determining expression of the sociopolitical reality. For example, a wave of kidnappings of businessmen took place in Rio de Janeiro towards the end of Governor Moreira Franco's incumbency, exposing the commonplace and pertinacious nature of this network of collusive relations between political and economic sectors, illegal gambling organizations (usually known as *jogo do bicho*), bank robbers, kidnappers, police officers, and drug traffickers, described by the press as a conviviality of "underworlds." At that time it was pointed out in Rio de Janeiro's case the danger of severe weakening of the state as a tendentious monopolizer of coercive resources and the predominance of sectors that privatized coercion and violence. The present situation is confirming those trends of chronic weakening of the state.

A Brazilian specificity also exists, constituted not only by the impunity that permeates the most different cases, but by the *resilience* of impunity that operates even in cases where the pressure of society or of determined groups guarantees as an outcome some type of limited punishment. This characteristic, already historically incorporated, is especially true at the highest echelons of the state's political and bureaucratic power as well as in significant portions of organized crime. The collusive transactions in the consolidation networks grant high levels of impunity to political, economic, or criminal felons. Political, economic, and influential citizens usually can delay punishment for many years using the resources available for the rich and powerful in the Brazilian system of criminal justice.

## MICRO-LEVEL ANALYSIS OF INFLUENCING FACTORS: SOCIAL FRAGMENTATION AND FACTIONS IN BRAZILIAN SOCIETY AS A FERTILE GROUND FOR MILITIAS

The fragmentation of Brazilian society was an always-present theme in literature, early cited as one of the most serious obstacles to the successful conclusion of the process of political democratization (Machado da Silva, 1990, 1991, 1993; Weffort, 1990).

This fragmentation of Brazilian society requires us not to reduce this question to a mere state–versus–civil society struggle, but rather to conduct research through the empirical confirmation of a multiplicity of sectors within a sociological tradition which we can refer to Weber (Weber, 1969, II:752). Specific social logics define each sector as is and oppose this sector to others, limiting the space of its self-reference. Weber's analysis of the bureaucratic sectors highlights the tight relation between the sector's specific logic and the bureaucratic and/or technical specific capabilities that characterized it.

Thus, we consider these sectors (business, the military, clerics, politicians, state bureaucracies, judiciary, state police, military police, federal police, etc.) not as spaces where the production of a sectorial consensus can be examined and evaluated, but as places of conflict and competition for political positions among the members of their own and other external sectors. This competition unfolds according to the specific logic of each one of these social sectors,[14] logic that determines the tactical activity of the sector, sustained by social mechanisms that guarantee its continued perception, comprehension, and practical use—constituting a real socialization process—by the members of a sector. This concept can be applied to analyze the case of the militias in Rio de Janeiro.

To exemplify this situation, let us consider a relevant Brazilian problem: factions. These groups are directly related to fragmentation processes in Brazilian society. As presented by Dobel, the characteristics of the factions analyzed in his paper are similar to those detailed by Ouchi (1980) and Abranches (1989): "The factions are objective centers of power: encompassing families, companies, unions, government bureaucracies and similar associations; their basic characteristics are autonomous power and enough internal cohesion to distort the government policies and provide semi-governmental services to its members . . . it turns rational to systematically work to corrupt the government in order to maintain the faction's power base" (Dobel, 1978:964).

Concerning these questions, other elements to be considered are the concept of the state as a collection of "resources" that can be captured by a faction and the propagation of the faction's dynamics: once initiated, they spread to other sectors of the state, resulting in a situation where only by aligning with a faction or creating a new one can citizens effectively influence politics. This is related to a structure of social relations developing to minimize the *cost of transactions* between individuals, sectors, or factions. Of course, the relations between factions are guided by dominance and control and not merely by competitive coexistence.

The "logic of factions" was adopted by the state in prison management. Prisons actually must specialize in prisoners belonging to a specific faction— the only way that proved feasible to impede killings among different factions when sharing the same prison facility.

## The Case of Rio de Janeiro: Demographics, Urbanization, and Development of Factions

The evolution of urbanization in the state of Rio de Janeiro during the development process shows differences from the whole picture for Brazil. By 1970, the state reached 75 percent urbanization, clearly ahead of other states of the federation. In 2000, 96 percent of the population of the state of Rio de Janeiro was urban (Brandão, 2006; Zaluar, 2004). Due to a mountainous geography, higher- and lower-income social groups inhabit the city of Rio de Janeiro in close proximity. A number of shantytowns, numbering between 516 and 752, depending on the sources,[15] are located on the mountain hillsides, with about 1 million residents. The most important slum complex in Rio de Janeiro is Maré, with 113,807 inhabitants.[16] In comparison, two additional well-known slum complexes consist of fewer residents (Complexo do Alemão [65,026] and Rocinha [56,338]). In these three slums, access to electricity, water supply, (precarious) sanitation, drainage, and waste collection— sometimes even curbside collection of recyclable materials—are available for nearly 100 percent of the households (Araújo, 2006).

These data show that the concept of "absence of the state" must be qualified, at least for these particular slums. This distinction suggests a more complex discussion about the problem of political control of important concentrations of low-income voters and the political and economic exploitation of the offering of urban commodities (cable TV, cooking LNG [liquefied natural gas], motorcycle taxis, etc.) in these areas.[17] During the 1980s and 1990s, the population which formed the slums in Rio de Janeiro and other metropolitan regions was usually an object of patronage and clientelistic vote control in the original places they inhabited. The original structure of social relations in Rio de Janeiro was responsible for developing new candidates to control the political, social, and economic rights of these populations. As a result, politicians, religious groups, drug gangs, and militias ally and compete for control in these slums.

## SLUMS AS STRONGHOLDS FOR LOWER-LEVEL DRUG TRAFFICKERS, DRUG KINGPINS, AND ARMS TRAFFIC DEVELOPMENT

"In addition to the many residents working at gainful employment outside the favela, Dona Marta, like most favelas, has *bocas-de-fumo*—places where drugs are sold. From where we are on the asphalt, this trade is invisible, but not inaudible. One of the aspects of life here at the foot of the hill that might be disturbing to the beginner is the fact that one hears fireworks from uphill on a regular basis. The general notion is that these are to signal the availability of drugs for sale, but one also gets the impression that it is not so uncommon to shoot these off just for the hell of it, to celebrate" (Moore, 2006).[18]

Recently in the *Washington Post* we can find a report on the occupation of a slum in Rio de Janeiro that is clear about the difficulties of the type of urban conflict that the police forces must deal with. Terrain characteristics are dominant in these cases. A slum is not a "strong and well-fortified place" on its own, but it can be a relatively safe area in which to establish control of retail for drugs sales, because its dense packing of jerry-built shanties, alleys, and gangplanks makes it difficult for police and other gangs to infiltrate.[19] In Rio de Janeiro, many slums are strategically located by the side of high-income consumers, minimizing the drug traffickers' potential logistic problems. This fact was perceived early on by drug dealers. Then in the 1980s and 1990s their strategy was oriented to establishing and maintaining control of specific slum areas. The three or four drugs gangs existing and competing in Rio de Janeiro divided control of hundreds of slums.[20] Our analysis of the problem looks at social actors competing for power in the Brazilian structure of social relations, with the state applying limited resources and feeble strategies. For reference on these approaches, see Crozier and Friedberg (1977), Lindblom (1978, 1980, 1995), and also Ministério da Justiça (2000, 2001).

Gangs and factions fight over terrain control in Rio de Janeiro, anticipated by the now-common reflection of military strategists on military operations on urbanized areas (MOUT). This will be of increasing importance in the coming years and is closely related to militias' development. Considering these possible scenarios, as we will see later, the Brazilian Army, since 2005, has been preparing a whole brigade for social control, basically in urban areas. This is the 11th Light Infantry Brigade–Law and Order Control (11a BIL–GLO) (Arruda, 2007).

As expected in all armed-conflict scenarios, both sides try to improve their availability of resources. Basic resources for armed conflict include human resources (recruits), arms, and funds. For the drug gang leaders at medium and low levels, the slum is the most important place where it is possible to find and stock resources. As a result of the young wave that affected Brazilian demographics in the 1990s, in the poor peripheries and slums there was—and still is—an ample offering of young dwellers who can be hired for traffic. Even considering that the absolute majority of the population of slums consists of honest workers, good citizens, and religious souls, a recruitment rate of 1 percent of the overall population of the Rio de Janeiro slums will provide the gangs with about 10,000 recruits. It was estimated that about 5,000 teens worked for drug traffickers in Rio de Janeiro city, with different tasks. In recent years, middle-class adolescents and young entrepreneurs have entered the drug business as well.

New resources escalate conflict. In the 1990s, heavy weapons arrived, mostly as AR-15 or AK-47 automatic rifles and Israeli Uzi machine guns, pushing the conflict to higher levels. In 1993, Brazilian Army intelligence services detected these changes, monitored in Rio de Janeiro since 1989.[21] The source was arms traffic, based on the almost endless possibilities of smuggling anything into Brazil due to absence of adequate border control and corrupt public officials. In the early 1990s, members of the United States Bureau of Alcohol, Tobacco and Firearms (ATF) declared that some of those rifles were purchased in Miami for US$250 and resold in Brazil at a price ten or twenty times higher.[22] Another important source of heavy weapons for the drug gangs is the corruption of police officers. Now and then, automatic rifles captured from one gang are resold to another for a big profit. Rifles from the police and the army are also sold to gangs by members of these institutions,[23] but in the case of the army this kind of corruption is still limited.

It must be noted some remarkable relations between demographics and the practical military organization of criminal factions. For the very young recruits, the drugs traffickers adopted the "baby rifle." The recruitment of young dwellers ("minors," not yet subject to the penal code) resulted in the more frequent use of weapons by children and adolescents. In 1997, 28.3 percent of the 5,011 adolescents under arrest were using firearms; two years later, this number climbed to 41 percent (2,642 out of 6,004 arrested). As the journals pointed out, it was "a brigade of adolescents early armed."[24] As evidence of the escalation of firepower by the drug gangs, new weapons were introduced and used by adolescents—a light version of the AR-15, the CAR-15, the submachine gun from Colt, which was called by the gangs "baby rifle."

Taking into account these facts, we can partially explain the increase in the number of homicides in Brazil previously examined. While public security can be thought of as a common good, it can also be thought of as a commodity. This conceptualization can help to explain the future development of militias in the city of Rio de Janeiro, the resigned acceptance of the slum and gritty suburbs residents, and the dubious and still limited treatment of the problem by the state, despite frequent pronouncements about the will to combat militias.

## MILITIAS ARE BASED ON AND BENEFIT FROM THE PROCESSES OF COLLUSION

In this chapter, the following definition of collusion is adopted: "The competitors operate in connivance when they decide to remove certain available resources from the conflict arena. To bring these resources into play means making the value of the game increasingly higher" (Bailey, 1970:170). The task consists of understanding in this context what it means for the value of the game to be "higher." It is related to a number of pragmatic rules that evolve and govern the type of resources—basically *legal* resources—that can or cannot be used in the contest between the parts.

Collusion has connotations of secrecy, deceit, and fraud. Many acts of collusion are tacit: the competitors don't want and don't need to admit they are not making use of resources, a very frequent situation when dealing with economic oligopolies. Analyzing the problem from another point of view, we can observe that pragmatic collusions and normative accords have almost the same meaning: restrictions in interest of stability (in the space of contest, which could be in the economic or political markets, etc.). Collusion implies that both competitors are limiting themselves in the use of resources. This situation was observed when we analyzed the army's repression of drug traffickers in the 1990s (Dellasoppa, 2000)[25] and again is present when inspecting the relations between militias and different areas of the state in all its levels. This is the way that confrontations are muffled. Collusion also includes those situations in which the contests involve an anticipation of the result: the no-contest situations or retreats. The challenges cannot be accepted and the weaker party will abandon the challenge, with the symbolic acceptance of his inferiority (Bailey, 1970:172–84).

External factors beyond the contest can be *argued* in all collusion situations (the public's well-being in a contest between parties or factions for the right to form part of the government, the stability of the national financial system when faced with the need to use the public money to sustain private banks, or the provision to the community of a common good, public security, for example). These external factors can be differentiated between pragmatic and normative, the last being alleged more frequently when collusion becomes of public domain (Bailey, 1970:176).

Similar situations can be observed in the political and social realms, being plentiful in violence and criminality areas. Certain practices that operate in the social relation between repression and criminality can be better explained by considering the concept of collusion as defined above. Not only are there clear interdependencies, as is the case in the use and trafficking of drugs, but there are also other interdependencies and complicities which manifest themselves in the specific forms of the fight against criminality. After that is established beyond the limits of legality, a perverse circle of reproduction of processes of pragmatic interactions, which permeate the whole society and which constitute a basic element of composition and permanence of a situation, reproduce restrictions of conduct, with stabilizing effects on the status quo.

Relations of complementarity imply establishing a web of mutual recognitions for the different subsectors/subsystems, which operate as a legitimating value for the political (economic, social, etc.) system and for the sectors involved. Differently, the collusive transactions and their associated mutual recognitions produce for their protagonists an additional objective, because on the *esquema montado* or "set deal" there is a *process of reification* (as defined by Berger and Luckmann, 1989) *which results in considering the product of the collusion a natural model that must be observed in relations with other sectors or be subject to sanctions.*

Then the collusion model is seen as "natural," and as a result, it attempts to include the greatest number from the most diverse autonomous sectors of the society in the consolidation networks, leading to the marginalization and weakening of the political importance of sectors which the dynamic of politics lead. In this way, a whole series of isomorphisms and homologies appear when observing what have been identified as *local consolidation groups.* Just as certain political structures are denominated "pressure groups," we can imagine the existence of numerous "collusion groups" disseminated through different consolidation networks, which operate according to the characteristics above.

Under such circumstances, the existence of organizations of collusion (collusion groups) is justified since they can mediate and enable transactions, economic or not, between different sectors at much lower costs. Socialization in this form of organization and mediation of relations in regard to values, norms, and common beliefs promote a harmony of interests which diminishes the possibility of opportunistic behavior between its members. Indeed, norms of reciprocity and solidarity are developed inside the collusion groups, there being a high degree of mutual trust among those who "are in the deal" (*estão no esquema*), maintaining a significant degree of trust between the middle and lower cadres and the political and bureaucratic cadres who represent the upper levels of the deal.

## PUBLIC SAFETY AND LAW ENFORCEMENT AGENCIES' CHANGING ROLES: PUBLIC SECURITY RELIES ON PRIVATE SUPPLIER

"From the changes experienced by police as a social control agency we can observe that the monopoly of legitimate violence by the state shows today a restricted form. The state delegates noncontractual forms of coercion to private groups, as a part of a 'policing forms' stock. At the same time, paramilitary forces are used in topical actions of level three and sporadically the Army" (Dellasoppa, 2005).

In Brazil there is no monopoly of legitimate violence by the state. Police forces are presently just *one* of the available forms of coercion/domestic repression of a diversified number available to the state (Monjardet, 2003; Giddens, 2001; Reiner, 2004; and Adorno, 2002). We can distinguish four levels of repression. The first level is negotiation: consensus construction without the use of force. The second level is policing: use of basic weapons without the use of military force. The third level is military organizations: National Guard (United States), Gendarmeria Nacional (Argentina), Força Nacional of Segurança (Brazil), topical and sporadic use of troops from the army. The fourth level is military repression on a large scale (example: the use of the army and Gendarmeria Nacional in Argentina for the repression of the Cordobazo, Córdoba, Argentina, 1969). It is also used in developed nations: Little Rock (Arkansas, 1959) under Eisenhower, the policing by the English army of Northern Ireland, the Canadian crisis of 1970 under Prime Minister Trudeau (Monjardet, 2003:37).

In Rio de Janeiro the army was used for repression at level three in November 1994 at the first of the so-called Operação Rio. The government of da Silva organized the Força Nacional de Segurança (National Security Force), a task force formed with police officials from several state military polices proposed to act in cases of emergency. The governor of the state of Espírito Santo claimed at that time that the use of the Força Nacional against organized crime was absolutely necessary. A former paper (Dellasoppa, 2005) analyzed the limitations of this proposal in terms of the political limitations that the intelligence of the army faces in fighting organized crime and the restrictions that operate on regulation proposals and planning in the public security area.

In the case of Brazil, Article 144 of the Brazilian constitution (Brazil, 1988) does not establish a definition of the concept of security nor of responsibility that is attributed to "all" (the citizens) in the double sense of right and responsibility.[26] This implies that the duties of the police are not more exclusive but are shared with "all" the citizens, communities, and organizations. From the point of view of the state, this concept means in practice the resignation of the monopoly of legitimate force and therefore a limitation of the duties and policies possible for the police agencies. Repressive action priorities for the police are submitted to a debate or with the participation of third parties ("all") (Monjardet, 2003:256).

As one of the stakeholders in the "public security problem," the Brazilian Army since 2005 has reorganized the 11th Brigade of Armoured Infantry based in Campinas, São Paulo, into the 11th BIL-GLO (11th Light Brigade–Law and Order). This brigade is less than twelve hours from any point in the Brazilian territory. Its training includes typical police operations and even the use of nonlethal arms. But, as even the army and the government admit, several blanks in the legislation remain to be filled. The experience of the Brazilian troops that are included in MINUSTAH, the United Nations Stabilization Mission in Haiti, is also being analyzed.[27]

From the available knowledge in economic science, we can suppose that the law of diminishing returns applies to policies in the public security area. We can expect this law to be exacerbated in the case of sequential interventions intended to control subjective variables. From this point of view, it appears evident the clear fragility of the police and security forces in terms of an "institution that should show results." The security forces are compelled to articulate a discourse in which responsibilities are credited to other institutions, or at least diluted among a great number of stakeholders, including the family, the school, the judiciary, the political system, and state and/or federal government, or, as it is usually called in Brazil, the "civil society." As discussed, the Brazilian constitution offers a good juridical argument for these strategies. Thus, the strategy of "social distribution of responsibilities" enters in Brazil into the complex interplay of political alliances at all political levels, with an always-growing participation of stakeholders entering the game. Within this scenario, militias in Rio de Janeiro city appear to be now one unexpected stakeholder.

## THE PROCESS OF THE FIGHT FOR CONTROL OF DRUG-RIDDLED SHANTYTOWNS: FROM DRUG TRAFFIC TO MILITIAS

There are antecedents and restricted experiences since the 1990s that evidence the *ambiguity* of public opinion, the state, and the journals about *ille-*

*gal* private security. In Rio de Janeiro, 1995, a journal reports that dwellers of the high-income borough Ipanema hired an illegal service of watchmen to take care of public security in several streets. They were civil police officers, military police members, and retired firemen working as illegal private security guards. The journalist tries to show himself and the journal as neutral, just reporting "facts."[28] Three years later, the problem of most of the private security firms, illegality, is qualified by a journal as "high-risk." But by the end of the 1990s, many boroughs of Rio de Janeiro and São Paulo were hiring cheaper illegal private security to patrol their streets. Payment is per capita, referring to individual residential apartments or shops, with differential taxes. Sometimes dwellers of a borough decide by voting, "democratically," if a private security firm is to be hired. As usual, there are conflicting opinions about paying for a service that should be the responsibility of the state. In most cases, illegal private security is approved in order *to cut costs*.[29]

As a part of the survey "Urban War," the *Folha de São Paulo* journal reported that in 1999 in São Paulo dwellers and shop owners of the downtown area hired guards to control and expel beggars from the area streets and parks. It was called by the journals "the anti-misery militia." These firms are usually owned by members of the PM (military police), which is illegal but not frequently prosecuted by the corporation. These militiamen earned about US$250–350 a month, and they provided twenty-four-hour protection in the (four) areas where the system was initially established.[30]

By 1999, illegal private security was sold in the high-income borough of Leblon, Rio de Janeiro, over the counter of a bakery established on a very important avenue.[31] The process of privatization of policing, both legally and illegally, has gotten momentum and is seen by the inhabitants of the metropolitan areas as perfectly normal, because security cannot rely on a state that has proven every time to be impotent in attempting to fight crime or prosecute illegalities in the public security area. This may be due to the fact that the federal police, who are responsible for the repression of illegal private security firms, have usually failed to control these activities.

In 2005, the middle classes in São Paulo and other Brazilian cities were hiring members of the military police. This service is also illegal (and usually known as *bico*) because a second job is not allowed by law. Middle classes prefer police officers working illegally as private security guards and not guards from illegal firms, because they believe risks are lower and the possibility always exists of an easier contact between the official working illegally and their colleagues legally on duty.[32]

One of the most interesting cases of illegal private security was the hiring, in Rio de Janeiro, of *slum dwellers* to work as security guards in the boundaries of middle- to high-class boroughs. This service was approved both by the drug gangs *and* the state. Some dwellers thought of this relation as "welfare," and the commander of the Special Areas Policing Group (GPAE), Major Antônio Carlos Carballo, thought of this project as a possible form to integrate "the slum and the city."[33] Ambiguity lingers about this method of illegal private security.

This ambiguity from all sectors about illegality and the acceptance and development of illegal services of illegal security firms, jointly with the skepticism about the possibility of the state to deliver its constitutional services in the area of public security, made it possible to accept—ambiguously—the presence and action of militias when these groups grew up and became another social actor and important stockholder in the public security problem.

## CHARACTERISTICS OF THE MILITIA-ASSOCIATED PHENOMENA IN RIO DE JANEIRO

Militias must be considered a development of previous trends: decay of the monopoly of legitimate violence by the state, private security growth and private group initiatives to cope with the increasingly serious security problem, and exploiting available areas—mainly in slums, but also in middle- and high-class areas—to demand protection money and to seek profit in a market for illegal services offered by the groups controlling these areas.

The first militia in Rio de Janeiro city began its operations in the slum Rio das Pedras at the end of the 1970s. The number of areas controlled by militias increased slowly, to about forty-two at the end of 2004. But in the last two years, another fifty shantytowns in Rio de Janeiro have been taken from drug gangs, or about one slum each twelve days.[34] A search performed in the archives of the newspaper *Folha de São Paulo* from December 2006 to November 2008 produced the following evolution in the number of areas in the state of Rio de Janeiro controlled by militias: December 2006, 40 (source: Military Police) or more than 60 (source: *Foha de São Paulo*); September 2008, 100 out of 513 officially recorded slums (source: Secretary of Public Security, State of Rio de Janeiro [SENASP/MJ]); and, finally, 170 in November 2008, as cited in the *Militias Report* of the Commission on Militias of the State Assembly of the State of Rio de Janeiro.[35]

Accordingly to the military police, these occupations are possible because they are supported by the local population and by the informal—and illegal—participation of military police units in these areas.[36] The basic claim of militias about their own legitimacy is related to the elimination of drug traffic and gangs in the communities.

## THE MILITIA AS A SOCIAL AGENT: AMBIGUITY AND COLLUSION IN THE PROCESS OF CONSTRUCTING LEGITIMACY

Let us now consider, under a Weberian approach, the *eigengeseztlichtkeit* (eigen social logic) of the militia groups. The system that brings the armed militia into power also deconstructs the legitimacy and availability of the state and all public security agencies by ensuring the state is powerless and incapable of offering security and clearly identifying the enemy and/or situation-problem. Militias in the Rio de Janeiro shantytowns have a clear answer to the question "Security against whom?" Everybody knows the answer, but only the militia can deliver the goods. *Also, we must note that in this process all the violence due to abuse of lethal force by the police vanishes as a legal problem related to the rule of law.*

Usually backed by policemen living in the target area, a militia is presented as the solution to the public security problem in the shantytown. The promise of security holds strong ground for the militia's legitimacy among dwellers, other policemen, and the public opinion. A policewoman, now federal representative Marina Magessi, has called the militia "the security of the poor," expressing again the fragmentation of Brazilian society.

The public and dwellers only recognize the militia as legitimate because it offers a solution against the gangs that impose their order and the chaos and insecurity that results from different gangs fighting. It is important to observe how the dwellers see the previous gangs creating the chaos compared to the militia, who will afterwards impose order. Some rules imposed by the gangs, like the prohibition on wearing red clothes (e.g., red might be the color of a rival faction), seem absurd to them. At times, it seems more absurd compared to the usual curfew at night.[37]

The militia's legitimacy depends on a number of factors, including collusion from state agency officials and widespread cynicism towards the "services" brought by the militia and the ideological structure of the client-based patronage system. The collusion processes explained above are necessary to ensure at least a state that closes its eyes to the action of these groups, despite some formal declarations of illegality and will to combat to the militias. This combat is actually restricted to a few slums in the state of Rio de Janeiro.

Another important point is the political control of poor populations. Political groups associated with militias aim to control grassroots civil societies' leading character within slums to obtain votes for their leaders. The militia plays effectively with client and patron relations: we observe here the higher efficiency of smaller groups. This kind of association, "police-politicians," was ironically described by some delegados of the civil police as if the policemen were playing the role of "Rex of the politicians," with reference to a German shepherd acting in a popular German television series.

But ironies aside, this association between policemen and politicians proved efficient, economic, and politically viable. The militia is not interested in any sense of community and trust, other than in itself. It guides its actions by patron-client values.

Fundraising for political campaigns can rely basically on protection money and economic exploitation of security-privatized areas. For the policemen, this is also a good deal. For example, free from extortion to drug traffickers to complement their salaries, they can obtain extra gains selling security as initial commodity—the protection money—and then "legal" benefits from illegal sales: cooking LNG, pirate cable TV, services (transportation taxes, private taxes on real estate operations, real estate development—usually illegal in state-owned areas). A military policeman member of a militia can increase his salary tenfold without additional pressure on public finances.

Business figures are impressive. It is estimated that in the Rio das Pedras slum, the monthly income of the militia is about US$500,000. Cable TV firms estimated that in this slum there are 11,200 clients for pirate cable paying R$15 each (US$6.50).[38] With such figures, a potential conflict between militias may arise when other groups can fight to offer the same "services" the militia has brought, attracted by economic considerations. This scenario was not yet verified, probably because there is an "internal frontier" represented by a great number of slums to be occupied and with big business opportunities also.

The militia maintains community passivity and silence, named "tranquility." As noted above, state and public cynicism and ambiguity related to private security solutions helps the militia to develop its control and be seen as a "minor damage" even by public officials.[39] With our model based on collusion processes, we have explored some of the mechanisms that contributed to constructing this cynicism. Obviously the militia ignores legal matters related to "the rule of law," perhaps cynically relying on the ambiguity of the Brazilian Constitution of 1988, art. 144.

## PROVISIONAL CONCLUSIONS

Democracy in its different forms, including the Latin American experience, implies a necessary subordination of force and coercion to the rule of law. In those democracies, a police force will act under the command of the political authority. Police forces are usually opaque in their organization and operation and usually opposed to external political regulations, an efficient inertia. But at the same time, the police force is an indicator of the structure of social relations that constitute the Brazilian society. In any case, Brazilian society will support the burden to define through democratic and institutional procedures the police it really wants, and to produce the constitutional mechanisms and policies to make these changes. To conclude, we must ponder the results of the public security plans that have been implemented up until now. If the null hypothesis (no observable effects) is applied in the case of the plans that have been implemented since 2000, we can affirm, without any doubt, that it would be fully verified. However, one cannot as yet definitively judge the plan that is now being implemented, even though events before carnival 2003, which culminated with the emergency use of the army to keep order in Rio de Janeiro, suggest some signs of what it has represented. We see a case where the presumed asymmetry of authority between state and civil society has broken down, the state's monopoly on legitimate violence within the rule of law has failed, and, in some places within Rio de Janeiro state, chaos (or control by drug traffickers) has been imposed as a social rule. Under such a scenario, in crisis situations, the regulator adapts by refusing to intervene or, as in the case of Rio de Janeiro, repeating military intervention (Donolo, 2001). Even though the Justice Ministry considered it to be an "emergency measure," it clearly shows that there is no hope for short-term control by state police forces. We are again faced with muddling through, a contingent adaptation in turn included within the framework of limited rationales of the involved regulators, both at the federal and state levels. But now there is no alternative except to increase the intensity of the army's operations (or of some "task force" that will come to replace them). All these factors favor the development of militias as a new—and illegal—form in the stock of policing forms.

## NOTES

1. The MOUT homepage, http://www.geocities.com/Pentagon/6453/usmcmouta .html (1/6/07).

2. Many of them are cited in the bibliography, in a list that doesn't pretend to be complete.

3. Data for this chapter were collected from the newspapers *Folha de São Paulo* (archives 1977–2008) and *O Globo* and also from interviews with police officers and dwellers of militia-controlled areas.

4. Fábio de Castro. "Inclusão urbana." *Boletim Agência FAPESP*, November 28, 2006.

5. Report "Mapa da Violência: os jovens da América Latina." 2008. Brasília: Rede de Informação Tecnológica Latino-Americana (Ritla), Ministério da Justiça, Instituto Sangari, November 25.

6. Report "Mapa da Violência dos Municípios Brasileiros." 2008. Brasília: Ritla. January 29.

7. *New York Times* (international). March 6, 2003, p. A12.

8. Source: PRO-AIM. "Programa de Aprimoramento das Informações de Mortalidade no Município de São Paulo—TABNET. Informações sobre Mortalidade." 2003. Instituto Brasileiro de Geografia e Estatística (IBGE), Censo de População 2000.

9. Ministry of Health. 1996.

10. International Survey by the United Nations on the Use of Firearms. Also, the *Folha de São Paulo*, May 6, 1997, p. 3–7. Considering the country at a global level, these same indicators in other countries remain at similar levels. For example, in the United States the homicide rate for every 100,000 inhabitants evolved from 9.9 in 1979 to 9.4 in 1994.

11. Here we can quote former minister José Dirceu (chief of the Home Office). He admits that "Brazil has nothing to fear, nothing to conceal. . . . We cannot hide the sun with a sieve. There is torture, there are murders and there are violations of the human rights in Brazil," said Dirceu commenting on the statements of the advisor to the UN for human rights, Asma Jahangir. That same day, the newspapers reported that a witness that had spoken with the UN advisor was shot to death in Bahia. The minister of justice, Márcio Thomaz Bastos, reluctantly recognizes that in some regions or areas in Brazil there is an intermittent form of a true "state of war." "Sem tapar o sol com a peneira" and "Dirceu admite que há tortura no Brasil e que inspeção no Judiciário não fere soberania." *O Globo*, October 10, 2003, p. 3.

12. This conception approaches the "social corporatism" as defined by Schmitter (Schmitter, 1974:85–131).

13. Report: "Estudo de conformidade do ambiente brasileiro com a Convenção Interamericana Contra a Corrupção da OEA." Transparência Brasil (Pedro Lehmann Baracui). São Paulo. March 2006. http://www.transparencia.org.br/index.html (1/6/2009). See also Dellasoppa (2000, 2003), O'Donnell (1999), and Méndez et al. (2000).

14. The concept of the *specific logic* of a sector is taken from the Weberian meaning of eigengesetzlichkeit (Weber, 1969:II, 752).

15. For the Instituto Brasileiro de Geografia e Estatística (IBGE), 516; for the Instituto Pereira Passos, 752. Both institutions differ in their criteria for defining a favela. See Faber Paganoto Araújo. 2006. *Favela: um conflito metodológico*. http://www.observatoriodefavelas.org.br/observatorio/acervos/mapas/favela.asp (12/16/2006).

16. IBGE, 2000 Brazilian census.

17. Low income is evident from the 2000 census data. In Maré, a household chief earned about 433 Brazilian reals (US$200). Illiteracy is also very high. Maré, Rocinha, and Complexo do Alemão have the worst rates in the city or Rio de Janeiro.

18. Things change: Dona Marta slum is now (November 2008) under military police control. According to the last reports, drugs traffickers were expelled from the slum.

19. Terrain characteristics are dominant in these cases, increasing the difficulties of the type of urban conflict that the police forces must deal with. Recently the mili-

tary police of Rio de Janeiro launched an occupation of a relatively small slum in a pilot test of new tactics to recover control over areas subjected to drugs traffic activity. "To Rid Slums of Drug Gangs, Police in Rio Try War Tactics." The police have regularly launched large operations in Brazil's favelas, or slums, in their battle against drug gangs over the years, but authorities say the occupation of Santa Marta, a relatively small, contained neighborhood, is part of a new approach, a pilot project for the future of crime fighting in this violent city. Brazilian police officers are attempting counterinsurgency tactics similar to those used by U.S. soldiers in Iraq—setting up small bases occupied around the clock inside violent neighborhoods, developing intelligence by living among their adversaries, and using government funds to rebuild broken areas and generate goodwill.

"Santa Marta is like a laboratory for policing a conflict area," said Antônio Roberto Cesário de Sá, a senior official in the office of the public security secretary of Rio de Janeiro. "The idea is to rescue a territory that until now has belonged to a drug-dealing gang" (http://www.washingtonpost.com/wp-dyn/content/article/2009/01/05/AR2009010502741_pf.html [01/07/2009]).

20. An academic debate was held in Brazil regarding the relationship between poverty and drug trafficking in the slums. Alba Zaluar discussed this topic from the very beginning. See, for reference, Zaluar (2004).

21. "Armas usadas pelo tráfico preocupam os militares." *O Globo* (Rio de Janeiro). October 3, 1993, p. 19.

22. "EUA dizem que contrabando aumentou." *O Globo* (Rio de Janeiro). October 3, 1993, p. 19.

23. "Mais 15 PMs são presos por extorsão, corrupção e venda de armas pesadas" and "Policiais iam vender a bando rival fuzil e pistola apreendidos com traficantes." *O Globo* (Rio de Janeiro). September 9, 1997, p. 11.

24. "Um batalhão armado desde cedo." *O Globo* (Rio de Janeiro). June 21, 1999, p. 8.

25. As in the Operação Rio in November 1994.

26. "Responsibility" is a polysemic concept: the state, quality, or fact of being responsible or something for which one is responsible; a duty, obligation, or burden (http://www.yourdictionary.com/ahd/r/r0182600.html [31/08/2005]).

27. Army ready to act. What does the law say? "You ask me: Is the Army ready to act [in urban cases like in Rio]? It is. But it is missing a change in the legislation for it to act with clarity. Our concern is to define this," stated Cel. Cunha Mattos, who worked for six months in Haiti and currently integrates the Army Communication Sector (CCOMSEx in Portuguese). In a telephone interview we did talk exactly about the possibility of action in Rio de Janeiro. Cunha Mattos explained that the army constantly performs training geared towards urban areas, be it for combat operations (war missions) or for operations to uphold law and order, which could even be called the "non-war mission."

Today's rules about the employment of the armed forces are article 142 of the Federal Constitution, from 1988, and the complementary laws 97, from 1999, and 117, from 2004. The latter was edited a few months after the ingress of Brazil in the Peace Force in Haiti. The legislation states that the military can act to "ensure the upholding of law and order" as long as there is formal recognition that the current available resources are inefficient. "The instruments related on article 144 of the Federal Constitution are considered extinguished when, on a certain moment, they are formally recognized by the Chief of Federal Executive Power or by the Chief of the State Executive Power as unavailable, inexistent or insufficient." The "assurance of upholding the law and order" has a long history in our constitutions, as Charles Pacheco Piñon shows in reporting the Magna Cartas of 1981, 1934, 1937, 1946, 1967, 1969, and 1988.

In Rio de Janeiro's panorama, where several military operations by BOPE, CORE, and Força Nacional already exist, military action could be utilized, as previously cited by government officials and the secretary of defense himself, based on the history of the Haiti slums. The expertise of the United Nations Peace Force would be used at this stage of legislation, preparation, and military strategizing. And it is at this level that the military asks for the solution for the judicial "fill-in-the-blanks." What would be the chain of command? Would the police forces be auxiliaries to the army? Would the army have the strength of the local police in the areas of operation? Is there authorization, like in Haiti, to search suspect houses, even if it is necessary to break into them? What are the rules of engagement for weaponry and types of shots? "All of this is necessary for the safety of the action and the complementary laws do not foresee," says Cunha Mattos (http://aloisiomilani.wordpress.com/2008/03/20/exercito-pronto-para-atuar-o-que-diz-a-lei/ [8/12/08]).

28. "Segurança nas ruas de Ipanema." Morador aceita firmas irregulares por temer pivetes." *Jornal do Brasil* 2. May 21, 1995, p. 20.

29. "Segurança privada toma conta das ruas. Associação boa Viagem faz plebiscito para saber se moradores aprovam guarda particular." *O Globo* (Niterói). April 5, 1998, p. 16.

30. "GUERRA URBANA. Já existe empresa especializada no serviço, que cobra até R$250 mensais e atua em 4 regiões do centro. Comércio contrata 'zeladores de rua' para expulsar mendigo de área pública." *Folha de São Paulo*. Segunda-feira, September 27, 1999.

31. "Os camelôs da segurança. Vigilantes clandestinos da Zona Sul vendem seus serviços até em balcão de padaria." *O Globo* (Rio de Janeiro). June 1, 1998.

32. "Classe média paga PM para proteger bairro." *Folha de São Paulo*. Cotidiano. October 26, 2005, p. C1.

33. "A segurança que vem da favela. Moradores de Ipanema, Copacabana e Gávea usam serviço de morros vizinhos." *O Globo* (Rio de Janeiro). March 11, 2001, p. 16.

34. "A polícia paralela. Milícias expulsam os traficantes de drogas e já controlam 92 favelas da cidade." *O Globo* (Rio de Janeiro). December 10, 2006, p. 19.

35. This report on militias in the state of Rio de Janeiro was concluded in November 2008 and was recently delivered to the congress in Brasilia and to the public prosecutor. Two representatives and a former police chief were indicted, a very small number for the total presumed related with militias.

36. BOPE commander Col. Mário Sérgio de Brito Duarte. *O Globo*. December 10, 2006, p. 19.

37. Personal interview with a dweller living in the West Zone. Here the militia was "promised" by a political candidate, who, when elected, "cleaned" the area of drugs traffickers. Even armed with rifles, the members of the Amigos dos amigos (ADA, "friends of our friends") group were killed or forced to leave the area. "Now, things are different: people are free to walk peacefully through the slum and there are no more fights," she said.

38. "Proteção imposta." *O Globo* (Rio de Janeiro). December 11, 2006, p. 10.

39. During the New Year's Eve celebration, military policemen sent by the radio communications system "greetings" to the militia members, a completely illegal use of resources.

# REFERENCES

AA.VV. 2000."Brazil: Burden of the Past, Promise of the Future." *Daedalus, Journal of the American Academy of Arts and Sciences* 129, no. 2, Spring.

Abranches, Sérgio H. H. de. 1989."O Leviatã anémico: dilemas presentes e futuros da política social." *Planejamento e Políticas Públicas* 1, July, Brasília: IPEA, p. 7–32.

Adorno, Sérgio. 2002. "Monopólio estatal da violência na sociedade brasileira contemporânea." In *O que ler na ciência social brasileira*. Edited by Sérgio Miceli. São Paulo: ANPOCS, Editora Sumaré; Brasília, DF: CAPES, p. 267–307.

Araújo, Faber Paganoto. 2006. *Favela: um conflito metodológico*. http://www.observatoriodefavelas.org.br/observatorio/acervos/mapas/favela.asp (12/16/2006).

Arruda, João Rodrigues. 2007. *O uso politico das Forças Armadas*. Rio de Janeiro: Mauad Editora.

Bailey, F. G. 1970. *Las reglas del juego político* [Stratagems and spoils: A social anthropology of politics]. Caracas: Ed. Tiempo Nuevo.

Berger, P., and Th. Luckmann. 1989. *La Construcción Social de la Realidad*. Buenos Aires: Amorrortu.

Brandão, Z. 2006. "Urban Planning in Rio de Janeiro: A Critical Review of the Urban Design Practice in the Twentieth Century." *City & Time* 2, no. 2, p. 4. Online, http://www.ct.ceci-br.org.

Brazil. Constituição. 1988. *Constitution 1988*. Translated and revised by Istvan Vajda, Patrícia de Queiroz Carvalho Zimbres, and Vanira Tavares de Souza. 1998 rev. ed. Brasília: Senado Federal, Subsecretaria de Edições Técnicas, 1998.

Bunge, Mario. 1999. *Social Science under Debate: A Philosophical Perspective*. Toronto: University of Toronto Press.

Crozier, Michel, and E. Friedberg. 1977. *L'acteur et le système*. Paris: Éditions du Seuil.

Debrun, Michel. 1983. *La Conciliação e outras estratégias*. São Paulo: Brasiliense.

Dellasoppa, Emilio E. 2008. "Rex non curat de re publica." *Delito y Sociedad* 17, no. 25, p. 35–62.

——. 2005. "Policing in Brazil at the Beginning of the 21st Century: Severe Challenges in Developing Countries." Paper presented at the International Police Executive

Symposium 12th Annual Meeting, "Challenges for Policing in the 21st Century: A Global Assessment." September 4–9, 2005. Prague, Czech Republic.

———. 2003. *"Corruption in Post-authoritarian Brazil: An Overview and Many Open Questions."* Institute of Social Science, University of Tokyo. Discussion Paper F-107 (February).

———. 2002a. "Estratégias e Racionalidade na Polícia Civil do Estado do Rio de Janeiro." In *Violencia, sociedad y justicia en América Latina.* Edited by Roberto Briceño-León. Buenos Aires: Consejo Latinoamericano de Ciencias Sociales (CLACSO), p. 201–28.

———. 2002b. "Violencia: Planos, oportunidades e o centro radical." *Polêmica 5* (May–June). http://www2.uerj.br/%7Elabore/violencia_dellasopa.htm (3/17/04).

———. 2000. "Structure of Social Relations and Collusion Processes in Brazilian Society." *Revista Internacional de Estudos Políticos* 2, no. 3, Rio de Janeiro: UERJ/Nuseg, p. 535–56.

Dellasoppa, Emilio E. et al. 2004. *Brazil's Public Security Plans: Rationality vs. the Politics of "Muddling Through."* Washington, DC: Georgetown University, the Mexico Project.

de Tocqueville, A. [1856] 1998. *The Old Regime and the French Revolution*, vol. 1. Chicago: University of Chicago Press.

Dobel, Patrick. 1978. "The Corruption of a State." *American Political Science Review* 72, September, p. 958–73.

Dobry, Michel. 1986. *Sociologie des crises politiques.* Paris: Presses de la Fondation Nationale des Sciences Politiques.

Donolo, Carlo. 2001. *Disordine.* Roma: Donzelli Editore.

Elias, Norbert. 1997. *Os Alemães.* São Paulo: Jorge Zahar Editores.

———. 1995. *O processo civilizador*, 2nd edition, vol. 1. São Paulo: Jorge Zahar Editores.

———. 1988. "Violence and Civilization: The State Monopoly of Physical Violence and Its Infringement." In *Civil Society and the State.* Edited by John Keane. London: Verso, p. 129–46.

Giddens, Anthony. 2001. *O Estado-nação e a violência.* São Paulo: Edusp.

Lindblom, Charles E. 1995. "The Science of 'Muddling' Through." In *Public Policy: The Essential Readings.* Edited by Stella Theodoulou and Matthew Can. New York: Prentice Hall, p. 113–17.

———. 1980. *The Policy-Making Process.* Englewood Cliffs, NJ: Prentice Hall.

———. 1978. "Defining the Policy Problem." In *Decisions, Organizations and Society.* Edited by F. G. Castles et al. New York: Penguin Books/The Open University.

Machado da Silva, Luiz A. 1993. "Violência e sociabilidade. Tenências da atual conjuntura urbana no Brasil." Seminário Globalização, fragmentação e Reforma Urbana. October 26–29, 1993. Itamonte, MG, Brazil.

———. 1991. "Violência Urbana: representação de uma ordem social." 15th Encontro Anual da ANPOCS. October 15–18, 1991. Caxambú, Brazil.

———. 1990. "Desdobramentos do Campo Temático dos Movimentos Sociais." 14th Encontro Anual da ANPOCS. October 22–26, 1991. Caxambú, Brazil.

Méndez, Juan, Guillermo O'Donnell, and Paulo Sérgio Pinheiro, eds. 2000. *Democracia, Violência e Injustiça. O Não- Estado de Direito na América Latina.* São Paulo: Paz e Terra.

Ministério da Justiça. 2001. *Balanço de 500 dias de PNSP—Balanço Consolidado de Destaques.* Brasília: Government of Brazil.

———. 2000. "Orientação Estratégica do Ministério da Justiça para a Elaboração do Plano Plurianual 2000–2003." Brasília: Government of Brazil.

Monjardet, Dominique. 2003. *O que Faz a Polícia.* São Paulo: Edusp.

Moore, Tom. 2006. *Dona Marta Favela, Rio de Janeiro: At the Foot of the Hill.* http://www.brazilmax.com/news.cfm/tborigem/pl_southcentral/id/41 (06/01/2007).

Mortara, G. (coord.). 1946. *Tábuas de Mortalidade e Sobrevivência Brasileiras. Distrito Federal e Município de São Paulo.* Rio de Janeiro: IBGE.

O'Donnell, Guillermo. 1999. "Horizontal Accountability in New Democracies." In *The Self-Restraining State.* Edited by Schedler et al. Boulder, CO: Lynne Rienner Publishers, p. 29–52.

———. 1997. *Contrapuntos. Ensayos escogidos sobre autoritarismo y democratización.* Buenos Aires: Paidós.

———. 1994. "Delegative Democracy." *Journal of Democracy* 5, no. 1, January 1994, p. 55–69.

Ouchi, William G. 1980. "Markets, Bureaucracies and Clans." *Administrative Science Quarterly* 25, no. 1, March 1980, p. 129–41.

Pinheiro, Paulo Sérgio. 2001. "Transição política e não-estado de direito na República." In *Brasil, un século de transformações.* Edited by Ignacy Sachs, Jorge Wilhem, and Paulo Sérgio Pinheiro. São Paulo: Companhia de las Letras, p. 260–305.

Plano Nacional de Segurança Pública. Ministério da Justiça. June 20, 2000. http://www.mj.gov.br/ (3/8/03).

Reiner, Robert. 2004. *A Política da Polícia.* São Paulo: Edusp.

Schmitter, P. C. 1974. "Still the Century of Corporatism?" *The Review of Politics* vol. 36, no. 1. pp. 85–131.

Secretaria Nacional de Segurança Pública (SENASP). SENASP/MJ. http://www.mj.gov.br/Senasp/senasp/inst_conceitos.htm (3/3/03).

United Nations Development Programme. 2005. *A Home in the City.* The Millennium Project.

Weber, Max. 1969. *Economia y Sociedad.* México: Fondo de Cultura Econômica.

Weffort, Francisco. 1990. "A América errada." *Lua Nova* 21, October 1990, p. 5–40.

Wievorka, 1997. *Une société fragmentée.* Paris: La Découverte.

Zaluar, Alba. 2004. *Integração perversa: pobreza e tráfico de drogas.* Rio de Janeiro: FGV Editora.

*Chapter Five*

# Australian Police Responses to Transnational Crime and Terrorism

Steve James and Ian Warren

Australia's geographic isolation and absence of shared international borders places it in a unique position regarding transnational crime and terrorism. Historically, even during two world wars and extensive global conflict, Australia has been largely immune from direct threats of invasion or attack. However, various facets of contemporary global life provide significant challenges to customary levels of domestic security. Increased air and sea travel, global communication technologies, strong and overt involvement in the "war on terror," a diverse multicultural population with migrants from all points of the globe, combined with often tense relationships with its most immediate neighbors in the South Pacific islands to the east and Indonesia and Southeast Asia to the west, all heighten the vulnerability of this southern nation to various transnational and terrorism-related threats.

Contemporary Australian life is built upon the foundations of English colonial settlement. Prior to federation in 1901, the six colonies had founded independent parliaments, courts, and law enforcement structures, which were overseen at a distance in Westminster (see James, 1994, pp. 1–12). By the turn of the twentieth century it was well recognized that a unified national system of government was required to deal with regulatory matters of collective interest. As in the United States, delegates from each governmental entity forged an agreement on a specific range of legislative, judicial, and executive powers to be transferred to the national level and enumerated in the *Commonwealth of Australia Constitution Act*, 1901, passed by the British parliament. This process identified various heads of Commonwealth lawmaking and enforcement responsibility, including postal and telecommunications law, intellectual property, customs, defense, the development of a national currency system, matrimonial law, and migration law (*Commonwealth of Australia Constitution Act*,

1901, section 51). The states retained residual lawmaking power over areas of responsibility not expressly conferred on the Commonwealth, including the passage and enforcement of most criminal laws dealing with offenses against the person and property crime (see *Crimes Act* Victoria, 1958; *Crimes Act* New South Wales, 1900; Findlay, Odgers, and Yeo, 2005). This has produced a highly fragmented series of laws and enforcement arrangements at the domestic level, with each state retaining a separate criminal code, police force, court system, and regime of criminal punishments (Finnane, 1987; 1994); federal laws and enforcement arrangements both duplicate and mirror existing state laws, but retain their primary focus on domestic cross-border crime, or the maintenance of order within Australia's non-self-governing domestic and international territories.

Since federation there have been persistent calls to nationalize various elements of Australian lawmaking and enforcement. However, obtaining agreement by the majority of people in the majority of states to confer the relevant power by referendum as required in the national constitution is almost impossible. Growing concerns over the threats to national security posed by transnational crime and terrorism, combined with the rather cumbersome nature of domestic cross-border legal and enforcement arrangements, have contributed to a radical sea change in national lawmaking, law enforcement, and crime prevention. Indeed, such is the extent and scope of change in this field that conventional methods for describing Australian policing and law enforcement practices, philosophies, and mandates are largely inappropriate in the twenty-first-century regulatory landscape.

Two main trends illustrate the nature and scope of one of the most profound shifts in the history of Australian policing. The first relates to the unprecedented growth of federal policing in terms of the range of enforcement agencies, their numbers, and their jurisdiction. The most notable agency to experience such growth is the Australian Federal Police (AFP), which has benefited from both a substantial restructuring of Commonwealth policing arrangements beginning in the mid-1970s (James, 2005, p. 81) and the growth of the illicit drug trade in subsequent decades (Chappell, 1996; Bryett et al., 1994). The AFP now boasts 5,435 sworn and unsworn personnel working in all states and territories of Australia and a gross operating budget of $1,086 million (Australian Federal Police, 2006, pp. 165 and 151). This represents an incremental annual increase of around 10.5 percent (James, 2005, p. 82 citing Keelty, 2004) making the AFP the fourth-largest police force in the country. This trend is mirrored within other federal enforcement and security agencies such as the Australian Customs Service (ACS) and the Australian Security Intelligence Organisation (ASIO). The creation of new strategic coordination bodies aimed at streamlining domestic interjurisdictional enforcement initiatives, such as the Australian Crime Commission (ACC), and the expansion of both internal and external bodies designed to enhance organizational accountability and operational efficiency within federal government departments add to the mix of contemporary interagency law enforcement arrangements at the domestic level.

The second trend stems logically from the first and relates to increased jurisdictional scope of the AFP and other enforcement and security agencies both within Australia and offshore. Part of the rationale for this expansion rests with an increased concern over the impact of transnational crime and terrorism on Australia in recent decades. However, a strong element of this shift is wedded in overtly preventative and security-driven activities. Therefore, rather than being characterized by a transferal of conventional state criminal law jurisdiction to the federal level, the expansion of federal law enforcement activity is characterized by a rapidly evolving security-centered focus. The range of initiatives emerging under this philosophy include the involvement of AFP personnel in international peacekeeping and disaster recovery missions in the South Pacific, Sudan, and Jordan (AFP, 2006, p. 59; James, 2005, p. 84); the secondment of AFP personnel to international criminal investigations involving Australian citizens or business interests on foreign soil; and the gathering of intelligence on or apprehension of Australian citizens involved in illicit transnational or terrorist activities.

Three explosions in Bali on 1 October 2005 resulted in 22 deaths including four Australians. Within one hour of this tragedy, the Indonesian National Police (INP) invited the AFP to participate in the response. The AFP provided 43 members to the INP investigation providing skills which included operations support, forensics, disaster victim identification, bomb data, protection and security, and counter-terrorism intelligence. The subsequent arrest of several key suspects by the INP is an indication of the robustness of this partnership. (AFP, 2006, p. 3)

While the AFP is by no means the only organization involved in these global, multilateral security and response arrangements, the scope of the jurisdictional and ideological shift demonstrated by this organization's recent evolution has a substantial filtration effect which seemingly redefines the idea of Australian policing. The most notable manifestation of this trend is the formation of the Australian Crime Commission (ACC), permanently chaired by the AFP commissioner (James, 2005, p. 83). The ACC's mandate focuses on the strategic assessment of national crime risks and brokering collaborative links between the various national and state policing agencies. This is indicative of a broader shift towards a "whole-of-government approach" to law enforcement and domestic security, driven by a strategic problem-solving agenda designed to coordinate disparate state policing activities through targeted oversight at the national level. When the ACC was first created through federal legislation in 2002, its original mandate included:

- a focus on criminal intelligence collection and the establishment of national intelligence priorities;
- access to task force investigative capabilities to give effect to its intelligence functions and to support its overall operations;
- the ACC board to include representatives from all states and territories with ministerial oversight retained by having the Board report to an intergovernmental committee of Commonwealth, state, and territory ministers;
- the process for obtaining investigation reference to be streamlined; and
- the ACC to retain the capability to use coercive powers to investigate criminal activity of national significance (Findlay, Odgers, and Yeo, 2005, p. 85; Australian Government and Australian Institute of Criminology, 2004, pp. 19–20).

The contemporary language of Australian policing and law enforcement emphasizes strategic risk identification and assessment, intelligence, domestic security, and crime prevention. Notions of interagency collaboration, networking, and nodal governance are prominent within a framework aiming to forge greater levels of civilian responsibility for the ongoing management of security risks and providing intelligence to the enforcement community (Palmer and Whelan, 2006; Brodeur and Dupont, 2006; Dupont, 2004). In practical terms, the viability of these functions is dependent on simultaneously targeting local and international activities impacting on Australia's domestic security or extensive offshore interests (see Australian Government/ Department of Foreign Affairs and Trade, 2004, p. 69). It is within this structural and ideological framework that our current understandings of transnational crime, terrorism, and the multiagency law enforcement responses to these problems are forged.


## TRANSNATIONAL CRIME

Australia's geographic isolation is no longer a barrier to transnational crime. Globalization, the mass movement of people, Internet culture, and the lucrative economies sustaining demand-and-supply patterns in the illicit drug trade have all had a profound impact on the Australian crime and law enforcement landscape since the end of World War II. Most contemporary academic and government literature specifies particular types of criminal activity which are of concern and which generate a range of targeted law enforcement responses by a combination of state and national enforcement agencies under the banner of transnational crime. Less clear is the frequency of this behavior, despite a range of currently available data from a growing number of diverse sources. Typologies of transnational crime focus broadly on the illicit drug trade, people smuggling, small-arms smuggling, and money laundering (see Goldsmith, 2006a, pp. 221–33). Other forms of transnational crime, which are either poorly understood or underresearched, include the piracy of copyrighted music, film, or computer software; child sex tourism and sex slavery; and the illicit trade in exotic animals and related environmental offenses related to fishing, toxic-waste dumping, and natural resource exploitation. The global accessibility and popularity of the Internet ensures cybercrime can also be added to this list (Smith and Grabosky, 2006). However, it is wrong in some respects to pigeonhole such typologies into rigid and discrete categories. For instance, illicit drug trafficking is often closely linked to money laundering. Equally, cybercrime has been linked to global Internet pedophilia networks, banking and credit card fraud, money laundering, identity theft, terrorism, and associated threats to the security of Australia's critical infrastructure (Parliamentary Joint Committee on the Australian Crime Commission, 2004). Therefore, the relationship between different types of transnational crime is extremely fluid, complicating attempts to precisely measure these phenomena under rigid definitional headings.

Some classes of activity, such as cybercrime, have a range of highly technical and qualitatively distinct subclassifications. This is illustrated by the following evidence presented by the Australian High Tech Crime Centre to a parliamentary joint committee into the ACC, which expands on the accepted law enforcement definition of cybercrime involving use of a computer "as a tool in the commission of an offence, as the target of an offence, or used as a storage device in the commission of an offence":

> We are not concentrating just on the Internet . . . and cyber is usually referred to as the Internet. We are looking at the misuse of technology in a more holistic sense. The danger is that we will miss other exploits or other criminal activities that fall outside the strict definition of the Internet. . . . We do not want to limit ourselves to just the Internet, while recognising that the Internet will form the backbone of a whole range of those activities . . . even things like telephony, with the move to IP telephone systems rather than switch systems, are becoming part of the Internet. That is the reason for drawing that distinction. (Parliamentary Joint Committee on the Australian Crime Commission, 2004, pp. 5–6)

These definitional issues are crucial in terms of measuring the nature and extent of such behavior, its impact on Australian law enforcement, and the evolutionary character of collaborative prevention arrangements in a multiagency environment. Cybercrime is particularly prone to complication given its capacity to incorporate a vast range of illegal conduct emanating from domestic or offshore sources. The wide variety of activities associated with cybercrime include organized consumer fraud scams (Smith, 2007), the dissemination of programs such as "botnets" and "zombies" aimed at disrupting or disabling computer systems (Choo, 2007), the predatory sexual behavior of adult men in online chat rooms (Krone, 2005) and the adoption of complex methods to conceal one's identity or source of transmission to avoid criminal detection (Smith, 2004). Further complexities emerge as new developments, such as the proliferation of wireless computer technologies, generate their own idiosyncratic problems, which in turn create new generations of targeted security, prevention, detection, and enforcement initiatives (see Urbas and Krone, 2006).

While cybercrime is arguably unique in terms of its scope, the sheer diversity of activities it encompasses, and its global reach, these characteristics are also prominent in other forms of transnational crime to varying degrees. The capacity to penetrate domestic and international geographic borders, often through complex organized, networked, and clandestine activity, is central to most transnational offenders (see Goldsmith, 2006a). Nevertheless, recent literature on "organized" crime reinforces the limitations of a typological approach by providing a more qualitative description of the range of behaviors, motives, and structure of certain groups, which reflect their criminal intentions. According to the Australian Institute of Criminology, organized crime in Australia involves a combination of:

- local criminal milieux which are typically loosely structured groups involved in a variety of illicit enterprises;
- networks or "secret societies" based in other countries which have local networks in Australia, and are characterised by shared ethnic backgrounds; and
- other criminal groups, such as paedophile networks and outlaw motorcycle gangs (Australian Government and Australian Institute of Criminology, 2004, p. 6).

The extent to which these groups or their operations in Australia involve transnational criminal behavior remains conjectural in the absence of further in-depth research into their structure, composition, and common activities. However, Morrison (2002) indicates many of the transnational organized crime groups stem from unstable political or social environments, or are relatively small-scale and opportunistic in their illicit behavior (see also Mackenzie, 2002). This contradicts much available yet anecdotal evidence on the highly organized nature of most transnational criminal activity. Moreover, Australia's geographic remoteness makes it quite possible any illicit transnational activity that occurs on Australian soil represents the end point in a global chain of law breaking across several international borders. This has significant implications for current law enforcement and crime prevention initiatives emanating from Australian state or federal agencies by heightening the need for strong collaborative links and increased financial resources to conduct strategic operations targeting organized criminal behavior either domestically or on foreign soil.

At a more legalistic level, transnational crime can encompass the illegal behavior of foreign nationals on Australian soil, or conduct which targets or threatens Australian business interests, government officials, or cultural activities in offshore locations. One recent trend in domestic criminal law involves the passage of a range of laws with extraterritorial application associated with major sporting and cultural events attracting a large influx of overseas visitors or dignitaries. The Sydney 2000 Olympic Games is a pertinent example which had profound implications for Australian federal and state law enforcement agencies in a range of areas, including event security, intelligence, border management, security at arrival and departure points, and the protection of international dignitaries (Australian National Audit Office, 1998). Extraterritorial legislation strengthens each of these risk management functions by enabling criminal prosecution in the host or "victim" jurisdiction if an unlawful act is planned or executed interstate or overseas but has a "real and substantial link" to the host region (see *Sports Event Ticketing (Fair Access) Act*, Victoria, 2002, section 6; *Crimes (Traffic in Narcotic Drugs and Psychotropic Substances) Act*, 1990). For example, Victorian laws dealing with theft or fraud can have extraterritorial application:

- if a significant part of the conduct relating to, or constituting the doing of the act or thing, or the omission, occurred in Victoria; or
- where the act or thing was done, or the omission occurred, wholly outside Victoria, if the act or thing was done, or omitted to be done, with the intention that substantial harmful effects arise in Victoria and such effects did arise (*Crimes Act*, Victoria, section 80A).

Australian state or federal law enforcers are increasingly involved in a range of information-sharing activities designed to assist overseas police during the investigative phase. Complex federal provisions allow for mutual assistance arrangements to be made with overseas jurisdictions to promote the gathering and sharing of intelligence or evidence or the arrest and transportation of criminal suspects to face trial in Australia, with reciprocal rights available to overseas states if such assistance is requested (see *Mutual Assistance in Criminal Matters Act*, Commonwealth, 1987). Crimes detected on Australian soil can be prosecuted under either the state or Commonwealth criminal law, but in rare cases where the offense is relatively minor and does not carry a term of imprisonment, a foreign national can be tried, convicted, and sentenced in absentia (Herald and Weekly Times, 2007). A further scenario with transnational implications involves a suspect fleeing Australian soil either before or during a criminal trial. Two high-profile examples, involving white-collar offender Christopher Skase (Goldsmith, 2006b, p. 427) and "fugitive crime boss" Tony Mokbel (Shanahan, 2007), highlight not only the variability of different bilateral extradition arrangements, but also the ease of contemporary global air travel in hampering the administration of justice at domestic level.

The complexities, contradictions, and enforcement responses brought about by recent developments in transnational crime are best illustrated by focusing attention on the fields of drug trafficking and terrorism. The range of federal and state legal, enforcement, policy, and crime-prevention initiatives under a whole-of-government approach in these particular areas exemplifies the perceived impact of transnational crime on contemporary Australian life more generally. Each example is also in some respects a unique counterpoint to the other. The transnational character of illicit drug trafficking has a relatively strong knowledge base, dating back to the first systematic governmental inquiries into this field in the late 1970s (Commonwealth of Australia, 1980). However, the nature, extent, and frequency of drug addiction and the availability of illicit drugs on the streets seriously brings into question the reach and effectiveness of recent domestic and transnational enforcement measures. In contrast, the body of knowledge on, and coordinated legislative and enforcement reaction to, terrorism on Australian soil or associated with Australian interests overseas is comparatively recent, extremely wide-reaching, and poorly understood. Events since September 11, 2001, and the bombing of the Sari Nightclub in the Kuta district of Bali on October 12, 2002, where eighty-eight Australians were killed, have arguably been the primary catalysts for most recent changes to Australia's transnational law enforcement landscape.

## TRANSNATIONAL DIMENSIONS OF ILLICIT DRUG TRAFFICKING

Most Australian laws identifying and prohibiting illicit drugs have been enacted at the state level (see *Drugs, Poisons and Controlled Substances Act* Victoria, 1981; *Drug Misuse and Trafficking Act* New South Wales, 1985). These provisions contain detailed definitions of the range of illicit substances and their derivatives which are subject to criminal regulation; various offenses relating to their trafficking, supply, or use; and offenses related to the possession and sale of paraphernalia used in the cultivation, manufacture, refinement, or consumption process (*Drugs, Poisons and Controlled Substances Act* Victoria, 1981, sections 4, 70–80H and schedule 11). A supplementary body of law deals with the forfeiture of prohibited items or the proceeds of illicit drug crime (*Confiscation Act* Victoria, 1997). This regime places the bulk of drug law enforcement activity in Australia squarely within the state policing realm. However, the *Criminal Code* (1995, part 9.1) creates a national criminal law enforcement regime working in tandem with existing state law, focusing on large-scale interstate criminal activity or illegal behavior detected in the Australian Capital Territory, the Northern Territory, or various offshore territories governed by Australia located in the South Pacific.

Australia's ratification of the 1961 "Single Convention on Narcotic Drugs" in December 1967 represents the first serious attempt to gain agreement amongst the six state governments for a unified national approach to curb the importation of heroin and opium into Australia (Commonwealth of Australia, 1980, book A, p. A358). From the late 1960s a series of reforms to the *Customs Act* of 1901 and various regulations under this legislation have expanded border protection arrangements, enabling federal authorities to search, seize, confiscate, and prosecute for a variety of activities associated with importing or exporting illicit substances into and outside Australian territory. Offenses include possession of a prohibited import, attempts or conspiracies to import or export a prohibited item, attempts to obtain possession of a prohibited import once it reaches Australian soil, and being in charge of an aircraft, ship, or boat used for an illicit purpose (*Customs Act* Commonwealth 1901, sections 233–233BA; *Customs [Prohibited Imports] Regulations* Commonwealth 1956, reg. 5; Commonwealth of Australia, 1980, book A, pp. A370–A371). The national *Criminal Code* (1995, part 9.1) also proscribes the cultivation, trafficking, and possession of various illicit substances, while the *Crimes (Traffic in Narcotic Drugs and Psychotropic Substances) Act* (1990) governs the offshore activities of Australian citizens intending to traffic prohibited substances into the country or dealing drugs on Australian seacraft or aircraft.

The intersections of Australian state and federal law in the drugs field are complicated by the existence of various prevention strategies developed through a national public health framework which targets vulnerable user populations. For example, the National Drug Strategy is formulated and overseen by a centralized national forum, the Ministerial Council on Drug Strategy (MCDS). The Council liaises closely with the Australasian Police Ministers' Council, the Australian Health Ministers' Council, and various other governmental bodies dealing with youth and indigenous affairs (Ministerial Council on Drug Strategy, 2004, p. 1). The primary responsibility of law enforcement within this whole-of-government framework emphasizes the role of forging interagency partnerships to "prevent and reduce the availability of drugs" by targeting drug supply emanating from local or international sources (Ministerial Council on Drug Strategy, 2004, p. 7). This approach endorses many existing state and federal initiatives focusing on transnational drug trafficking, with the Council facilitating ongoing policy guidance, research and knowledge building, interagency coordination and oversight, and increased levels of international cooperation designed to:

- disrupt the manufacture and supply of illicit drugs;
- enhance efforts to control the inappropriate supply and diversion of pharmaceutical drugs and precursor chemicals;
- dismantle organized crime;
- implement effective legislation and regulatory regimes and education programs for key justice and health professionals;
- implement effective legislation and regulation of alcohol, tobacco, and other substances to reduce associated harms to the community; and
- examine mechanisms to ensure that all relevant stakeholders participate in implementing law enforcement strategies in all jurisdictions (Ministerial Council on Drug Strategy, 2004, p. 7; Intergovernmental Committee on Drugs, 2006, p. 5; Parliamentary Joint Committee on the Australian Crime Commission, 2007, pp. 30–31).

Despite this wide range of initiatives and the increasing number of studies conducted into illicit drug trafficking and usage patterns in recent decades, the overall size of the illicit drug market in Australia remains largely unknown (ANAO, 2002, pp. 11 and 34). According to Homel and Willis (2007), recent estimates to measure total direct and indirect expenditure on drug law enforcement and related interdiction policies are highly varied, but are in the general vicinity of 2 billion Australian dollars. In part, this level of imprecision is fuelled by different federal, state, and local agency priorities, which produce conflicting methods of defining, measuring and analyzing the nature and extent of the illicit market and its various social impacts. This is particularly evident in a recent federal parliamentary joint committee review into the manufacture and importation of "amphetamines and other synthetic drugs" (AOSD) in Australia, which recommended the various federal and state agencies needed to "standardise the terms being used to describe amphetamines and other synthetic drugs, particularly for research and statistical purposes" (Parliamentary Joint Committee on the Australian Crime Commission, 2007, p. 7). The evolving nature of drug manufacture in recent decades also contributes to inaccurate measurement, with new substances generating new consumption patterns and associated prevention and enforcement priorities. Nevertheless, widespread recognition of the "global drug problem" (Ministerial Council on Drug Strategy, 2004, p. 13) and the need to develop coordinated preventative measures helps to drive the contemporary knowledge base in Australia, with a range of studies conducted by national, state, and local enforcement and public health agencies providing insight into how this problem has evolved in recent decades.

Most available data focuses on particular substances, their geographic source of cultivation and their various effects on user populations, and law enforcement priorities at the domestic level. The starting point for systematic data gathering on this issue is the Williams Royal Commission into drugs undertaken during the late 1970s (Commonwealth of Australia, 1980). The six-volume report identified and synthesized a range of local, national, and international data on illicit drug use and supply patterns to paint a contextual picture of each level of the illicit production and consumption chain. This in turn helped to inform the contemporary law enforcement response within the whole-of-government approach.

There is little to suggest that the starting points in the transnational supply chain for the range of illicit substances have changed significantly since the Williams Royal Commission. What has altered is the need for more sophisticated theoretical and conceptual tools with which to strategically identify the principal risks, based on available production, supply, and cost trends (Morrison, 2003). The most notable shifts relate to the evolution of the types of substances produced in each region and the effectiveness of border inspection procedures to curb importation into Australia. Cocaine supply trends offer the most pertinent illustration of the stability in the global production market and the effectiveness of recent supply reduction methods at the domestic level. The Williams Royal Commission reported no domestic cocaine production in Australia during the 1970s (Commonwealth of Australia, 1980, book A, p. A184), with the global supply chain concentrated in South America. By 2005, Bolivia, Peru, and Colombia were identified as the primary sources of global coca leaf cultivation, with production in Colombia increasing despite a government-sponsored "eradication and alternative development" policy (Australian Crime Commission, 2007, p. 52). The remaining South American nations were important transit locations for illicit supply into the global consumption market. Notably, in recent years the amount of cocaine detected and seized by the ACS has dropped markedly from just under one thousand kilograms in 2001–2002 to eighty-three kilograms in 2005–2006 (Australian Crime Commission, 2007, p. 53). The number of annual seizures is also declining from around 650 in 2003–2004 to 367 in 2005–2006, indicating most illicit importation detected by the ACS involves only small amounts. This could be classified as a success in restricting the supply of cocaine into Australia, with the reduction of large-scale seizures demonstrating "an absence of large, professionally organized seaborne shipments sent to Australia as sea cargo, by motherships meeting pickup vessels at sea, by seagoing small-craft, or with crew of merchant ships" (Australian Crime Commission, 2007, p. 53).

Throughout the 1970s and well into the 1990s the prevalence of heroin in Australia was perhaps of most concern due to its addictive properties, the rates of use amongst the domestic population, and the extensive cultivation of opium within the Golden Triangle region of Southeast Asia (Commonwealth of Australia, 1980, book A, p. A176). The geographic proximity of this region to Australia is notable for a variety of reasons and highlights the fusion of issues underpinning the contemporary transnational crime focus. In the immediate aftermath of the Vietnam War, Australia's Vietnamese-born population was around 700. By the 2001 national census, a combination of refugee settlement programs and family reunion initiatives in subsequent years saw this population rise to 155,000, or 1 percent of the total Australian population (Australian Bureau of Statistics, 2005). Recent reports indicate contemporary heroin importation trends are not currently "ethno-specific," but also suggest the strong involvement of both highly organized and more "opportunistic" ventures through air, sea, and mail carriage emanating from Vietnam, Cambodia, Thailand, Singapore, Hong Kong, India, and Pakistan. Global seizure data reported by the ACC indicates heroin and opium seizures began to increase in 2005 (Australian Crime Commission, 2007, p. 45), with embarkation points beginning to widen and incorporating nations such as Tanzania, the United Arab Emirates, South Africa, Nigeria, Kyrgyzstan, and Canada (Australian Crime Commission, 2007, p. 45). However, Morrison (2003) indicates the market is far from stable, with cost and production variations making consistent predictions of likely importation trends in Australia extremely difficult. This is compounded by the numerous transit points from the original production sources in the Golden Triangle region to the end point in Australia. In short, heroin is characterized by a highly fluid supply pattern, with recent intelligence-led border controls in Australia having some, albeit an imprecise, impact in reducing importation levels in recent years.

The strategic targeting of consistent supply sources can also produce false leads for law enforcers, with the production and distribution of new substances in global drug markets disturbing the accuracy of the existing knowledge base upon which interception and related preventative targets are identified. This is exemplified by the shift towards the production of high-grade methamphetamine. Recent estimates indicate approximately 50 percent of global amphetamine manufacture is concentrated in Asia, with the drug's ease of production, marketability, and lucrative profit margin making it a logical replacement for heroin amongst Asian organized crime gangs (Parliamentary

Joint Committee on the Australian Crime Commission, 2007, p. 17). There is a considerable methamphetamine supply market originating in North America, with the Czech Republic and Baltic states involved in most production throughout Europe. Other drugs, such as Methylenedioxymethamphetamine (MDMA or ecstasy), are commonly classified alongside methamphetamine but have a very distinct production and supply market. Evidence provided by the AFP to the 2007 parliamentary joint committee investigation highlights not only this point, but also the sophistication underpinning the production and exportation process, including the importance of the street-level demand and price.

> Global MDMA manufacture and trafficking is generally controlled by European syndicates emanating from the Netherlands. Information received from the AFP Liaison Officer in the Hague has identified that these groups operate in a manner similar to that employed by multinational companies including conducting cost benefit analyses on MDMA trafficking which took into consideration factors such as foreign exchange rates in the transhipment of drugs. This level of sophistication is alleged to exist within the transnational MDMA market while similar opportunistic importation attempts continue to occur. The street price of MDMA in Australia is considerably higher than in other countries, ensuring that Australia will remain an attractive target for MDMA trafficking syndicates. (Parliamentary Joint Committee on the Australian Crime Commission, 2007, p. 17 [reference omitted])

A crucial focus of recent federal enforcement involves targeting "the inappropriate supply and diversion of pharmaceutical drugs and precursor chemicals" (Intergovernmental Committee on Drugs, 2006, p. 34) to prevent the manufacture of MDMA at the domestic level. More recent evidence indicates that despite several large-scale seizures through incoming sea cargo, the domestic consumption market has remained relatively stable, with around 84 percent of detections in 2004–2005 being of moderate size and discovered through the Australian postal system. Nevertheless, the scale of illicit international trafficking in processed ecstasy and the coordinated efforts adopted by Australian law enforcement agencies to curb its supply are clearly demonstrated by the following seizures:

- a joint Customs/AFP operation which led to the detection in Melbourne in April 2005 of more than one tonne of MDMA in a shipping container. This was one of the world's largest seizures of MDMA and resulted in the arrest of four men;
- Australia's second largest seizure of MDMA in Melbourne, with an air cargo screener detecting 818 kilograms of MDMA in the shell on an industrial baker's oven; and

- approximately two tonnes of MDMA precursors in a sea cargo consignment from China. This operation involved cooperation between Customs, the AFP, the ACC, Victoria Police and NSW Police (Intergovernmental Committee on Drugs, 2006, p. 36).

Collaborations with regional enforcement agencies in countries such as New Zealand (New Zealand Customs Service, 2006) and Fiji (AFP, 2004a, p. 4) have also led to significant seizures of MDMA or ecstasy in recent times.

Finally, cannabis is by far the most popular and widely available illicit substance in Australia, accounting for just over 70 percent of all drug arrests for trafficking and consumption throughout the nation (Australian Institute of Health and Welfare, 2007, pp. 71–72; ACC, 2007, p. 90). The difficulty with cannabis from a transnational law enforcement perspective is its ease of cultivation and broadening supply base. The global industry is no longer confined to specific geographic regions such as Afghanistan, Turkey, Lebanon, South Africa, and the West Indies, which were common points of supply during the 1980s (Commonwealth of Australia, 1980, Book A, pp. A187–194). There is also extensive cannabis production within Australia, facilitated by the use of hydroponic technologies by those growing for personal use or commercial distribution. Most transnational supply emanates from Papua New Guinea to the immediate north of Australia (see McCusker, 2006) and the United States, although ACS data indicates several points of embarkation including Germany, India, and Singapore. Most seizures in 2005–2006 were discovered through the postal system, in air cargo, or in the luggage of air passengers (see ACC, 2007, pp. 32–34).

Three additional forms of data add to the knowledge base on the illicit drug trade in Australia. Table 5.1 provides an overview of the number of illicit drug detections and quantities of each substance seized by the ACS between 2003 and 2006. The statistics demonstrate some constancy in seizure patterns for certain substances, but also some notable fluctuations in the transnational supply trends from year to year. Part of this variability could be directly attributable to targeted enforcement initiatives directed at transnational supply operations and the increased risk of detection this produces. This could be viewed as a strong measure of the effectiveness of the whole-of-government approach advocated by the MCDS and the various enforcement agencies. However, other factors, including varying patterns in the illicit offshore production and supply chain, are undoubtedly at play.

Domestic usage and accessibility data provide a further indicator of the various benefits and problems of contemporary transnational enforcement initiatives. It is clear that Australia remains a lucrative market for organized drug trafficking networks based on current domestic consumption and

Table 5.1. Australian Customs Service Drug Detections and Amounts Seized 2003–2006

| | Detections | | | Weight (kg) where confirmed | | |
|---|---|---|---|---|---|---|
| | 2003–2004 | 2004–2005 | 2005–2006 | 2003–2004 | 2004–2005 | 2005–2006 |
| Cannabis | 658 | 476 | 504 | 708.92 | 4.48 | 47.27 |
| Cocaine | 652 | 443 | 376 | 138.16 | 196.98 | 83.4 |
| Heroin | 64 | 192 | 300 | 61.29 | 172.54 | 47.11 |
| MDMA (ecstasy) | 294 | 171 | 135 | 873.42 | 2,377.71 | 413.31 |
| Amphetamine-type stimulants | 141 | 206 | 423 | 5.94 | 156.9 | 89.67 |
| Precursors (prohibited raw materials) | 782 | 282 | 563 | — | — | — |
| Performance- and image-enhancing drugs | 1,216 | 1,054 | 1,089 | — | — | — |
| Other | 2,899 | 1,568 | 2,012 | — | — | — |

Source: Australian Customs Service, 2006, p. 46.

availability figures. In the twelve months preceding the most recent self-report survey into national drug consumption patterns conducted by the Australian Institute of Health and Welfare in 2004, projection calculations indicated around one in six or 2.5 million Australians had used an illicit substance in the previous twelve months (AIHW, 2005, p. 33). For certain substances such as cannabis, self-report data indicates patterns of experimentation and regular usage amongst teenagers have been declining since the mid-1990s (see Victorian Department of Human Services, 2006a, pp. 94–96). However, poly–drug use amongst older age groups appears to be increasing, with certain substances such as ecstasy, methamphetamine, and cocaine becoming more popular and more readily available amongst the Australian public (Victorian Department of Human Services, 2006b, pp. 89–92; Johnston, Quinn, and Jenkinson, 2006, pp. 10–12; AIHW, 2007). Given lower rates of detection and lower seizures by ACS inspectors in recent years, these rates of availability could be due to a time lag or extensive stockpiling between the time of importation and the ultimate point of use.

Table 5.2 is based on a self-report study involving injecting drug users in the state of Victoria and offers some guidance on current market availability, purity, and cost trends for a range of illicit substances at their end point in the domestic or global supply chain (Jenkinson and Quinn, 2007, p. xi). This information is one measure of the impact of global supply patterns on local consumers (see also O'Brien et al., 2007). Notably, despite recent whole-of-government approaches and the range of successful transnational enforcement initiatives, including the recent large-scale ecstasy seizures, most substances are relatively easy to access at the local level through stable domestic markets and informal social networks.

A final measure which is useful to consider is drawn from a recent report into the sentencing of federal offenders conducted by the Australian Law Reform Commission (ALRC) (2006). A detailed appendix prepared by the Australian Institute of Criminology provides an extensive statistical review of the current federal offender muster for all offense categories. While the majority of incarcerations for summary offenses involve breaches of the national *Criminal Code* (1995) or related social security, fisheries management, taxation, bankruptcy, and migrations laws, incarceration patterns "are dominated by serious drug importation offences" (ALRC, 2006, appendix 1, paragraph 54). Of a total of 695 offenders in federal custody, 460 were convicted of major drug offenses under the *Customs Act* (ALRC, 2006, appendix 1, paragraph 55 and figure A1.14). In fact, only one person was incarcerated for a federal customs offense not involving drugs (ALRC, 2006, appendix 1, figure A1.14). Over 65 percent of federal customs drug offenders were serving sentences in New South Wales (ALRC, 2006, appendix 1, paragraph 58 and figure A1.15), the

**Table 5.2. Price, Availability, and Purity of Illicit Substances, Melbourne, Victoria, 2006**

| | Heroin | Methamphetamine | Cocaine | Cannabis |
|---|---|---|---|---|
| **Price** | | | | |
| **Cap/Point** | $40 | $35–50 | $50 | Gram $20 (hydro) |
| **Gram** | $350 | $200 | $350 ($300–500) | Ounce $200 (hydro) |
| | Stable–increasing | Stable | Stable | Stable–decreasing |
| **Availability** | Very easy/easy to obtain; stable market; mostly accessed through known dealers | Speed and crystal meth/ice generally easy/very easy and stable market | Stable market; sourced from friends or known dealers | Readily available; stable market; accessed through social networks |
| **Purity** | Average purity 17% (0–69% range); average purity stable/decreasing; purity medium to low | Average purity 19% (range 5–46%); purity variable | Average purity 37% (range 15–77%); average purity relatively stable in the past six years | Purity medium to high; stable potency |
| **Use** | Mostly rock form (94%); decreasing prevalence and frequency of use | Prevalence of use of speed and base stable among injecting drug users; crystal meth/ice increased; frequency of use stable–increasing | Cocaine use remains infrequent among injecting drug users (median two days use) | Most common illicit drug; frequently used with other drugs |

*Source:* Jenkinson and Quinn, 2007, p. xi (prices in Australian dollars).

most populous Australian state with the nation's largest international air and sea transit points. The mean sentence for a customs drug offense was 10.6 years, with twenty-nine prisoners currently serving life sentences excluded from this calculation (ALRC, 2006, appendix 1, paragraphs 61–62 and figure A1.16). Available statistics do not pinpoint the country of birth of convicted federal drug offenders, but 43 percent of the overall federal prison population is of Australian origin; 23 percent are from Asian nations including Indonesia, China, Hong Kong, and Vietnam; 13 percent from mainland Europe, the British Isles, and North America; 4 percent from Africa; and 2 percent from the Middle East (ALRC, 2006, appendix 1, paragraphs 49–50 and figure A1.13).

The available data on illicit drug supply and consumption patterns in Australia paints a mixed picture. While there are notable successes stemming from tighter and more-targeted border control aimed at restricting supply from known international embarkation points, how these are influenced by the current whole-of-government approach, greater strategic targeting, and increased multiagency collaboration remains unclear. The number of seizures and amounts of specific types of drugs seized underscores a more complex series of issues in terms of the evolving profiles of and methods used by illicit drug traffickers and the overall stability of the supply market at the domestic level. For instance, it is unclear whether existing detection and prosecution methods are meeting the MCDS objective of reducing domestic or international organized crime (see Homel and Willis, 2007) or whether they are simply notable chinks in a more elaborate and enduring global supply chain which will continue despite more strategic target identification, detection, and criminal prosecution under Australian law. Further, while the size and number of recent drug seizures paints a quite impressive picture of the effectiveness of recent targeted enforcement initiatives, there are doubts over whether they are actually engaging both domestic and international agencies and the broader communities they are policing in meaningful collaborative processes to reduce transnational production and supply trends despite considerable mutual assistance legislation, increased extraterritorial enforcement capacity, and the commitment to Australia's international obligations. While many criticisms of community policing are directed at local crime prevention and interdiction strategies (see Fielding and Innes, 2006; James and Sutton, 1998), they can be easily translated to the transnational context given the strategic "problem-solving" mandate promoted in contemporary Australian illicit drug policy. This approach conveys the appearance of a more strategic and knowledge-based enforcement paradigm; however, further investigation and evaluation is required to assess the actual effectiveness of current border control methods, particularly in light of the stability in local availability and consumption patterns. As the next section illustrates, similar concerns arise over the effectiveness of recent legal and enforcement responses to terrorist activity under the whole-of-government approach, despite their wide-ranging impact on the Australian law enforcement and security milieu.

## TERRORISM

Historically, Australia's national security and law enforcement functions have been independent. The security role focuses on gathering intelligence on potential threats to "peace, order and good government" of the nation, while the enforcement function deals with various related preventative initiatives and gathering evidence or initiating prosecutions under the criminal justice system. Understandably, the covert nature and military origins of national security functions ensures they have a lengthy but relatively poorly documented public history (cf. Hocking, 1993). As Hocking (2004, pp. 13–26) illustrates, measures designed to preserve national security predate the outbreak of World War I and became solidified in their current form with the establishment of the ASIO thirty years before the AFP, Australia's first national policing body, in 1949. During this period most domestic security functions involved covert military-styled intelligence gathering directed against left-wing labor organizations such as the International Workers of the World and the Communist Party during the Cold War. ASIO's formation stemmed from the desire to maintain defensive national security from external Cold War threats, rather than the systematic monitoring of dissenting internal political groups per se. However, this mandate has remained extremely fluid, as Australia's domestic and international political culture has been characterized by close and ongoing ties with the United Kingdom and the United States, and postwar immigration patterns have attracted refugees and legal settlers from all regions of the world, many of which have unstable political cultures and more established traditions of terrorism, sedition, and violent civil dissent.

As with transnational drug offending, terrorism is characterized by a wide variety of activities, which precludes accurate legal definition (Golder and Williams, 2004) or the development of precise behavioral typologies. Many authors distinguish between terrorism and other behaviors such as conventional or guerrilla warfare to add meaning to the term. For example, Schmid (2004) indicates terrorism generally involves individuals or small groups engaged in clearly illegal, strategically targeted violent activity aimed at having a widespread destabilizing effect on governments or the broader public. The communication of these activities is a central motive aimed at violently inducing fear and behavioral or policy change, with common illegal domestic or international tactics including kidnapping, assassinations, car bombings, hijackings, and hostage taking. Providing financial support for terrorist activity has also received increased legal and academic attention in recent times (*Criminal Code* Commonwealth, 1995, part 5.3, division 103; McCulloch and Pickering, 2005; McCulloch and Carlton, 2006). In contrast to conventional warfare, terrorism is both clandestine and prohibited under domestic and international law. It is also devoid of the standard territorial motives characteristic of war, which heightens its concern in a contemporary world where conventional geographic borders are increasingly perceived as irrelevant to transnational crime groups and accepted law enforcement principles (see Pickering and Weber, 2006).

With these definitions in mind it is safe to say Australia's direct exposure to terrorism either on domestic soil or internationally has been confined to a few isolated incidents since the mid-1960s, at least until events at the World Trade Center in New York on September 11, 2001, and the Bali bombing on October 12, 2002. A series of violent threats and small-scale bombings against travel agencies and other small Croatian-owned businesses were attributed to extremist Ustashi nationalists during the early 1970s (Hocking, 2004, pp. 40–43). This led to a fundamental review of domestic security arrangements after ASIO viewed these incidents as a series of isolated coincidences committed by radical or disturbed individuals rather than the organized and planned activities of the Ustashi movement (Koschade, 2007). However, the extent to which these incidents were local manifestations of a more strident transnational terrorist organization seeking to violently overthrow the Yugoslav government remains to be investigated.

The most notable incident was the detonation of a bomb outside the Hilton Hotel in Sydney on February 13, 1978, which killed two council workers emptying the bin where the device was located and a police officer (Hocking, 2004, p. 83). The incident coincided with the commencement of the first Commonwealth Heads of Government Regional Meeting and eleven visiting heads of government were staying at the hotel at the time. As Hocking (2004, pp. 84–100) indicates, the decision by then–Prime Minister Malcolm Fraser and various ministerial and security advisers to call in the military to deal with an essentially civil policing responsibility in the immediate aftermath of the incident created widespread concern over the trajectory for domestic counterterrorism policies throughout the subsequent period. The catalyst was the characterization of the incident as an act of terrorism rather than a case of civil disorder (Hocking, 2004, p. 93). Attention focused on the activities of the Ananda Marga sect, "a spiritual and social movement" (Hocking, 1993, p. 133) which was previously identified by the Protective Services Coordination Centre as a national security threat. However, after over a decade of criminal trials and appeals against conspiracy and murder convictions, based largely on the evidence of paid police informers; a Royal Commission investigation; and several related inquiries, the true identity of the bomber remains unknown (see Hocking, 2004, pp. 129–34; Koschade, 2007).

While a series of sporadic incidents and inquiries into Australian national security was conducted in the aftermath of the Hilton Hotel bombing, two significant events appear to be the most prominent catalysts for the systematic examination and review of the nation's contemporary security and law enforcement arrangements. The first was the hosting of the Sydney 2000 Olympic Games and the specter of terrorism after the detonation of a pipe bomb at Olympic Park during the Centennial Olympic Games in Atlanta on July 27, 1996 (Cable News Network [CNN], 1996). As with many terrorist incidents, this event heightened both Australian and international concern over the capacity of the Sydney Organising Committee for the Olympic Games and Australian law enforcement agencies to guarantee security at major Olympic venues during the sixteen days of competition. A detailed report conducted by the Australian National Audit Office (ANAO) into Commonwealth security preparations for the Sydney 2000 Olympic Games released two years before the event highlighted the complexity of Australia's security arrangements and the need for greater role delineation between a range of federal and state agencies given the projected influx of international athletes, dignitaries, and tourists expected at the event (Warren, 2002, pp. 73–74). While primary responsibility for law enforcement at the games rested with the New South Wales Police Service, the report found both the size and character of this event led to a highly complex network of arrangements between various federal bodies, including the Attorney General's Department Protective Security Coordination Centre, the ACS, the AFP, the Australian Protective Service, the Australian Quarantine and Inspection Service, the ASIO, and the Department of Defence. Greater clarity in the delineation of roles and responsibilities between these agencies was seen to facilitate more efficient and targeted planning and "a more formal and systematic reporting process" covering the breadth of security activities under the multiagency framework (ANAO, 1998, p. 15). The ANAO endorsed the formation of a coordination task force to oversee a range of core functions, including security planning and coordination, intelligence gathering and threat assessment, border management, security at international entry and departure points, protective security, and crisis management.

At the time of the audit, there was no consolidated statement of activities being undertaken by Commonwealth security agencies in preparation for the Olympics. Similarly, there was no particular timeframe set for completing different stages of these preparations or a formal mechanism to ensure regular progress reporting against these timeframes. In view of the number of different committees and agencies involved in Commonwealth Olympic security preparations, a Sydney 2000 Games Coordination Task Force was established recently within the Department of the Prime Minister and Cabinet. This is a significant step in facilitating a consolidated commonwealth approach to key policy and planning aspects and in monitoring the subsequent implementation of plans to finality. (ANAO, 1998, p. 14)

World events since Sydney 2000 have reinforced Australia's status as a global terrorist target. The destruction of the World Trade Center towers in New York on September 11, 2001, where ten Australians were reported killed (National Museum of Australia, 2004; News.com.au, April 11, 2007) and the further eighty-eight deaths resulting from the Bali bombings the following year (Griffiths, Hilton, and Lain, 2003; AFP, 2004b) thrust counterterrorism into both the global and Australian national consciousness. Australia has affirmed its allegiance to the United States and the United Kingdom in the "war on terror" swiftly and emphatically. A raft of contentious legal reforms aimed at strengthening domestic security, largely at the expense of conventional due-process rights, expanded the definitions of terrorism, sedition, and related crimes; extended the powers of ASIO and AFP agents to detain and interrogate terror suspects; and restricted judicial review and media scrutiny through tighter "secrecy provisions" (see, generally, McCulloch and Tham, 2005; Head, 2002; Tham, 2004). In this legal milieu, a number of government reports and policy documents reasserted the immediacy of the terror threat to Australia and its foreign interests (Australian Government, 2006; Australian Government/Department of Foreign Affairs and Trade, 2004), reviewed existing domestic and international security arrangements amongst a range of national agencies (Australian Government/Flood, 2004), and examined security procedures at a range of sites including airports (Australian Government/Airport Security and Policing Review, 2005; ANAO, 2003) and other major critical infrastructure locations (Palmer and Whelan, 2006).

Understandably, the organized and targeted character of terrorist activity represents the foundation for most strategic and preventative initiatives through extensive coordination of and collaboration between state and federal agencies. However, official reports also identify the response to critical incidents as crucial to contemporary counterterrorism arrangements. The most recent incarnation of the national policy has four key emphases.

- **Prevention:** to hinder, deter, mitigate and disrupt terrorist activity, while maintaining readiness to deal with a terrorist incident

- **Preparedness:** to protect our people, assets, infrastructure and institutions from terrorist activity and planning; and to establish, train for and exercise arrangements to respond to, and recover from a terrorist incident
- **Response:** to respond rapidly and decisively to a terrorist incident, should one occur, and manage its immediate consequences
- **Recovery:** to return national and community life to normal as quickly as possible after a terrorist incident, through the restoration of social, economic, physical and environmental wellbeing (Australian Government, 2006, p. 13).

The Council of Australian Governments and the National Counter-Terrorism Committee are the two primary "intergovernmental bodies" which link the Commonwealth, states, and territories under the current National Counter-Terrorism Plan (Australian Government, 2006, pp. 14–15). Within this broad structure, ASIO, the AFP, and the various state policing agencies retain their conventional mandates to investigate and prosecute for criminal offending on domestic soil, with the AFP involved in a growing number of multilateral and bilateral international arrangements and domestic coordination initiatives aimed at identifying discernible threats and rapid crisis management in the event of a terrorist incident. Relevant initiatives at the juncture of domestic and international regional security and law enforcement include:

- interjurisdictional Joint Counter Terrorism Teams (JCTTs) to coordinate investigations across states/territories that impact on national security;
- validating and assessing Australia's domestic and international counterterrorism capacity and capabilities through national and offshore exercise regimes;
- international counterterrorism liaison officers that undertake operational- and capacity-building activities, working closely with the AFP's broader International Network;
- rapid-response capability to manage crises and the consequence of such events impacting on the economic, social, and political stability of Australia's local and global interests;
- regional counterterrorism cooperation and operations support teams that encourage the transferability of skills and knowledge; and
- enhancement of the Jakarta Centre for Law Enforcement Cooperation through the delivery of technical, specialist, and leadership programs that encourage transformational change within the region (AFP, 2007).

A lengthy document outlining the core domestic and international threats to Australia's global civilians, military, businesses, and nongovernment humanitarian activities identifies Islamic extremism as the source of most concern (Australian Government/Department of Foreign Affairs and Trade, 2004, pp. vii–xii). This is a direct legacy of the 9/11 disaster and a series of express references to Australia as a potential al-Qaeda target by Osama bin Laden and Ayman al-Zawahiri between November 2001 and October 2003 (Australian Government/Department of Foreign Affairs and Trade, 2004, p. 66). However, since the first Bali bombing in 2002, the threat has become more immediate:

> Terrorists associated with Jemaah Islamiyah (JI)—the regional group responsible for the 2002 and 2005 Bali Bombings, as well as the 2004 bombing of the Australian Embassy in Jakarta—remain a great threat to Australians and Australian interests in our region. Under pressure from counter-terrorism operations, JI appears to have become more decentralised in its structure and operational planning. However, it remains resilient and dangerous. It retains links with Al Qaida, but is not dependent on it for either funding or operational support. JI also has links with other terrorist groups in South-East Asia, such as the Abu Sayyaf Group in the Philippines. (Australian Government, 2006, p. 9)

Precise information about the nature of these threats is not publicly released. However, JI, al-Qaeda, the Abu Sayyaf Group, and Lashkar-e-Taiba are amongst the nineteen listed terrorist organizations under the new legislative regime (see *Security Legislation Amendment [Terrorism] Act* Commonwealth, 2002). All are extremist Islamist organizations, many of which are based in Southeast Asia or the Middle East and are also outlawed in the United States, the United Kingdom, and Canada.

The contemporary security environment in Australia means public knowledge about the nature and extent of domestic feeder activity into these or other suspect organizations, including the existence of training camps or transnational terrorist financing, is confined to press reports, highly generalist government inquiries, or the outcomes of criminal investigations which have reached trial. As such, it is impossible to measure the nature or extent of internal threats based on current federal or state risk assessments. Nevertheless, in recent years concern has been expressed over the blurred boundaries between humanitarian financial assistance and terror financing in relation to separatist Tamil groups in Sri Lanka (Liberty Victoria, 2006; Parliament of Australia, 2002; Dunn and Bice, 2007) and Hezbollah in Lebanon (Kearney, 2006). Concern has also spread towards Sudan given its previous links with al-Qaeda (McGeough, 2004) and related concerns over "the trafficking of people for sexual servitude and other serious (transnational) crimes" (Australian Government/Attorney General's Department, 2007). Australia has a long, intergenerational history of Sri Lankan and Lebanese settlement, while the new wave of African immigration contains a large population of Sudanese refugees fleeing the humanitarian crisis in that region. This conforms to the small yet increasing body of research indicating nationalist and terrorist groups have been active amongst some Australian migrant populations in recent decades, with the notable example involving militant training activities by the Croatian Ustashi (see Koschade, 2007). However, the nature and extent of the domestic or offshore activities of such groups remains highly speculative and subject to further research.

The secrecy of most counterterrorism operations means there is limited publicly available data through which to measure the effectiveness of current domestic or international enforcement initiatives. One possible, albeit imperfect, measure is the rate of successful prosecutions for terrorism offenses. However, the recency of Australia's counterterrorism law reforms and their impact ensures only a handful of prosecutions have been initiated (*R. v. Jack Roche* [2005] WASCA 4), with most trials pending or still in progress at the time of writing. Nevertheless, guidance on the dilemmas experienced in the field of counterterrorism law enforcement can be gleaned from the highly publicized deportation of French terror suspect Willy Brigitte.

Brigitte was arrested and deported from Australia in October 2003 for a series of planned terrorist activities targeting military facilities and a nuclear installation after a series of images were dumped by one of his associates in a rubbish bin (Sexton, 2004). French authorities suspected Brigitte had planned terrorist activities targeting the 1998 Rugby World Cup (Carne, 2004, p. 574) and communicated their suspicions Brigitte was in Australia and was planning terrorist activities. However, the first communication was not received by ASIO and a subsequent communication was not immediately acted upon (Carne, 2004, pp. 574–75). Brigitte was deported on October 17, 2003, and later admitted his involvement with the Lashkar-e-Taiba organization in Pakistan. While in Australia, Brigitte married a former Australian soldier who had converted to Islam and persistently supported his denials prior to his trial in Paris (Connolly, 2004).

In early 2007 Brigitte was convicted in Paris of "criminal association with a view to committing a terrorist act" and sentenced to a nine-year jail term (News.com.au, March 16, 2007). However, evidence revealed at trial suggests the case against him was circumstantial and insufficient to secure a conviction under Australian law (Button, 2007; Fairfax Digital, 2007). After his deportation, AFP agents traveled to Paris seeking to interview Brigitte regarding his potential prosecution in Australia, but Brigitte declined to speak (House of Representatives, 2005, p. 178). While an ASIO media release in 2005 indicates many of Brigitte's associates in Australia are subject to ongoing investigation (Australian Government/Australian Security Intelligence Organisation, 2005a) and Bilal Khazal, who allegedly collected Brigitte from the Sydney airport, has been charged along with four others for terror-related offenses in Australia (Legislative Council New South Wales, 2005, p. 17,165), according to the deputy director-general of ASIO the mere fact of Brigitte's capture and deportation prior to a large-scale terrorist act being executed is evidence of the success of Australian law enforcement in this case: "Perhaps no one person better illustrates the global nature of the challenge than Willy Brigitte; born in the Caribbean, introduced to militant Islam in France, trained as a terrorist in Pakistan, Brigitte came to Australia to carry out a terrorist attack. And, but for the cooperative work of the French authorities, ASIO, the AFP and the NSW Police, he may have succeeded" (Australian Government/ Australian Security Intelligence Organisation, 2005b).

Carne (2004) identifies several problems emerging from the Brigitte incident. The first involves the failure of intelligence exchange on Brigitte between French and Australian authorities, which in turn has been used as a justification for tightening Australia's counterterrorism legislation despite concerns over the erosion of civil liberties and due-process rights. Indeed, the overt politicization of this issue becomes a shroud for more immediate concerns regarding the effectiveness of Australia's entry policies and the enforcement of existing counterterrorism laws. The second involves the "differentiation of criminal law and intelligence" (Carne, 2004, p. 611) and the difficulties this creates in terms of detention, questioning, and the rights of the accused. This problem is symptomatic of widespread concern over the classification of activities prohibited under domestic and national criminal law as security-related and the impact this has on the expansion of covert surveillance procedures (Hocking, 2004). Finally, the cumulative effect of these issues stifles public accountability for security operations through restricted media reporting and limited grounds for judicial review. Greater ministerial oversight and agenda-setting can be seen as a broader theme in many areas of transnational policing in contemporary Australia, which in turn heightens the political character of these issues, yet in many ways stifles informed public or law enforcement input into this process under the current whole-of-government approach. Indeed, Carne's assessment of the political dimensions of the Brigitte case is scathing, with the political response to the issue reinforcing tighter executive control over counterterrorism law and policy at the expense of forging greater and more meaningful international law enforcement links with a real preventative focus. Whether this is an accurate appraisal of current relations between Australian law enforcement and security agencies in a transnational policing environment remains subject to further research. Nevertheless, the fusion of political, legal, and enforcement concerns under this national security focus raises serious doubts about the efficacy of a whole-of-government approach which continually reasserts its power through increased executive expansion and the erosion of conventional notions of judicial review, due process, and criminal responsibility.

## POLICE AND JUSTICE RESPONSES

There is no doubt transnational crime has generated a wave of legislative reform and policy change in Australia in recent times with immense bearing on both national and state policing agencies. Under a preventative problem-solving and intelligence-led philosophy, Australian police agencies are now required to be more strategic in focus. Underpinning this model is a greater level of external oversight or accountability from nonconventional sources. As the counterterrorism example illustrates, ministerial responsibility rather than judicial review becomes the driving mechanism for setting both the new policing agenda under a whole-of-government approach and, seemingly, for validating the effectiveness of current transnational law enforcement and security measures. This is occurring in tandem with the rapid expansion of national law enforcement and security capacity, both in terms of legal obligations and manpower, to produce a situation where both state and federal enforcement agencies have parallel laws, powers, and jurisdiction over substantively similar areas. This is compounded in the terrorism field, with the tendency for the classification of these issues as matters of national security rather than generic crime problems creating an additional layer of complexity in the domestic interagency and law enforcement equation.

Figure 5.1 provides a general illustration of the contemporary Australian law enforcement structure. The most notable component is the creation of a series of strategic priority and coordination bodies, which have a crucial role in setting the national and transnational law enforcement agenda under the current whole-of-government approach. The role of this diverse range of oversight bodies is to help promote and coordinate greater information sharing and strategic problem solving amongst the state and national enforcement agencies, while feeding information back to the relevant ministers at the state or federal level to promote various policy goals. At one level, these organizations are driving the contemporary law enforcement agenda in Australia. At another, they are crucial in helping to coordinate the disparate state and federal enforcement agencies by enhancing communication flow and streamlining diverse organizational priorities within a complex two-tiered multiagency law enforcement structure. However, the extent to which these organizations are actively feeding into an improved and collaborative problem-solving agenda focusing on identified domestic and

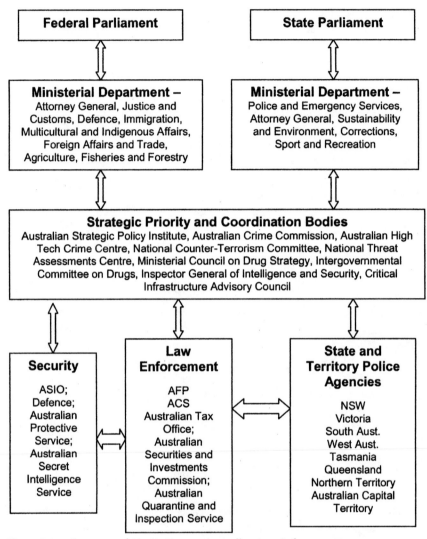

**Figure 5.1.  Structure of Contemporary Australian Law Enforcement**

transnational law enforcement problems and associated strategic knowledge building remains to be examined.

Part of the shift towards a more sophisticated, proactive, intelligence-based, and cooperative system of law enforcement is the devolution of responsibility for large-scale crime prevention back onto Australian citizens. Palmer and Whelan (2006, p. 450) illustrate that the characteristics of "new federalism" stretch well beyond law enforcement per se and include, amongst other things, a combination of "planning, legislative and media initiatives," all influenced by a profound shift towards collective responsibility to counter new terrorism threats. Expert security and law enforcement agencies, overseen by a growing number of ministerial committees, now play a key role in advising the community on how to counter recognized threats as part of the ongoing implementation of a strategic domestic, national, and transnational crime-prevention model. While state policing agencies retain various threads of jurisdiction to deal with risk assessment and the protection of "essential service" infrastructure on "social, economic, and defence and security grounds" (Palmer and Whelan, 2006, p. 455), the new "multilateralisation" aimed at protecting public or privately-owned critical infrastructure is contingent on the formation of networks of expertise involving specialist divisions within the state police forces; a series of new federal initiatives helping to coordinate risk identification, information sharing, and preventative functions; and the education of both the corporate and private sector to enhance the level of responsibility for the day-to-day management of these risks (see Beare, 2000). Therefore, the important shift is not necessarily in law enforcement per se but rather in its coordination at the national level through expert committees acting on the advice of and advising members of Parliament.

The Australian Government has declared that the fostering of "effective partnerships with state and territory governments and the private sector" is central to protecting critical infrastructure. To facilitate these partnerships, the government formed the Trusted Information Sharing Network (TISN) for Critical Infrastructure Protection. The TISN is a forum for owners and operators of critical infrastructure to exchange information on matters related to security. It has a Critical Infrastructure Advisory Council (CIAC) which advises the (federal) Attorney-General on matters relating to critical infrastructure protection. The CIAC comprises representatives from the Infrastructure Assurance Advisory Groups (IAAGs), expert advisory groups, each of the states and territories, relevant agencies of the Commonwealth Government, and the National Counter-Terrorism Committee (the committee responsible for coordinating counter-terrorism arrangements nationwide). Thus, not only does TISN enable communication between business and government on matters pertaining to the protection of critical infrastructure, through the CIAC it has a direct link to high-level policy makers on matters of security. The TISN thus is a form of security network that cuts across state and non-state boundaries to shape security risk awareness. (Palmer and Whelan, 2006, p. 458)

These multiagency preventative arrangements have become emblematic of the contemporary Australian security landscape and are also characteristic of the whole-of-government approach dealing with a range of transnational crime problems including drug trafficking and Internet crime. This security-centered preventative focus ultimately magnifies the complexity of the contemporary law enforcement role, which is in turn further complicated by the split between federal and state jurisdictions on the one hand and law enforcement and security functions on the other. Therefore, functions including risk assessment, intelligence, and crisis response involve extensive collaborative planning and knowledge gathering by the range of state and federal agencies, each with a specific role to play within the broader tapestry of functions involving security management, incident prevention, strategic policy advice, multiagency cooperation, and information sharing. No longer do state-based agencies retain a monopoly on retrospective investigations with a view to successful criminal prosecutions targeting harmful behaviors once they have occurred. Rather, the focus is on the management of risks to prevent their realization, with intricate, multi-leveled networks dealing with a variety of problem identification functions which transcend conventional notions of policing delineated under the criminal law or confined by geographically determined jurisdictional limits.

Within this domestic context viable transnational enforcement arrangements must be developed and sustained. This is primarily the responsibility of federal law enforcement agencies in general, but is driven largely by the AFP. State police agencies will also have an important preventative or investigative function depending on the issue. However, as the Brigitte case indicates, there can be numerous barriers to fostering viable and effective interagency enforcement cooperation at the international level. This can stem from the fusion of political, cultural, legal, and enforcement issues, which are emblematic of transnational communication practices on sensitive crime and security issues. While there is little available data examining the effectiveness of Australia's contemporary bilateral and multilateral law enforcement initiatives, one highly publicized case involving a midlevel drug trafficking venture into Australia highlights the stark effects of these issues in light of the disparate legal and criminal justice traditions operating in the Southeast Asian region.

In the aftermath of the Bali bombings and the conviction of three Islamic extremists under Indonesian law, nine young Australian citizens were arrested in Bali on April 17 and 18, 2005, while attempting to traffic over four kilograms of heroin into Australia. Indonesia has long been recognized for its harsh drug laws, but the tense political environment in the region at the time appeared to fuel mutual levels of antagonism between these nations over the combined impacts of terrorism, drug trafficking (ABC, 2005), contrasting religious philosophies, and Australia's extensive tourism in the region. After being tried under Indonesian law, seven members of the Bali Nine were sentenced to life imprisonment, while two organizers of the failed trafficking venture were sentenced to death. After a series of prosecution and defense appeals against the sentences imposed, the death penalty was extended to six of the group (Forbes, 2006; Lewis, 2006). The nature of Australia's interagency cooperation with the INP on questions of transnational drug-law enforcement was a central and highly contentious element of this case, and was subject to unsuccessful legal proceedings in Australia focusing on the attempts by the father of one of the Bali Nine to encourage the AFP to prevent the departure of his son on the suspicion he might become involved in illegal activity.

The case demonstrates two tiers of problematic enforcement communication links: those between the Queensland Police Service, the AFP, and the ACS prior to Scott Rush departing from Australia and the international links between Australian federal law enforcers and the INP once the Bali Nine had left Australia. Much public debate in Australia over this case is highly critical of the AFP's conduct on the basis that the suspects would have received fairer treatment if apprehended in Australia at the end point of their illegal transaction rather than at the Indonesian transit point where the death penalty is in operation. The verdict in *Rush v. Commissioner of Police* ([2006] FCA 12) documents part of the trail of correspondence between AFP Agents and the INP leading to the apprehension of the Bali Nine in Indonesia. Amongst a variety of legal grounds, it was claimed the AFP breached their legal obligations under the *Mutual Assistance in Criminal Matters Act* (1987) by failing to obtain the approval of the attorney general prior to making the various communications to senior INP personnel that led to the offshore arrests (*Rush v. Commissioner of Police*, 2006, paragraph 59).

At the time of his departure Scott Rush was on bail, had prior convictions for a series of minor crimes committed in the state of Queensland, and was listed on a passport alert service administered by the ACS aimed at gathering intelligence and "preventing certain targeted individuals from entering or leaving the country" (*Rush v. Commissioner of Police*, 2006, paragraph 19). However, this listing was not deemed sufficient to prevent his departure. Once Rush left Australia a series of written communications took place between AFP agents and the INP under various memoranda of understanding between the Australian and Indonesian governments aimed at combating transnational crime and enhancing mutual police cooperation (*Rush v. Commissioner of Police,* 2006, paragraph 44). There was no evidence Indonesian police made any formal request for assistance from the AFP that could be construed under the provisions of Australia's mutual assistance laws. The AFP's requests were clearly intended to encourage the INP to gather and communicate more evidence on the activities of Scott Rush and his associates given available intelligence on their suspected illegal activities, with an express instruction that "no action" should be taken until "interdiction commences in Australia" to secure the identification of the organizers and recipients of the drugs (*Rush v. Commissioner of Police*, 2006, paragraph 22). However, the INP issued a formal "Investigation Order" for each of the suspects listed in the AFP communications directing their personnel to commence a formal criminal investigation under the relevant Indonesian narcotics laws. The Australian Consul was subsequently informed of the arrest and detention of one of the Bali Nine, while a dossier of evidence against each of the suspects was completed and delivered to Indonesian prosecutors by August 15 on the eve of the remaining arrests.

Rather than evidence of multiagency cooperation, this example suggests in the transnational environment, where highly distinct political, cultural, and legal factors are at play, multiagency competition can have potentially devastating results. In absence of a more consistent series of international guidelines, preferably under a unified international criminal law, it is unlikely many of the bilateral or multilateral arrangements currently involving Australian federal law enforcement agencies will produce a truly collaborative transnational criminal regime. How this example conforms to claims by the AFP which praise the effectiveness of various regional transnational enforcement partnerships aimed at stemming illegal drug trafficking remains highly conjectural.

> For the past decade, the AFP has concentrated on taking the fight against the illicit drug trade offshore. Working with our international partners, the organisation is targeting drug syndicates and their points of vulnerability in source or transit countries. The benefits of this approach include greater opportunities to arrest criminal syndicate leaders, larger seizures, greater disruption and limited safe havens for syndicate operations. Ultimately it means less drugs reaching Australian streets. (AFP, 2004a, p. 4)

Goldsmith (2006b) indicates that an international criminal law is a necessary ingredient in fostering meaningful transnational law enforcement in distinct intercultural settings, but creating a unified global criminal law is highly unlikely because the very strength of these diverse international political, cultural, and legal factors prohibits agreement between nation states. This in turn compromises true interagency cooperation at the transnational level under an agreed series of institutions and basic law enforcement principles. The Rush case illustrates that political reality dictates it could be preferable for some offshore policing agencies to use shared intelligence communications as a means of strengthening their own law enforcement records, even if this might compromise the discovery of more intricate organized crime networks on foreign soil. While this might be offset by a range of community development and peacekeeping initiatives involving the AFP and other federal and state agencies in overseas jurisdictions (AFP, 2006), further research and evaluation of the effectiveness of these endeavors is clearly required.

A range of additional questions also remain open for further investigation. These include the need to examine the effectiveness of electronic data-sharing initiatives such as CrimTrac (ANAO, 2004) in targeting serious offenders within Australia's state borders and the need to evaluate the range of targeted law enforcement arrangements at Australian airports (ANAO, 2003; Australian Government/Airport Security and Policing Review, 2005), on its extensive sea borders (ANAO, 2000), and in searching incoming air and sea cargo (ANAO, 2002). In addition, while legislative powers in relation to law enforcement and security issues have expanded considerably in recent years (see *Australian Security Intelligence Organisation Act* Commonwealth, section 4; Carne, 2004; Tham, 2004), their real effects in producing more sophisticated or interventionist preventative efforts remain to be examined. As Homel and Willis (2007) indicate in relation to the illicit drug market, part of the task ahead involves rationalizing the range of diverse performance indicators from the high end of transnational production, supply, and importation to the consumer level at the community level. Writing almost a decade ago after obtaining data from a range of state and federal law enforcers, James and Sutton issued a skeptical prognosis on the effectiveness of complex interagency preventative measures aimed at curbing illicit drug supply or reducing local demand for these substances, despite their increased sophistication under a strategic problem-solving model.

[Our report to the National Police Research Unit] recommended more systematic national and inter-jurisdictional cooperation between Commonwealth, state and other relevant enforcement agencies in their efforts to reduce the flow of illicit drugs into Australia and their production here, and to dismantle organised production and trafficking groups. However, like many of our expert informants in the enforcement sector, we were not optimistic about the likelihood that even the most highly skilled and resourced task-forces would be able significantly to reduce the supply of illicit drugs and to target the most important organised crime elements. All evidence seemed to suggest that it may simply be too easy for the more resourceful (e.g. wealthy) operators to put themselves beyond the reach of the law. (James and Sutton, 2000, p. 259)

A final issue warranting further investigation relates to the nature of law enforcement culture under the multitiered and multiagency whole-of-government approach. Traditionally, research into police culture in Australia has focused on the characteristics of police officers in state policing agencies working in a variety of operational and managerial roles (Chan, 1997; Chan, 2001; Coady, James, Miller, and O'Keefe, 2000). Little is known about the organizational cultures of Australia's national law enforcement agencies either in their own right or in the context of the "pluralised fields of security governance" (Wood, 2004; Gill, 2006). In this respect, two pertinent sites of investigation are required. The first relates to cultural manifestations of domestic interagency relationships forged within a specific problem-solving model and incorporating the voices of federal and state law enforcers, security personnel, and strategic policy implementation bodies. The second is the more complex task of investigating crossnational interagency enforcement and intelligence networks involved in curbing transnational crime. As the experience in the Rush case indicated, crosscultural legal and political variables are likely to produce a mixed assessment of the effectiveness of these arrangements, but these issues will invariably be contingent on which jurisdiction is driving the law enforcement or research agenda. What is clear is that global cultural networks are being promoted in a variety of policing fields to assist with transnational law enforcement efforts and to help promote cultural change within otherwise staid policing agencies and their conventional hierarchical structures (Heidensohn and Brown, 1999). The extent to which conventional cultural analyses built upon qualitative understandings of the working personality of police officers in the domestic setting can illuminate these complex transnational enforcement networks remains a fruitful site of further investigation.

While much remains unknown about the effectiveness of recent Australian multiagency policing and law enforcement initiatives, it is clear transnational crime and terrorism present fundamental challenges for conventional notions of policing in Australia. The focus on strategic problem solving, crime prevention, and complex domestic and international cooperative measures between multiple policing, security, and policy agencies represents a marked shift in Australian law enforcement that is poorly understood or evaluated through independent research. The complexities associated with transnational crime offer many potential sites for further critical analysis, in light of both the expanding size and power of federal policing agencies and the conventional dominance of state police forces on the Australian law enforcement landscape. It is clear there is no shortage of information to drive the contemporary whole-of-government approach in the areas of drug law enforcement, counterterrorism, and allied transnational crime areas. Less clear is the value of this information in providing agreed evaluation criteria on the effectiveness of law enforcement and security arrangements, or in rectifying existing problems identified in the foregoing discussion.

## REFERENCES

ABC. "Corby Sentenced to 20 Years Jail." *ABC News Online*, 27 May 2005, http://www.abc.net.au/news/newsitems/200505/s1378668.htm (18 June 2007).
Australian Bureau of Statistics. "Australia's Top Four Overseas Birthplace Groups," *Year Book Australia, 2005*, section 1301.0. Canberra, ACT: Australian Bureau of

Statistics, 21 January 2005, http://www.abs.gov.au/Ausstats/abs@.nsf/Previous products/1301.0Feature%20Article72005?opendocument&tabname=Summary& prodno=1301.0&issue=2005&num=&view= (8 June 2007).

Australian Crime Commission. *Illicit Drug Data Report 2005–2006.* Canberra, ACT: Commonwealth of Australia, 2007, http://www.crimecommission.gov.au/content/ publications/iddr_2005_06/IDDR_2005-06.pdf (7 June 2007).

Australian Federal Police. "Business Strategies." Australian Federal Police website, 2007, http://www.afp.gov.au/about/framework/business_strategies.html (13 June 2007).

Australian Federal Police. *Annual Report 2005–2006.* Canberra, ACT: Commonwealth of Australia, 2006.

Australian Federal Police. *Fact Sheet: The AFP Fight against Illicit Drug Trade.* Canberra, ACT: Australian Federal Police, 2004a, http://www.afp.gov.au/__data/assets/ pdf_file/3853/factsheetafpfightillicitdrugtrade.pdf (5 June 2007).

Australian Federal Police. *Fact Sheet: AFP Assists in Tracking Down Bali Bombers.* Canberra, ACT: Australian Federal Police, 2004b, http://www.afp.gov.au/__data/ assets/pdf_file/3858/factsheettrackingdownbalibombers.pdf (13 June 2007).

Australian Federal Police. "Transnational Crime, Police Peace Operations and Asia-Pacific Security." Australian Federal Police, 2001, https://afp.gov.au/media/national _media/speeches/archive_of_speeches/2001/transnational_crime,_police_peace _operations_and_asia-pacific_security (24 May 2007).

Australian Government. *Protecting Australia against Terrorism 2006: Australia's National Counter-Terrorism Policy and Arrangements.* Canberra, ACT: Commonwealth of Australia, 2006.

Australian Government (prepared by Flood, Phillip, Queen's Counsel). *Report of the Inquiry into Australian Intelligence Agencies.* Canberra, ACT: Commonwealth of Australia, July 2004.

Australian Government/Airport Security and Policing Review (prepared by Sir John Wheeler). *An Independent Review of Airport Security and Policing for the Government of Australia.* Canberra, ACT: Commonwealth of Australia, September 2005.

Australian Government/Attorney General's Department. "Listing of Terrorist Organisations." Canberra, ACT: Attorney General's Department, 2007, http://www.national security.gov.au/agd/www/nationalsecurity.nsf/AllDocs/95FB057CA3DECF30CA 256FAB001F7FBD?OpenDocument (13 June 2007).

Australian Government/Attorney General's Department. "Law and Justice Overview: Joint Media Release, Attorney-General The Hon Phillip Ruddock MP and Minister for Justice and Customs Senator the Hon David Johnson." Attorney General's Department website. Canberra, ACT: Attorney General's Department, 8 May 2007, http://www.ag.gov.au/www/agd/agd.nsf/Page/RWP6EA7D29118E543CECA2572 D30082D5D5 (13 June 2007).

Australian Government and Australian Customs Service. *Australian Customs Service Annual Report 2005–2006.* Canberra, ACT: Commonwealth of Australia, 2006, http://www.customs.gov.au/site/page.cfm?u=5667 (9 June 2007).

Australian Government and Australian Institute of Criminology. *The Worldwide Fight against Transnational Organised Crime: Australia*. Technical and Background Paper no. 9. Canberra, ACT: Commonwealth of Australia, 2004.

Australian Government/Australian Security Intelligence Organisation. "Australian Strategic Policy Institute Address, *Australia's Security Environment*, 2 November 2005." ASIO press release. Canberra, ACT: Australian Security Intelligence Organisation, 2005a, http://www.asio.gov.au/Media/Contents/aspi_address.aspx (14 June 2007).

Australian Government/Australian Security Intelligence Organisation. "Address of ASIO Deputy Director-General, Security in Government Conference, Canberra, Tuesday 10 May 2005." ASIO press release. Canberra, ACT: Australian Security Intelligence Organisation, 2005b, http://www.asio.gov.au/Media/Contents/sec_in_government2005.aspx (14 June 2007).

Australian Government/Department of Foreign Affairs and Trade. *Transnational Terrorism: The Threat to Australia*. Canberra, ACT: Commonwealth of Australia, 2004.

Australian Institute of Health and Welfare. *2004 National Drug Strategy Household Survey: Detailed Findings*, Drug Statistics Series no. 16. Canberra, ACT: Australian Institute of Health and Welfare, 2005, http://www.aihw.gov.au/publications/index.cfm.title/10190 (11 September 2006).

Australian Institute of Health and Welfare. *Statistics on Drug Use in Australia 2006*, Drug Statistics Series no. 16. Canberra, ACT: Australian Institute of Health and Welfare, 2007, http://www.aihw.gov.au/publications/phe/soduia06/soduia06.pdf (6 June 2007).

Australian Law Reform Commission. *Same Crime, Same Time: Sentencing of Federal Offenders*, ALRC Report 103. Canberra, ACT: Australian Law Reform Commission, 2006, http://www.austlii.edu.au/au/other/alrc/publications/reports/103 (5 June 2007).

Australian Law Reform Commission. *Sentencing of Federal Offenders*, ALRC Issues Paper no. 29. Canberra, ACT: Australian Law Reform Commission, 2005, http://www.austlii.edu.au/au/other/alrc/publications/issues/29/ (5 June 2007).

Australian National Audit Office. *The Implementation of CrimTrac*. Audit Report no. 53, 2003–2004. Canberra, ACT: Australian National Audit Office, 2004.

Australian National Audit Office. *National Marine Unit: Australian Customs Service*. Audit Report no. 37, 2003–2004. Canberra, ACT: Australian National Audit Office, 2004.

Australian National Audit Office. *Aviation Security in Australia: Department of Transport and Regional Services*. Audit Report no. 26, 2002–2003. Canberra, ACT: Australian National Audit Office, 2003.

Australian National Audit Office. *Fraud Control Arrangements in the Australian Customs Service*. Audit Report no. 35, 2002–2003. Canberra, ACT: Australian National Audit Office, 2003.

Australian National Audit Office. *Drug Detection in Air and Containerised Sea Cargo and Small Craft: Australian Customs Service*. Audit Report no. 54, 2001–2002. Canberra, ACT: Australian National Audit Office, 2002.

Australian National Audit Office. *Coastwatch: Australian Customs Service.* Audit Report no. 38. Canberra, ACT: Australian National Audit Office, 2000.

Australian National Audit Office. *Commonwealth Agencies' Security Preparations for the Sydney 2000 Olympic Games.* Audit Report no 5. Canberra, ACT: Australian National Audit Office, 1998.

Australian Security Intelligence Act, 1979. Office of Legislative Drafting and Publishing, Attorney General's Department, Canberra.

Beare, Margaret. "Structures, Strategies and Tactics of Transnational Criminal Organizations: Critical Issues for Enforcement." Paper presented at the Transnational Crime Conference convened by the Australian Institute of Criminology in Association with the Australian Federal Police and Australian Customs Service, Canberra, ACT, 9–10 March 2000, http://www.aic.gov.au/conferences/transnational/bearesst .pdf (18 June 2007).

Brodeur, Jean-Paul and Dupont, Benoît. "Knowledge Workers or 'Knowledge' Workers?" *Policing and Society* 16, no. 1 (March 2006): 7–26.

Bryett, Keith; Harrison, Arch; and Shaw, John. *The Role and Functions of Police in Australia.* Sydney, NSW: Butterworths, 1994.

Button, James. "I Am Not a Terrorist: Brigitte." *The Age,* 8 February 2007, http://www.theage.com.au/news/world/i-am-not-a-terrorist-brigitte/2007/02/07/ 1170524170036.html?s_cid=rss_age (14 June 2007).

Carne, Greg. "Brigitte and the French Connection: Security *Carte Blanche* or *A La Carte?" Deakin Law Review* 9, no. 1 (2004): 573–619.

Chan, Janet. *Changing Police Culture: Policing in a Multicultural Society.* Cambridge, UK: Cambridge University Press, 1997.

Chan, Janet. "Negotiating the Field: New Observations on the Making of Police Officers." *Australian and New Zealand Journal of Criminology* 34, no. 2 (August 2001): 114–33.

Chappell, Duncan. "A Review of Federal Law Enforcement Arrangements," in *Australian Policing: Contemporary Issues*, 2nd ed., edited by Duncan Chappell and Paul Wilson. Sydney, NSW: Butterworths, 1996.

Choo, Kim-Kwang Raymond. "Zombies and Botnets." *Trends and Issues in Crime and Criminal Justice* no. 333. Canberra, ACT: Australian Institute of Criminology, March 2007.

CNN. "ACOG President: Bomb Will Not Ruin Olympic Spirit." *CNN Interactive,* 27 July 1996, http://www.cnn.com/US/9607/27/payne.reaction/index.html (30 May 2007).

Coady, Tony; James, Steve; Miller, Seumas; and O'Keefe, Michael (eds). *Violence and Police Culture.* Melbourne, Vic.: Melbourne University Publishing, 2000.

Commonwealth of Australia (prepared by the Honorable Mr. Justice E. S. Williams). *Australian Royal Commission of Inquiry into Drugs.* Six volumes (books A–F). Canberra, ACT: Commonwealth of Australia, 1980.

*Confiscation Act* Victoria, 1997.

Connolly, Ellen. "Wife Visits Brigitte in Jail." *Sydney Morning Herald,* 4 February 2004, http://www.smh.com.au/articles/2004/02/04/1075776071800.html (14 June 2007).

*Crimes Act* NSW, 1900.

*Crimes Act* Victoria, 1958.

*Crimes (Traffic in Narcotic Drugs and Psychotropic Substances) Act* Commonwealth, 1990.

*Criminal Code* Commonwealth, 1995.

*Customs Act* Commonwealth, 1901.

*Customs (Prohibited Imports) Regulations* Commonwealth, 1956.

*Drug Misuse and Trafficking Act* NSW, 1985.

*Drugs, Poisons and Controlled Substances Act* Victoria, 1981.

Dunn, Mark and Bice, Katie. "Tsunami Aid to Tigers, Says AFP." *Herald Sun*, 2 May 2007, http://www.news.com.au/heraldsun/story/0,21985,21656730-661,00.html (13 June 2007).

Dupont, Benoît. "Security in the Age of Networks." *Policing and Society* 14, no. 1 (March 2004): 76–91.

Fairfax Digital. "Brigitte Verdict Leaves Questions Unanswered." *Brisbane Times*, 16 March 2007, http://www.brisbanetimes.com.au/news/world/brigitte-verdict-leaves -questions-unanswered/2007/03/16/1173722744322.html (14 June 2007).

Fielding, Nigel and Innes, Martin. "Reassurance Policing, Community Policing and Measuring Police Performance." *Policing and Society* 16, no. 2 (June 2006): 127–45.

Findlay, Mark; Odgers, Stephen; and Yeo, Stanley. *Australian Criminal Justice*, 3rd ed. Melbourne, Vic.: Oxford University Press, 2005.

Finnane, Mark. *Police and Government: Histories of Policing in Australia*. Melbourne, Vic.: Oxford University Press, 1994.

Finnane, Mark, ed. *Policing in Australia: Historical Perspectives*. Sydney, NSW: University of New South Wales Press, 1987.

Forbes, Mark. "Execution Shock for Four of the Bali Nine." *The Age*, 6 September 2006, http://www.theage.com.au/news/national/execution-shock-for-four-of-the-bali -nine/2006/09/05/1157222131815.html (18 June 2007).

Gill, Peter. "Not Just Joining the Dots but Crossing the Borders and Bridging the Voids: Constructing Security Networks after 11 September 2001." *Policing and Society* 16, no. 1 (March 2006): 27–49.

Golder, Ben and Williams, George. "What Is 'Terrorism'? Problems of Legal Definition." *University of New South Wales Law Journal* 27, no. 2 (2004): 270–95.

Goldsmith, Andrew. "Crime across Borders," in *Crime and Justice: A Guide to Criminology*, 3rd ed., edited by Andrew Goldsmith, Mark Israel, and Kathleen Daly. Pyrmont, NSW: Thomson/Lawbook Company, 2006a.

Goldsmith, Andrew. "Transnational Law Enforcement and Counter Terrorism," in *Crime and Justice: A Guide to Criminology*, 3rd ed., edited by Andrew Goldsmith, Mark Israel, and Kathleen Daly. Pyrmont, NSW: Thomson/Lawbook Company, 2006b.

Griffiths, Christopher (Group Captain, AM, RFD, DPH(D), FICD); Hilton, John (Group Captain, RFD, MB ChD, FRCPA); and Lain, Russell (Lieutenant, BDS, DipForOdont, RANR). "Disaster Response: Aspects of Forensic Responses to the Bali Bombings." *ADF Health* 4, no. 2 (2003): 50–55, http://www.defence.gov.au/ dpe/dhs/infocentre/publications/journals/noids/adfhealth_sep03/ADFHealth_4_2 _50-55.html#authors (13 June 2007).

Head, Michael. "'Counter-Terrorism' Laws: A Threat to Political Freedom, Civil Liberties and Constitutional Rights." *Melbourne University Law Review* 26, no. 3 (December 2002): 666–89.

Heidensohn, Frances and Brown, Jennifer. "Global Networks and Women in Policing." Paper presented at the Second Australasian Conference on Women and Police, Brisbane, QLD, July 1999, http://www.aic.gov.au/conferences/policewomen2/Heidensohn.pdf (18 June 2007).

Herald and Weekly Times. "Sylvester Stallone Cops Fine." *Herald Sun*, 22 May 2007, http://www.news.com.au/heraldsun/story/0,21985,21772112-5006023,00.html (6 June 2007).

Hocking, Jenny. *Terror Laws: ASIO, Counter-Terrorism and the Threat to Democracy*. Sydney, NSW: University of New South Wales Press, 2004.

Hocking, Jenny. *Beyond Terrorism: The Development of the Australian Security State*. St. Leonards, NSW: Allen and Unwin, 1993.

Homel, Peter and Willis, Katie. "A Framework for Measuring the Performance of Drug Law Enforcement." *Trends and Issues in Crime and Criminal Justice* no. 332. Canberra, ACT: Australian Institute of Criminology, February 2007.

House of Representatives (Commonwealth). *Hansard* (Questions in Writing). 23 May 2005, http://www.robertmcclelland.com/speeches/qRuddock23may05.htm (14 June 2007).

Intergovernmental Committee on Drugs. *Intergovernmental Committee on Drugs National Drug Strategy 2004–2009: Annual Report July 2004–June 2005 to the Ministerial Council on Drug Strategy*. Canberra, ACT: Commonwealth of Australia, 2006, http://www.nationaldrugstrategy.gov.au/internet/drugstrategy/publishing.nsf/Content/2A301D32A3142681CA25724B001C366A/$File/igcd-annrep2005.pdf (4 June 2007).

James, Stephen. "Police in Australia," in *Police Practices: An International Review*, edited by Dilip K. Das. Netuchen, NJ: The Scarecrow Press Inc., 1994.

James, Steve. "New Policing for a New Millennium?" in *Issues in Australian Crime and Criminal Justice*, edited by Duncan Chappell and Paul Wilson. Chatswood, NSW: LexisNexis/Butterworths, 2005.

James, Steve and Sutton, Adam. "Developments in Australian Drug Law Enforcement: Taking Stock." *Current Issues in Criminal Justice* 11, no. 3 (March 2000): 257–72.

James, Steve and Sutton, Adam. "Policing Drugs in the Third Millennium: The Dilemmas of Community-based Philosophies." *Current Issues in Criminal Justice* 9, no. 3 (March 1998): 217–27.

Jenkinson, Rebecca and Quinn, Brendan (Turning Point Alcohol and Drug Centre Inc.). *Victorian Drug Trends 2006: Findings from the Illicit Drug Reporting System (IRDS)*, NADRC Technical Report No 274. Sydney, NSW: National Drug and Alcohol Research Centre, University of New South Wales, 2007, http://notes.med.unsw.edu.au/NDARCWeb.nsf/resources/TR+273-277/$file/TR.274.pdf (4 June 2007).

Johnston, Jennifer; Quinn, Brendan; and Jenkinson, Rebecca (Turning Point Alcohol and Drug Centre). *Victorian Trends in Ecstasy and Related Drug Markets 2006:*

*Findings from the Ecstasy and Related Drugs Reporting System (EDRS)*, NDARC Technical Report No. 282. Sydney, NSW: National Drug and Alcohol Research Centre, University of New South Wales, 2006, http://notes.med.unsw.edu.au/NDARCWeb.nsf/resources/TR+278-282/$file/TR.282.pdf (4 June 2007).

Kearney, Simon. "Two Suspected over Hezbollah Cash." *The Australian*, 17 November 2006, http://www.theaustralian.news.com.au/story/0,20867,20771991-2702,00.html (13 June 2007).

Koschade, Stuart. "Constructing a Historical Framework of Terrorism in Australia: A Concise Examination from the Fenian Brotherhood to 21st Century Islamic Extremism." *Journal of Policing, Intelligence and Counter-Terrorism* 2, no. 3 (2007): 54–76.

Krone, Tony. "Queensland Police Stings in Online Chat Rooms." *Trends and Issues in Crime and Criminal Justice* no. 301. Canberra, ACT: Australian Institute of Criminology, July 2005.

Lain, Russell; Griffiths, Chris; and Hilton, John M. N. "Forensic Dental and Medical Response to the Bali Bombing: A Personal Perspective." *E-Medical Journal of Australia* 179, no. 7 (6 October 2003): 362–65, https://www.mja.com.au/public/issues/179_07_061003/lai10499_fm.html (13 June 2007).

Legislative Council NSW. *Hansard*. 22 June 2005, http://parliament.nsw.gov.au/prod/parlment/hanstrans.nsf/V3ByKey/4BC8F3186058813CCA2570280059C892/$File/531lc143.pdf (14 June 1007).

Lewis, Julie. "Explore International Legal Options for Bali Nine Now, Says Professor." *Law Society Journal* 44, no. 10 (November 2006): 18–19.

Liberty Victoria. *Submission in Relation to Anti-Money Laundering and Counter-Terrorism Financing Bill, 2006 (Cth)*. Melbourne, Vic.: Liberty Victoria, 10 November 2006, http://www.aph.gov.au/Senate/committee/legcon_ctte/aml_ctf06/submissions/sub01.pdf (13 June 2007).

Mackenzie, Simon. "Organised Crime and Common Transit Networks." *Trends and Issues in Crime and Criminal Justice* no. 233. Canberra, ACT: Australian Institute of Criminology, July 2002.

McCulloch, Jude and Carlton, Bree. "Preempting Justice: Suppression of Financing of Terrorism and the 'War on Terror.'" *Current Issues in Criminal Justice* 17, no. 3 (March 2006): 397–412.

McCulloch, Jude and Pickering, Sharon. "Suppressing the Financing of Terrorism: Proliferating State Crime, Eroding Censure and Extending Neo-Colonialism." *British Journal of Criminology* 45, no. 4 (July 2005): 470–86.

McCulloch, Jude and Tham, Joo-Cheong. "Secret State, Transparent Subject: The Australian Security Intelligence Organisation in the Age of Terror." *The Australian and New Zealand Journal of Criminology* 38, no. 3 (December 2005): 400–415.

McCusker, Rob. "Transnational Crime in the Pacific Islands: Real or Apparent Danger?" *Trends and Issues in Crime and Criminal Justice* no. 308. Canberra, ACT: Australian Institute of Criminology, March 2006.

McGeough, Paul. "Planting the Seeds of Terror." *Sydney Morning Herald*, 19 June 2004, http://www.smh.com.au/articles/2004/06/18/1087245107862.html (13 June 2007).

Ministerial Council on Drug Strategy. *The National Drug Strategy: Australia's Integrated Framework 2004–2009*. Canberra, ACT: Commonwealth of Australia, 2004.

Morrison, Shona. "Researching Heroin Supply." *Trends and Issues in Crime and Criminal Justice* no. 257. Canberra, ACT: Australian Institute of Criminology, July 2003.

Morrison, Shona. "Approaching Organised Crime: Where Are We Now and Where Are We Going?" *Trends and Issues in Crime and Criminal Justice* no. 231. Canberra, ACT: Australian Institute of Criminology, July 2002.

*Mutual Assistance in Criminal Matters Act* Commonwealth, 1987.

National Museum of Australia. "Australian Flag Home from World Trade Centre." *National Museum of Australia*, 10 September 2004, http://www.nma.gov.au/media/media_releases_index/2004_09_10/ (13 June 2007).

New Zealand Customs Service. "Praise for Customs Officers in Major Trans-Tasman Drug Seizure." New Zealand Customs Service, 26 October 2006, http://www.customs.govt.nz/about/News/cocaineseizure2610061.htm (4 June 2007).

News.com.au. "DNA Confirms Aussie 9/11 Victim." *The Australian*, 11 April 2007, http://theaustralian.news.com.au/story/0,20867,21538130-23109,00.html (13 June 2007).

News.com.au. "Willy Brigitte May Appeal Terror Plot Jail Sentence." *News.com.au*, 16 March 2007, http://www.news.com.au/story/0,23599,21391322-2,00.html (14 June 2007).

O'Brien, Susannah; Black, Emma; Degenhardt, Louisa; et al. (National Drug and Alcohol Research Centre). *Australian Drug Trends, 2006: Findings from the Illicit Drug Reporting System (IDRS)*, NDARC Monograph no. 60. Sydney, NSW: National Drug and Alcohol Research Centre, University of New South Wales, 2007, http://ndarc.med.unsw.edu.au/NDARCWeb.nsf/resources/Mono_7/$file/Mono.60.pdf (4 June 2007).

Palmer, Darren and Whelan, Chad. "Counter-terrorism across the Policing Continuum." *Police Practice and Research* 7, no. 5 (December 2006): 449–65.

Parliament of Australia. "Bills Digest No. 127 2001–02: Suppression of the Financing of Terrorism Bill 2002." *Parliamentary Library*. Canberra, ACT: Parliament of Australia, 2002, http://www.aph.gov.au/library/pubs/bd/2001-02/02bd127.htm (13 June 2007).

Parliamentary Joint Committee on the Australian Crime Commission. *Inquiry into the Manufacture, Importation and Use of Amphetamines and Other Synthetic Drugs (AOSD) in Australia*. Canberra, ACT: Parliament of the Commonwealth of Australia, February 2007, http://www.aph.gov.au/Senate/committee/acc_ctte/aosd/report/index.htm (1 June 2007).

Parliamentary Joint Committee on the Australian Crime Commission. *Cybercrime*. Canberra, ACT: Parliament of the Commonwealth of Australia, 2004, http://www.aph.gov.au/senate/committee/acc_ctte/completed_inquiries/2002-04/cybercrime/report/report.pdf (6 June 2007).

Pickering, Sharon and Weber, Leanne. *Borders, Mobility and Technologies of Control*. The Netherlands: Springer, 2006.

*R. v. Jack Roche* (2005) WASCA 4.

*Rush v. Commissioner of Police* (2006) FCA 12.

Schmid, Alex, P. "Frameworks for Conceptualising Terrorism." *Terrorism and Political Violence* 16, no. 2 (Summer, 2004): 197–221.

*Security Legislation Amendment (Terrorism) Act* Commonwealth, 2002.

Sexton, Elisabeth. "Brigette Tells of Band of Brothers Planning Sydney Terrorist Strike." *Sydney Morning Herald*, 9 February 2004, http://www.smh.com.au/articles/2004/02/08/1076175033542.html (14 June 2007).

Shanahan, Luke. "Mokbel Caught 'Living the High Life.'" *The Age*, 6 June 2007, http://www.theage.com.au/news/national/mokbel-caught-living-the-high-life/2007/06/06/1181089114901.html (7 June 2007).

Smith, Russell. "Consumer Scams in Australia: An Overview." *Trends and Issues in Crime and Criminal Justice* no. 331. Canberra, ACT: Australian Institute of Criminology, February 2007.

Smith, Russell. "Impediments to the Successful Investigation of Transnational High Tech Crime." *Trends and Issues in Crime and Criminal Justice* no. 285. Canberra, ACT: Australian Institute of Criminology, October 2004.

Smith, Russell and Grabosky, Peter. "Crime in the Digital Age," in *Crime and Justice: A Guide to Criminology*, 3rd ed., edited by Andrew Goldsmith, Mark Israel, and Kathleen Daly. Pyrmont, NSW: Thomson/Lawbook Company, 2006.

*Sports Event Ticketing (Fair Access) Act* Victoria, 2002.

Tham, Joo-Cheong. "Casualties of the Domestic 'War on Terror': A Review of Recent Counter-Terrorism Laws." *Melbourne University Law Review* 28, no. 2 (August 2004): 512–31.

Urbas, Gregor and Krone, Tony. "Mobile and Wireless Technologies: Security and Risk Factors." *Trends and Issues in Crime and Criminal Justice* no. 329. Canberra, ACT: Australian Institute of Criminology, November 2006.

Victorian Department of Human Services (report prepared by Victoria White, Edith Szabo, Jane Hayman, Bernice Webster, Angela Hain, and Andrew Fairthorne). *Victorian Secondary School Students' Use of Licit and Illicit Substances in 2005: Results from the 2005 Australian Secondary Students' Alcohol and Drug Survey.* Melbourne, Vic.: Government of Victoria, 2006a, http://www.health.vic.gov.au/drugservices/downloads/assad_part1a.pdf (11 September 2006).

Victorian Department of Human Services (report prepared by Mark Stoové, Rebecca Jenkinson, Stefan Cvetkovski, Sharon Matthews, Brendan Quinn, Paul Dietze, and Paul McElwee of the Turning Point Alcohol and Drug Centre Inc.). *The Victorian Drug Statistics Handbook 2006: Patterns of Drug Use and Related Harm in Victoria.* Melbourne, Vic.: Government of Victoria, 2006b, http://www.health.vic.gov.au/drugservices/downloads/hbook_2006.pdf (4 June 2007).

Warren, Ian. "Governance, Protest and Sport: An Australian Perspective." *Journal of Entertainment and Sports Law* 1, no. 1 (Spring 2002): 67–94.

Warren, Ian and James, Steve. "The Police Use of Force: Contexts and Constraints," in *Violence and Police Culture*, edited by Tony Coady, Steve James, Seumas Miller, and Michael O'Keefe. Melbourne, Vic.: Melbourne University Publishing, 2000.

Wood, Jennifer. "Cultural Change in the Governance of Security." *Policing and Society* 14, no. 1 (March 2004): 31–48.

*Chapter Six*

# Police Response in the Russian Federation

Yakov Gilinskiy

Russia's total area is 17,075,400 square kilometers. Its population grew from 101.4 million in 1950 to 148.7 million in 1991 and fell to 143.5 million in 2002 (there is so-called depopulation now). Approximately 78.6 percent of the population live in the European sector and 21.4 percent in the Asiatic sector (West and East Siberia and the Russian Far East); 47 percent are male and 53 percent female; 73.0 percent living in urban and 27.0 percent in rural areas (Vishnevsky, 2002: 11, 14, 20).

The contemporary Russian Federation (Russia) came into existence in 1991 after the break up of the Union of Soviet Socialist Republics (USSR). Russia includes twenty-one republics as part of the Russian Federation, six *krai* (large regions, territories), fifty *oblast* (provinces, regions), one autonomous area (Chukotsk), and two cities under federal administration (the capital, Moscow, and the former capital, St. Petersburg). Moreover seven Federal Okrugs (central, northwestern, southern, of the Volga, Ural, Siberian, and far eastern) were recently constituted. Every Federal Okrug includes some regions. There is a president who is the head of each Federal Okrug.

According to the constitution of the Russian Federation there is "division of powers." The president of the Russian Federation is head of state. The Russian Federation is a presidential republic with powerful presidential power. Following Vladimir Putin, Dmitry Medvedev, the current president of the Russian Federation, has a reputation for law and order and believes in intensification of central power ("power's vertical line"). Moreover, there are presidents of the republics in each part of the Russian Federation (Bashkiria, Dagestan, Tatarstan, and others).

The federal legislature is the parliament of the Russian Federation (the so-called Federal'noe Sobranie—Federal Assembly) consisting of two chambers: upper chamber Sovet Federatsiy (Council of Federation) and lower chamber Gosudarstvennaja Duma (State Duma).[1] There is a regional legislature—zakonodatel'noe sobranie (legislative assembly)—or parliament in each of the republics of the Federation.

Federal executive power is the central government with a prime minister at its head. Regional executive power is a governor or mayor in a city who is in charge of that branch of government.

## CRIME AND ITS CONTEXT

The level and structure of crime common with all types of so-called deviance (drug and alcohol addiction, prostitution, corruption, suicide, etc.) and police activity is wholly dependent upon the social, economic, political, cultural, and demographic processes taking place in society. Therefore, one must understand the social situation in contemporary Russia to study crime.

Former Soviet leader Mikhail Gorbachev's perestroika was an attempt to save the Communist regime's power structures by way of reform. A similar attempt was made by Nikita Khrushchev, former Soviet leader after the death of Joseph Stalin (the "Thaw"). However, these attempts ended with the political death of their propagators and were followed by "Stagnation" or "Reaction."

With all due credit to Gorbachev, his reforms turned out to be the most radical and democratic (freedom of speech, freedom of the press, the multiparty system, the right to hold private property, the lifting of the Iron Curtain, the release of those states occupied by Stalin [Latvia, Lithuania, and Estonia], etc.) However, these reforms did not bring an end to the turbulent nature of Russian reform.

Difficulties in the Russian economy continue today. Power has shifted to new "oligarchs" and criminals. Corruption, while not unusual in Russia, has taken on a monumental, total scale in all organs of power, including the government and its law enforcement bodies. There are crises in health, education, transport, and other social services. Compounding these issues are difficulties in dealing with spirituality, morality, and the militarization of economics and politics. Technological backwardness and the incompetence of domestic production and service sectors have manifested themselves in the course of the reforms. A consequence of this is the inferiority complex of employees, their dequalification and marginalization. These issues form the social basis for deviance, including crime and organized crime (Lenoir, 1974; Finer and Nellis, 1998; Young, 1999).

The growth of the role (importance) of the so-called power structures— FSB (former KGB), MVD (Ministry of Internal Affairs) including police, and others—is not helping the situation. The war in Chechnya is terrifying evidence of neototalitarianism. The country also permits human rights abuses on a massive scale. It is particularly evident in the army and penal institutions, where tyranny and torture dominate (Abramkin, 1998; Christie, 2000: 79–90; Gilinskiy, 1998; *Index on Censorship*, 1999; Walmsley, 1998: 358–86; Walmsley, 2002). Nationalist, anti-Semitic, neofascist, and skinhead groups (there are more than fifty thousand skinheads in contemporary Russia) have widespread activity that meets with no resistance. Attacks against mass media in opposition began in 1999–2000 and continue today. Censorship was reestablished de facto, although there is no official policy on it (so-called internal censorship). "Spy mania" has also increased since 1999.

## Organized Crime

Organized crime is the functioning of stable, hierarchical associations engaged in crime as a form of business, and setting up a system of protection against public control by means of corruption. Criminal associations are a *kind of social organization* of a "working (labor) collective body" type. The growth of the organizational aspect of crime is a natural process; it is a manifestation of the growth of the organizational aspect of the social systems as well as of their subsystems (economy, politics, culture, etc.). It is a worldwide process. The high degree of criminal associations' adaptivity (resulting from their strict labor discipline, their careful selection of staff, the high profit, etc.) ensures their great vital capacity.

I consider that the three models of organized crime acknowledged in the literature (hierarchical, local or ethnic models, and organized crime as a business enterprise) complement each other in practice. "Business enterprise" is the *content* of the organized crime activities, whereas hierarchical (including "bureaucratic/corporate model" and "patrimonial/patron-client model"), local (including "alien conspiracy model"), and ethnic models reflect the organizational forms of this activity. As we have already suggested, the literature of criminology throughout the world is increasingly recognizing organized crime as a form of business enterprise (Abadinsky, 1994; Albanese, 1995; Arlacchi, 1986; Kelly, Chin, and Schatzbery, 1994) or "illicit enterprises" (Smith, 1975).

In my view criminal business arises, exists, and develops under the following conditions: (1) demand for illegal wares (drugs, arms, etc.) and services (sexual, etc.), (2) dissatisfied demand for legal wares and services (for example, total "deficit" in the Soviet Union), (3) unemployment and other sources of dissatisfaction as a social basis of deviance, and (4) defects of tax policy, customs policy of the state, and so on.

The growth of organized crime is an objective process. But in the Russian case, it is also important to recognize the way in which organized crime, through lobbying and direct infiltration, directly attempts to influence the government. Russian criminal organizations are very careful in their selection of staff and very demanding in the discipline they impose on this newly selected workforce. Generally speaking, they employ only the youngest, bravest, and most enterprising of people with strong character.

The criminal organization (syndicate) is defined by the following indispensable characteristics: (1) a *stable* association of people, designed for *long-term* activity; (2) the *criminal nature* of the activity (financial pursuits dependent on criminal activity); (3) the derivation of *maximum profits* as the key goal of the activity; (4) the complex *hierarchical structure* of the organization with its functions clearly delineated; (5) the *corruption* of power bodies and law enforcement bodies as the main means of the criminal activity; and (6) the aspiration to *monopolization* in a certain sphere of trade or in certain territories.

The main fields of activity of criminal organizations in Russia are bank speculation (illegal transactions); fictitious real estate transactions; stealing and reselling cars; illegal export of nonferrous metals; production of, and traffic in, fake hard liquor; arms sales; control over gambling; agencies for supplying sexual services; drug trafficking; human trafficking; and laundering money.

## Gambling

Illegal gambling is particularly prevalent. "Dens" (*katran*) function in the city, where clients play in uncomplicated gambling (card playing, dice, backgammon, etc.). Play goes on for very large sums of money. Half or more of the clients are representatives of the "criminal world." Another big part of this business is street gambling. There are "thimbles," "three cards," and street raffles. Independent from the rules of play, the client never wins. Modern organizers of street raffles pay about 20 percent of their criminal group (*krysha*—roof) and contractually pay a percent to patrol service of police (PPS). Casinos also enter into the organization of gambling.

I. (interviewer Dr. Kostjukovsky): What about the organization of gambling?

R. (respondent from criminal group): If we are talking about a casino as an organization of gambling. . . . This is very suitable to criminal activity. I can invite to the casino an "interesting" person and he will win. He can win as much as I want. This situation works purely and beautifully—no bribes, no corruption. The person appears lucky, no problems. It is possible to realize through the casino great amounts of money without any interference by authorities. It is possible to find law violations, however, what officer will check it if some high ranking politician is gambling?

## Human Trafficking

Human trafficking is a global problem (Glonti, 2003; Kangaspunta, 2003). The definition of "trafficking in persons" includes three main elements: (1) recruitment, transportation, transfer, harboring, or receipt of persons; (2) the threat or the use of improper means, such as force, abduction, fraud, or deception; and (3) the objective of exploitation, such as sexual exploitation, forced labor, servitude, or slavery (Protocol to Prevent, Suppress and Punish Trafficking in Persons, Especially Women and Children, supplementing the UN Convention against Transnational Organized Crime, November 2000). There are several kinds of human trafficking: trafficking of women ("white slavery"), trafficking of children (for prostitution, for pornography, for illegal adoption), slavery, trafficking of internals, and so on. The smuggling of migrants is also widespread.

All kinds of trafficking exist in Russia. Moreover, Russia leads the world in the list of world trafficking (Erokhina and Buryak, 2003: 36). "Considering the global inequalities in affluence, it is not surprising that Africa, Asia and the CIS member states were the main regions where victims of trafficking were recruited" (Kangaspunta, 2003: 91). Russia is a country with a great number of the victims of trafficking (in descending order: Ukraine, Russia, Nigeria, Albania, Romania, Moldova, Bulgaria, China, and so on) and a great number of the offenders, who were suspected of being involved in trafficking as criminals or had been found guilty (in descending order: Russia, Nigeria, Ukraine, Albania, Thailand, Turkey, China, Poland, and so on) (Kangaspunta, 2003: 94, 99).

This is no surprise, because there are very many poor unemployed, especially women and children. For example, full employment in the Irkutsk region (Eastern Siberia) in the year 2000 was only 65.2 percent of men and 52.3 percent of women. At the same time, 60 percent of the population has an income below the living wage (Repetskaya, 2003: 31). More than 50 percent of the Russian population is "excluded" (Borodkin, 2000). More than 30 percent of the people have an income of lower than the living wage. About 24 percent of the Russian population lives below the international poverty line (World Bank, 2005: 261). Unfortunately, official data on different forms of trafficking in Russia is absent, therefore we must use local information and examples.

## Trafficking of Women

There are various kinds of prostitution in Russian cities: street prostitution (the prostitutes' average age being 16–17 years), highway prostitution (very young girls, including children of 12–15 years of age), railway station prostitution, hotel prostitution, club prostitution (14–17 years of age), "public house" (illegal, underground in Russia), "call services," and others (Gurvich et al., 2002: 15–17).

"White slavery" is the prevailing kind of trafficking. The International Organization for Migration names four "waves" of trafficking. The first wave is white slavery from Thailand and Philippines; the second wave is from the Dominican Republic and Colombia; the third wave is from Ghana and Niger; and the fourth wave is from countries of Central and Eastern Europe, including Russia (Stoecker, 2000: 58). According to selected data, more than five thousand prostitutes from the Russian Far East "work" in Thailand. Slavic women are a "symbol of social prestige" for Asiatic businessmen from Japan, China, and Thailand (Stoecker, 2000: 59). Many Russian women prostitute in Europe and the United States. For example, the main topic "From Russia with Sex" was in a special issue of the magazine *New York* (August 10, 1998). The author saw the Russian prostitutes in the red-light district of Amsterdam, on the Reeperbahn in Hamburg, and in Antwerp's harbor.

Russian criminal organizations realize that the export of prostitutes across the border occurs regularly (Europe, the U.S., Asia, some countries of Latin America, Israel, and some other countries). One piece of evidence for this is seen in interviews conducted by social scientist Dr. Yakov Kostjukovsky (the Center of Deviantology of the Sociological Institute of the Russian Academy of Sciences) with representatives of criminal organizations about this activity.

I. (Interviewer): What about the organization of prostitution?

R. (Respondent): Prostitution in St. Petersburg is currently operating on a regular basis. . . . There are hundreds *kontor*.[2] It is more developed in Moscow. . . . In our city the most expensive women are in pubs, hotels, casinos. Then there are "call girls," girls in saunas, girls in "centers of leisure." So . . . massage salons, make-up salons. Street girls are the cheaper . . .

I.: And what about children's prostitution?

R.: Sure. This is practiced as well. There are many drunkards, who are selling their own children. Then it is possible for the bottle of vodka literally too. If we speak of prostitution in general, certainly, there is male prostitution and gay prostitution too. And males are higher in cost.

I.: What can you say about "business trips"?

R.: Yes, it happens. Moreover girls are not always whores. It can be the team of girls for the striptease work, or in the scope of service in general. But they are exported to, for example, Turkey and they are forced to work as whores.

## Trafficking of Children

The trafficking of children is a terrible and widespread phenomenon in the world and in Russia. Trafficking of children is realized for prostitution (male and female), pornography, and illegal adoption. The social basis for children's prostitution is more than 2 million children homeless and in orphanages, children of drunkard parents, and children who want money for the "sweet life."

The Center of Deviantology of the Sociological Institute of the Russian Academy of Sciences has published studies of the commercial, sexual exploitation of children in St. Petersburg and northwest Russia, including Vyborg, Petrozavodsk, and others (see Gurvich et al., 2002). The main users of children's sex are the "new Russian" city's "authorities" and foreign visitors, particularly from Finland and also from Sweden, Germany, Norway, and England. Oral sex, which is the service most widely offered by minors, costs 100–150 rubles (US$3–5). Sexual intercourse costs 200–250 rubles ($7–8). A night with a client costs from 500–600 rubles to 1,000 rubles (from $17–20 to $30–35). If the child's parents are alcoholics, then the payment is often a bottle of vodka (about $3). The boys are more expensive: 3,000–7,000 rubles ($100–250) for spending the evening with a client.

Child pornography is the least studied and highly profitable sphere of the commercial sex trade. "The street children are the most vulnerable to exploitation as models in pornographic video and other materials. The individuals involved in the production of pornography seek out such children in the streets, marketplaces, and near metro and railway stations and other places of the city. After feeding them, they ask the children whether they would like to 'make good money.' The minors, who are in an extremely hard economic situation, believe that it will be an easy way to make money, get food, clothes, or sometimes drugs, alcohol, cigarettes. . . . Cadets of military boarding schools of St. Petersburg are often used for the shooting of homosexual porno-materials" (Gurvich et al., 2002: 27).

## Forced Labor or Slavery

Strange as it may seem, forced labor is widely practiced today. Of cases where men were reported to be the victims, 24 percent involved trafficking for forced labor and 60 percent of cases included both types of exploitation: sexual and slavery. Among cases of trafficking of women 2 percent involved trafficking for forced labor and 13 percent for both types (sexual and forced labor), and among children 70 percent were trafficked for sexual exploitation, 13 percent for forced labor, and 18 percent for both types of exploitation (Kangaspunta, 2003: 95).

Contemporary Russian slaves work in the Caucasian region of Russia and even in the central regions. Moreover, Russia is a "consumer" of "slaves" from the members of the Commonwealth of Independent States (CIS), especially from Tajikistan, Uzbekistan, Kazakhstan, and Moldova, as well as from China, Vietnam, Afghanistan, North Korea, and from some African and Latin American countries. Russian and international criminal groups take part in unlawful transit of illegal immigrants. The forced labor is very hard and dangerous. Many slaves of the twenty-first century see "life-saving" in suicide (Repetskaya, 2003: 34).

### Trafficking of Internal Organs

This type of the trafficking is the most secret and cryptic. Many people in the world need transplants of different internal organs (hearts, kidneys, and others). There is a deficit of internal organs and they can be bought on the black market. The Russian press sometimes informs about cases of illegal trafficking of internal organs, but trustworthy information is absent.

## CONNECTION TO INTERNATIONAL
## ORGANIZED CRIMINAL ACTIVITY

Russian criminals are very aggressive, as are most young representatives of new structures. However, Russian bandits are getting more "civilized." They prefer to penetrate legal and semilegal structures; pay by credit card, not cash; and wear haute couture clothes. Of course, "wild" criminals (so-called *otmorozki*—"frost-bitten") remain too. Russian organized crime will fight for its "place under the sun" on the international organized crime scene.

There are various connections between Russian and foreign organized crime, for example, drug traffic from Afghanistan, Azerbaijan, Kyrgyzstan, Turkmenistan, and countries of Latin America (especially cocaine) to Russia and from Russia to Western Europe; joint stealing and reselling cars with foreign "colleagues" from the Netherlands, Poland, and Germany; sex business and traffic of prostitutes to Europe, the U.S., countries of Latin America, Israel, China, and Korea; and illegal selling of arms to Europe, Africa, and Asia (this business involves not only criminals, but army authorities, too). As a result of the international cooperation of criminals, there are greater amounts of adulterated strong drinks produced. These drinks appear authentic and, therefore, get high prices on sale in Russia. They often come from Poland, Hungary, Holland, or Germany.

For example, in part of an interview:

I.: Do you get in touch with foreigners?

R. (criminal): Yes, of course. We have joint business of cars. It is exchange. Somebody drive away car here, in St. Petersburg, and car going to Holland, and from Holland also to here. . . . Generally, it is a whole system in Germany, Poland, France, Hungary, Holland and Russia. Just so, it is OK! There is international contact.

There is a special police unit in Russia that fights against organized crime: the Board of Fight against Organized Crime (in Russian Upravlenie po bor'be s organisovannoi prestupnost'ju [UBOP]). This board includes the special department "prompt response" (SOBR) for the taking of criminals.

It is a shame that Russian police on the one hand battle with organized crime yet, on the other hand, exacerbate the illegal activity of criminal organizations by their corruption. I present below some parts of my interviews with police officers (February–March, 2005).

I. (interviewer): What you can tell about news of the contemporary organized crime?

R. (respondent, officer from UBOP): Organized crime is not. There are *menty*.[3] Who *kryshuet* (make "roof")[4] of different stalls, shops, markets? Who *kryshuet* of *tochki* ("points")?[5] *Menty*. Let's see: that is stall. Policeman will come sometimes and get money from owner of stall. *Tochka* is on fourth floor of house across the street. It is under control of *X* department of police. . . . All shops, stalls, small and middle business are today under *mentovskaja krysha* (roof of police).

I.: Who is "patron" of prostitution?

R.: *Menty*, of course.

I.: Who is "patron" of gambling?

R.: It is FSB. It is too hard for police. . . . Gambling business is very profitable. FSB *kryshuet* of these.

Another interview:

I.: It is said, that "roofs" of police change of criminal "roofs." Is it really?

R. (police officer from the Board of Own Security): Yes, of course. It is a practice not only single policemen, but different police units. For example, new café appears on local police office (department). Head of police department send some officer to owner of café for "conversation." And owner of café pay "tribute" every month for police office after such "visit."

In sum, our main points on Russian contemporary organized crime include the following:

- For organized crime authorities striving for the combination of legal and illegal forms of business, the amalgamation of legal and illegal business is a fact.
- Striving for influence over power structures and legal authority, they reach it by directly entering the power bodies, lobbying, and bribery of state bureaucrats at all levels. Today, criminal authorities are elected to federal and regional power bodies and finance the election campaigns of "useful" persons (corrupted bureaucrats).
- There is a confluence of criminal, economic, and power "elites" who govern.
- There is an internationalization of Russian organized crime activity. Interaction and cooperation with foreign and international criminal organizations is rampant.


## TERRORISM

Terrorism (terror—*lat.* fear, horror) is one of the most serious global social problems, potentially or actually touching every inhabitant of our planet. At the same time, as often happens, the more serious, real, and obvious the problem, the more the myths and misunderstandings that surround it.

There is no single definition of terrorism in the social sciences. Here are some of the typical ones (there are more than a hundred in all [Cassesse, 1989: 3]).

- "The threat of violence or the use of violence for political motives" (*Das neue taschen Lexikon*, 1992: 59–60).
- "The use of violence or the threat of violence against individuals of property in order to achieve political goals"(Schnaider, 1994: 439).
- "Violent actions or threats to use violence made by political subjects when pursuing their political objectives" (Kabanov, 2000: 40).
- "Systematic use of murder, bodily harm and destruction, or the threat of these in order to achieve political goals" (Laqueur, 1977: 79).
- "Method of political war, a systematic use of physical compulsion which is unlimited, unconnected with military action and with the aim of [achieving]

certain determinate results by creating fear in its opponents" (Dmitriev and Zalysin, 2000: 53).

From the above definitions we can isolate two basic indicators of terrorism:

1. the threat to use or the actual use of *violence*, and
2. its political *motivation*.

Terrorism is a social phenomenon and not an individual act of political murder. This is indicated by *the indeterminate circle of immediate objects* of a terrorist act, the use of violence in relation to an indeterminate group of people ("innocent people") for the sake of achieving an ultimate objective— the satisfaction of political (economic, social) demands. For "of terrorism we can speak only when the sense of an act is defined as the creation of fear and horror. This is the fundamental characteristic of terrorism" (Antonyan, 1998: 8).

Laqueur saw the complexity and subjectivity inherent in the definition of terrorism: "One man's terrorist is another man's freedom fighter" (Laqueur, 1987: 302). This theme is treated similarly in an article by B. Ganor (Ganor, 2002), member of the International Police Counter-terrorism Institute. How can we differentiate terrorism and partisan conflict, terrorism and revolutionary violence, terrorism and the battle for national liberation? Much depends on the position of the subject judging various violent, politically motivated acts. In addition, Ganor suggests a distinction between analyzed phenomena. In his scheme he delineates first of all declared war between states and undeclared war between organizations and states. The latter includes primarily terrorism and partisan conflict. Besides these, we can also add the activities of anarchists, freedom fighters, and revolutionaries and also ad hoc actions (in specific situations). The most important distinction—that between terrorism and partisan conflict— lies in the fact that partisan conflict is carried out *against combatants, that is, armed forces*, military units, and equipment, whereas terrorism is directed *against a peaceful population of non-combatants* and has political motives for its aggressive actions. This distinction strikes me as highly relevant and allows us to make more concrete some of our evaluations. On the other hand, the suggested difference is somewhat conditional (a peaceful population could become the victim of partisan activity as, for example, in the use of "smart bombs" or "limited strike"). In any case, Ganor cites three very important elements of terrorism: (1) the use of or the threat of *violence*, (2) the *political goal or motive of the act*, and (3) the *real objective* being the *peaceful population*, the citizenry.

Terror and terrorism are usually distinguished as follows:

1. *terror* is on the part of the ruling power structures (or "violence of the strong against weak," which is inherent, in particular, in totalitarian regimes); 2. *terrorism* is in the form of violence and intimidation used by "the weak against the strong," "the weapon of the weak, the victim of state terror" (Chalikova, 1989: 310; Ferro, 1989: 314).

In other words "terror is violence and intimidation objectively used by the stronger in relation to the weaker" (Berngard, 1978: 23).

Terrorist organizations and individual terrorists working alone represent—tacitly or not—the interests of a mass of *excluded* people in the contemporary world (Finer and Nellis, 1998; Lenoir, 1974; Young, 1999). The polarization between the very rich and powerful minority of "included" and the really impoverished and powerless majority of "excluded" (and the relative erosion of "the middle class," the guarantor of a social system's solidity) is leading, in conditions of global economics, to a worldwide split into inclusive/exclusive people, which is dangerous for humanity. There are included/excluded people and countries. Thus, we have the "Gold Billion" countries (included) and all the rest (excluded). This polarity of people and groups is expressed in the writing of N. Luhmann.

> The worst of all possible scenarios is that society of the next century [i.e., the present twenty-first century—Y.G.] will have the metacode inclusion/exclusion. This would mean that certain people would be personalities and the others only individuals, that some would be included in the functional system, others excluded from it remain creatures who just try to survive another day; . . . that care and scorn will lie on different sides of the border, that the tight bond of exclusion and the loose, freer ties of inclusion will distinguish Fate from Fortune, that two forms of integration will be completed negative integration of exclusion and the positive integration of inclusion. (Luhmann, 1998: 107)

Is not the negative integration the major social base of terrorism (and, we could say, of other forms of deviant behavior—crime, drug addiction, alcoholism, etc.)?

The ruling elites are insufficiently aware of this global process. As examples we can cite American aggression in Iraq (no matter how "bad" Saddam Hussein may have been) and the actions of Russia in Chechnya (no matter how ruthless the Chechen fighters can be). *Terror incites terrorism.* Or, as the St. Petersburg economist D. Travin wrote, "Don't wet on others, so that you don't get wet on yourself!"[6] No matter who started it, humanity is now paying for its political games with mountains of corpses.

Human rights are primary and inalienable (Articles 1, 2, and 3 of the General Declaration of Human Rights, 1948). Violations of human rights breed violent reactions, in particular, terrorism. *Demands for the curtailment of human rights for the sake of the war with terrorism are absurd.* Firstly, these right themselves constitute the ideological basis for justifying terrorism (as a response to state terror). Secondly, there is an increased risk that citizens will become victims of human rights violations. This is happening in contemporary Russia: *we are all to a large extent hostages, not of terrorists, but of the power structure.*

Former president of Russian Federation Mr. B. Yeltsin and present president Mr. V. Putin transmute the fight against terrorists to an unjust war against the Chechen nation. It is genocide. It is a shame, but the police and army are obliged to realize the criminal battle-order. Terror by those in power generates terrorism. In my view every Chechen, for example, has a moral (not legal!) right to take revenge. The rights of man and the risk of crime are interdependent: *the more reliable the defense of human rights, the smaller the probability of the risk of terrorism.*

The history of political repression (terror) and terrorist acts in the form of political assassinations goes back centuries.[7] However, the majority of researchers have noticed that essential distinctions of contemporary terrorism are its being "an integral part of state terror—one of the forms of state power" (Ferro, 1989: 313) and a systematic violent intimidation of society, its having a mass character (sometimes to the point of genocide perpetrated by the power structures), a constantly growing number of terrorist acts and their victims, and the globalization (internationalization) of terrorism.

The New York tragedy of September 11, 2001, has become a terrible symbol of the new reality of the twenty-first century (as Auschwitz was a symbol of the twentieth century).[8] It is significant that the chosen objects of the most monstrous act in world history were in New York (how can we not recall M. Gorky's "City of the Yellow Devil"?)[9] and the World Trade Center, symbol of the country of the "Golden Billion" (the *included*).

The new methods of terrorism are innumerable: hijackings of transport and hostage taking; the destruction of transport communications; explosion and arson; military force, including partisan actions; poisoning the food and water supplies; the use of poisonous substances or threatening to use them; and other measures and means.

Leaving the juridical (criminal) aspect of the terrorism problem, we will go on to consider some sociopolitical questions.

Terrorism, leading to innumerable victims and bringing unimaginable suffering, is a form of *criminal* activity (a crime) and deserves severe punishment. But the sociopolitical essence of terrorism and the desire to battle it demand a much wider approach than the simply juridical. Yes, from the point of view acceptable to the world community there is no justification for terrorism. But terrorism is nevertheless a special type of crime. From the point of view of terrorists and organizations and movements resorting to terrorist methods, their demands and asserted ideas are "just" and have no less value than those of the people against whom they perpetrate their acts. Therefore, the armed war on terrorism, which has a political (ethnic, confessional, ideological) character, is not effective. As proof of this we can cite the protracted, bloody experience of Ulster in the Irish conflict and the wars with Basque separatists in Spain, Algerian terrorists in France, Albanians in Serbia, and Chechens in Russia.

Violence and hate breed violence and hate, and form the ideology and perpetrators of "hate crimes" (Jacobs and Potter, 1998). Therefore "the art of civilized life . . . consists in not breeding unhappy, resentful 'martyrs' but in building the well-being of people in the context of their long-term relations with one another" (Dmitriev, V. Kudryavtsev, and S. Kudryavtsev, 1993: 171).

The international community as a whole and each state in particular must first of all take political (economic, social) steps towards *preventing the conditions* which breed terrorism and finding nonviolent means of dealing with interethnic and interreligious social conflicts. Of course, it is much easier to propose nonviolent, preventive measures to counter long-standing problems and conflicts than it is to actually make them work in practice. But a "simple solution" to complicated social problems does not exist. So-called simple solutions ("liquidation," "suppression," "extermination") are either unworkable or lead to a further complication of the situation. It is possible (and necessary) to do battle with individual perpetrators of terrorist acts—skyjackers, assassins, bombers, and so on. But we cannot use the law and prisons to eradicate the causes and sources of terrorism when it is used as a method of "solving" social (ethnic, religious, political, ideological) conflicts. Obviously, it is not by chance that in the postwar world, terrorist organizations arose first of all in post-Fascist, posttotalitarian, post-Communist countries—Italy (the Red Brigade), Germany (Red Army Faction, neo-Nazis), Japan (the Japanese revolutionary Red Army), Spain, Yugoslavia, and Russia—and in countries with totalitarian regimes (Latin America, the Near and Middle East), where there was no experience of solving social problems and conflicts through democratic political methods. In 1990, out of seventy-nine well-known terrorist organizations, thirty-seven belonged ideologically to Marxism, Leninism, Trotskyism, or Maoism; nine represented various strands of Pan-Arabism and Islamic fundamentalism; seven were a remarkable mix of Pan-Arabism and Marxism; and four were relabeled as right-wing extremism and neo-Fascism (Long, 1990). Of course this correlation has undergone certain changes up to the present day. The number of prominent terrorist organizations has grown and the number of left-wing groups has fallen on account of the growth of rightists and Islamic movements.

There is no universal medicine for preventing terrorism and solving the complex problem that lies at its roots. Certain general approaches have been suggested in the conflictological and politological literature (Dmitriev, V. Kudryavtsev, and S. Kudryavtsev, 1993: 162–208; Dmitriev and Zalysin, 2000: 242–96). It is important to understand that

- a world without violence is impossible in the foreseeable future;
- the fundamental antiterrorist problem is, as much as possible, to curtail the scale of terrorism (understood as violence of the weak used against the strong); and
- the main path to this curtailment is the prevention of, or at least the regulation of, social problems and conflicts by nonviolent, nonrepressive, political methods.

"An absolutely non-violent world is an unreal prospect. The task of reducing political violence to the minimum looks much nearer to reality. The evidence for this is in the political life of developed, democratic countries, where violence is more often than not a secondary means of power" (Dmitriev and Zalysin, 2000: 296).

Many tragedies occurred in Russia due to terrorism. The world knows about acts of terrorism on the musical *North-East*, in Beslan's school and others. My hypothesis is that the war in Chechnya is the main source of these tragedies.

There were many killed in the Caucasian region, including policemen. The hunt for policemen exists in different Caucasian republics now. The reciprocal fight of terrorists and police and the army constitutes a vicious circle. Only political decisions can cut the knot.

## OTHER CRIMES

First, we present some common data about crime in Russia (see tables 6.1, 6.2, and 6.3). We can see the main tendencies.

- The rate (per 100,000 inhabitants) of registered crime decreased in 1963–1965 (the time of Khrushchev Thaw) and in 1986–1988 (the time of Gorbachev's perestroika), increased from 816.9 (1987) to 1887.8 (1993), and after a short stable period (1996–1998) increased again to 2051.4 in 1999 (2016.6 in 2004).

**Table 6.1. Crimes, Offenders, and Convicts in Russia (1961–2005)**

| Year | Crimes | Rate (per 100,000 Population) | Offenders | Convicts |
|------|--------|-------------------------------|-----------|----------|
| 1961 | 534 866 | 446,5 | — | — |
| 1962 | 539 302 | 446,1 | — | — |
| 1963 | 485 656 | 397,7 | — | — |
| 1964 | 483 229 | 392,2 | — | — |
| 1965 | 483 550 | 388,7 | — | — |
| 1966 | 582 965 | 464,5 | 596 764 | — |
| 1967 | 572 884 | 452,5 | 628 463 | — |
| 1968 | 618 014 | 483,6 | 626 129 | — |
| 1969 | 641 385 | 497,6 | 659 607 | — |
| 1970 | 693 552 | 533,1 | 700 685 | 554 589 |
| 1971 | 702 358 | 536,6 | 652 763 | 574 350 |
| 1972 | 706 294 | 536,3 | 698 964 | 575 056 |
| 1973 | 695 647 | 524,6 | 682 399 | 538 156 |
| 1974 | 760 943 | 570,4 | 718 161 | 579 642 |
| 1975 | 809 819 | 603,4 | 753 005 | 581 035 |
| 1976 | 834 998 | 618,0 | 770 473 | 599 652 |
| 1977 | 824 243 | 606,5 | 746 354 | 525 984 |
| 1978 | 889 599 | 650,7 | 782 099 | 557 564 |
| 1979 | 970 514 | 705,8 | 818 746 | 590 538 |
| 1980 | 1 028 284 | 742,2 | 880 908 | 645 544 |
| 1981 | 1 087 908 | 779,7 | 919 001 | 682 506 |
| 1982 | 1 128 558 | 803,1 | 988 946 | 747 865 |
| 1983 | 1 398 239 | 988,1 | 1 077 802 | 809 147 |
| 1984 | 1 402 694 | 984,4 | 1 123 351 | 863 194 |
| 1985 | 1 416 935 | 987,5 | 1 154 496 | 837 310 |
| 1986 | 1 338 424 | 929,9 | 1 128 439 | 797 286 |
| 1987 | 1 185 914 | 816,9 | 969 388 | 580 074 |
| 1988 | 1 220 861 | 833,9 | 834 673 | 427 039 |
| 1989 | 1 619 181 | 1098,5 | 847 577 | 436 988 |
| 1990 | 1 839 451 | 1242,5 | 897 299 | 537 643 |
| 1991 | 2 173 074 | 1463,2 | 956 258 | 593 823 |
| 1992 | 2 760 652 | 1856,5 | 1 148 962 | 661 392 |
| 1993 | 2 799 614 | 1887,8 | 1 262 737 | 792 410 |
| 1994 | 2 632 708 | 1778,9 | 1 441 568 | 924 754 |
| 1995 | 2 755 669 | 1862,7 | 1 595 501 | 1 035 807 |
| 1996 | 2 625 081 | 1778,4 | 1 618 394 | 1 111 097 |
| 1997 | 2 397 311 | 1629,3 | 1 372 161 | 1 013 431 |
| 1998 | 2 581 940 | 1759,5 | 1 481 503 | 1 071 051 |
| 1999 | 3 001 748 | 2026,0 | 1 716 679 | 1223255 |
| 2000 | 2952367 | 2028,2 | 1741439 | 1183631 |
| 2001 | 2968255 | 2045,6 | 1644242 | 1244211 |
| 2002 | 2526305 | 1760,5 | 1257700 | 859318 |
| 2003 | 2756398 | 1924,8 | 1236733 | 767371 |
| 2004 | 2893810 | 2016,6 | 1222504 | 793918 |
| 2005 | 3554738 | 2477,6 | 1297123 | 878893 |

*Source:* Annual "Crime and Delinquency" (1991–2006). Moscow: MVD RF, MJ RF.

**Table 6.2.** Rate (per 100,000 Inhabitants) of Serious Violent Crimes in Russia (1985–2005)

Homicide

| 1985 | 1986 | 1987 | 1988 | 1989 | 1990 | 1991 | 1992 | 1993 | 1994 | 1995 | 1996 | 1997 | 1998 | 1999 | 2000 | 2001 | 2002 | 2003 | 2004 |
|------|------|------|------|------|------|------|------|------|------|------|------|------|------|------|------|------|------|------|------|
| 8.5 | 6.6 | 6.3 | 7.2 | 9.2 | 10.5 | 10.9 | 15.5 | 19.6 | 21.8 | 21.4 | 19.9 | 19.9 | 20.1 | 21.1 | 21.8 | 23.1 | 22.5 | 22.1 | 22.1 |

Grievous bodily harm

| 1985 | 1986 | 1987 | 1988 | 1989 | 1990 | 1991 | 1992 | 1993 | 1994 | 1995 | 1996 | 1997 | 1998 | 1999 | 2000 | 2001 | 2002 | 2003 | 2004 |
|------|------|------|------|------|------|------|------|------|------|------|------|------|------|------|------|------|------|------|------|
| 19.9 | 14.7 | 13.9 | 18.2 | 25.0 | 27.7 | 27.8 | 36.2 | 45.1 | 45.7 | 41.7 | 36.2 | 31.4 | 30.8 | 32.4 | 34.1 | 38.4 | 40.7 | 39.9 | 40.1 |

*Source:* Annual "Crime and Delinquency" (1991–2006). Moscow: MVD RF, MJ RF.

**Table 6.3.  Rate (per 100,000 Inhabitants) of Crimes against Property in Russia (1985–2005)**

| | 1985 | 1986 | 1987 | 1988 | 1989 | 1990 | 1991 | 1992 | 1993 | 1994 |
|---|---|---|---|---|---|---|---|---|---|---|
| Theft | 324.7 | 264.4 | 251.1 | 327.2 | 512.1 | 616.8 | 837.3 | 1110.2 | 1065.2 | 888.4 |
| Robbery | 29.9 | 21.8 | 21.0 | 29.9 | 51.0 | 56.3 | 68.8 | 110.9 | 124.3 | 100.4 |
| Assaults with robbery | 5.8 | 4.2 | 3.9 | 5.5 | 9.9 | 11.2 | 12.4 | 20.4 | 27.0 | 25.6 |
| | 1995 | 1996 | 1997 | 1998 | 1999 | 2000 | 2001 | 2002 | 2003 | 2004 |
| Theft | 924.6 | 818.0 | 716.3 | 779.2 | 966.2 | 900.0 | 879.2 | 645.8 | 803.6 | 892.3 |
| Robbery | 95.0 | 82.2 | 76.2 | 83.4 | 95.0 | 91.0 | 102.8 | 116.5 | 138.3 | 175.7 |
| Assaults with robbery | 25.5 | 24.3 | 23.3 | 26.2 | 27.9 | 27.0 | 30.9 | 32.8 | 33.9 | 38.7 |

*Source:* Annual "Crime and Delinquency" (1991–2006). Moscow: MVD RF, MJ RF.

- The rate (per 100,000 inhabitants) of homicide (with attempt) decreased in 1986–1988 (6.3 in 1987), increased from 6.3 (1987) to 21.8 (1994), and after a short time period of cutting down in 1996–1997 increased to 23.1 in 2001 (22.5 in 2003).
- The dynamic of rate of other kinds of crime is analogous: it was at a minimum during the Gorbachev period, increased again from 1994 to 1995, decreased for a short period, and increased again from 1999 to 2003. The period of the Khrushchev Thaw also saw a reduction in the crime rate.

But we must consider the following facts to get a real picture:

- The real number and rate of crime is much higher than official statistical data in all countries.
- Since 1993–1994 there has been in Russia a mass criminal cover-up of crimes from registration (Gilinskiy, 2000: 146–48; Luneev, 1997: 145; and others).

## VIOLENT CRIME

Violent crimes and corruption are a great concern in the Russian situation. The *rate of violence is very high* in Russia. The official rate (per 100,000 population) of homicide increased from 6.6 in 1987 up to 23.2 in 2001. Russia is ranked third in world in homicide after Colombia and South Africa. But the data on homicide from *medical* statistics (World Health Organization, 1996; Questions of Statistics, 2004: 33) is more exact than *police* data:

| date | medical data | police data |
|------|-------------|-------------|
| 1992 | 22.9 | 15.5 |
| 1993 | 30.4 | 19.6 |
| 1994 | 32.3 | 21.8 |
| 2002 | 30.8 | 22.4 |
| 2003 | 29.5 | 22.1 |

For comparison, the rate of homicide in some countries was (average per year, 1999–2001, from Barclay and Tavares, 2003: 10):

| | | | |
|-----------|-----|---------|-----|
| Australia | 1.9 | Canada | 1.8 |
| Austria | 1.2 | Denmark | 1.0 |

| Estonia | 10.6 | Norway       | 0.9  |
|---------|------|--------------|------|
| Finland | 2.9  | Poland       | 2.0  |
| France  | 1.7  | South Africa | 55.8 |
| Germany | 1.1  | Spain        | 1.1  |
| Hungary | 2.3  | Sweden       | 1.1  |
| Italy   | 1.5  | Switzerland  | 1.1  |
| Japan   | 1.0  | USA          | 5.6  |

The number of victims in contemporary Russia is huge. Official statistics indicate that the number murdered in Russia is staggering (*Crime and Delinquency*, 1991–2006):

| date | no. of persons | date | no. of persons |
|------|---------------|------|---------------|
| 1987 | 25,706        | 1997 | 65,598        |
| 1988 | 30,403        | 1998 | 64,545        |
| 1989 | 39,102        | 1999 | 65,060        |
| 1990 | 41,634        | 2000 | 76,651        |
| 1991 | 44,365        | 2001 | 78,697        |
| 1992 | 213,590       | 2002 | 76,803        |
| 1993 | 75,365        | 2003 | 76,921        |
| 1994 | 75,034        | 2004 | 72,317        |
| 1995 | 75,510        | 2005 | 68,554        |
| 1996 | 65,368        |      |               |

The total number of persons murdered in 1987–2005 was 1,331,223. In addition, twenty-five to forty thousand people are declared missing every year and are never found (42,643 in 2003). In the military, from five to six thousand of those who *do not participate in wars* die every year. Most of them die due to the violent "uncommissioned (unregulated) relationships" (*dedovshina*, the abuse of power by the older soldiers that often has sadistic forms),[10] accidents related to military service, and suicide.

Moreover, latent criminality is great. A national victimization survey is absent, but there are local studies. Our victimization study in St. Petersburg (1999–2002) shows the following:

- The rate of victimization in St. Petersburg is relatively stable at a little over 25 percent (1999–2002: 26.5%, 27.0%, 25.9%, 26.1%).
- 28–36 percent of respondents from all victims were victims two or more times in a year.
- A high, stable percentage do not make a police report about their victimization (1999–2002: 70.3%, 69.2%, 73.7%, 73.5%).

- Reasons for refusing to report were: "police will do nothing" (34–38%), "police could not do anything" (17–19%), "did not want to have contact with police" (7–8%), "injury was insignificant or there was no injury" (26–32%), and so on.
- Reaction of police to report: "did not react at all" (12–18%), "responded but a long time afterward" (5–8%), and "do not know anything about actions of police"—11–15 percent (!). Police reaction was immediate for only 29–38 percent of victims.

Similar results were found in the city Volgograd and the town Borowitchy (2001).

We have shown that the Russian people have little defense against crimes and police activity is low. What are the causes of this Russian situation (see Tsytsarev and Gilinsky, 2004)?

The first cause is a *geographical* factor. Russia was and is a very large country. Second is a *historical* factor, including the Byzantine heritage and the former Soviet regime. Third is a *political* factor. Russia has never been a democratic state, under the rule of law. There is a centuries-long tradition of despotism and totalitarianism.

Fourth is an *economic* factor. Russian people were always poor. Considerable social and economic inequality always existed in Russia, but exist especially now: the ratio of incomes between the 10 percent least prosperous and the 10 percent most prosperous increased from 1:4.5 in 1991 to 1:15 in 1999. This is based on official data, but the opinion of experts is that the real difference in incomes may be as much as 1:23–25 (*Human Development Report in the Russian Federation, 1999*, 2000: 46, 152) and in Moscow, up to 1:60. It is a reason for conflicts, envy, spite, and hatred.

Fifth is a *cultural* factor. Historical, political, and economic factors have caused Russian culture to be intolerant. Sixth is a "juridical" factor. Contemporary criminal legislation and practice of the police, criminal justice, and prisons are very strict, unjust, and repressive.

## CORRUPTION

There are many definitions of corruption (Heidenheimer, Johnston, and Le Vine, 1989; Rose-Ackerman, 1996; Wewer, 1994; and others). Perhaps the shortest (and the most precise) of them is "the abuse of public power for private profit" (Joseph Senturia, see Wewer, 1994: 481). The United Nations (UN) offers an analogous definition (Resolution 34/169 of the General Assembly UNO, 12.17.1979).

There is corruption in all countries. It is a world problem. But the dimensions of corruption are diverse. Corruption, common in Russia, has taken on a *total scale* in all organs of power and establishments. The Index of Perception of Corruption—2004 (from Transparency International) for Russia is 2.8; it is in ninetieth place from 146 countries (maximum corruption is in Haiti, index 1.5; minimum is in Finland, index 9.7).

The damage from corruption is about $20–25 billion per year. The export of capital from Russia abroad mounts to $15–25 billion per year and $300–350 billion from 1988 to 1999 (*Corruption and Combat Corruption*: *Role of Civil Society*, 2000: 18–21; 72–73). But this is old data. The head of the Russian foundation Information Science for Democracy (INDEM), Dr. G. Satarov (former assistant of former president Boris Yeltsin) advises in an interview that about $319 billion is lost to corruption per year. This is from the latest study by INDEM. G. Satarov comments: "It is fantasy. . . . There is feeling that it is a blind alley" (*Novaya Gazeta*, 2005a: 3). The sum total of bribery in 2004 was more than 2.6 times the sum total of the Russian budget! (*Novaya Gazeta*, 2005b: 6–7).

Every day the Russian and foreign mass media produce facts on Russian corruption and corrupt activity. Every day different Russian newspapers and journals are publishing who (name, position), when, and how much money or "service" was gotten as bribe, and this gets no reaction from authorities. *Novaya Gazeta* (*New Newspaper*) published in July 2003 (N49) the price for training in St. Petersburg's universities: from $2500 to $4000. *Novaya Gazeta* published in December 2002 (N93) data about a booklet of the Duma's deputy Professor G. Kostin. There were published prices for buying the highest state positions in the booklet: head of department of the Supreme Court of Justice—$400,000; deputy of head of Moscow's Arbitration Tribunal—$1.3 million; deputy of Ministry of Power Engineering—$10 million; and so on. *Novaya Gazeta* expected some reaction from law enforcement officials (excuse, refutation, inquiry) but—nothing! It is said that in Russia "silence is the sign of consent" . . . most of the highest officials have inviolability de jure (deputies, judges, and others) or de facto.

There are spacious *corruption networks* including ministries, police, and FSB (former KGB) (Satarov, 2002; Sungurov, 2000: 72–82*). Corruption in contemporary Russia is an element of the political system, a mechanism of the political regime.* There are two levels of forms of corruption: "lower" ("face-to-face") and "upper," the great corruption networks. A study by INDEM (head Dr. G. Satarov) shows that the great corruption networks exist in the Ministry of Internal Affairs, Federal Service of Security, and State Committee of Customs Service. Moreover, the military is also very corrupt. Every corruption network includes three structures: commercial or financial, state officials, and a "group of defense"—police, FSB, prosecutor's office (Sungurov, 2000: 8).

The mean value of a bribe on the "lower" level (for police, doctors, teachers, and so on) is $20–120, on the "upper" level, $1,000–5,000 (Gilinskiy, 2003: 63). However, this is for one time use only. The dimensions of a bribe on corruption networks are greater. Moreover there is system of *otkat* (recoil, delivery, or return). It is 3 percent to 10 percent (Satarov, 2002: 8) or 40 to 60 percent of the sum of agreement for official corruption (*Novaya Gazeta*, 2003: 12).

Corruption paralyses any positive, creative activities. It is absolutely impossible to develop production, market economics, or social reforms if the whole depends on corrupt officials. Corruption of police, the prosecutor's office, and judges are particularly dangerous. "Corruption of judges is one of the most powerful corruption markets in Russia. Corruption of judges penetrates the different corruption networks on different level of power" (Satarov, 2003). Arbitration courts are particularly corrupted.

The police are very corrupted as well. For example, there are fixed prices of bribes for obstructing an investigation (bringing an action) in a criminal case—$1,000–10,000; for commutation of arrest for pledge or engagement— $20,000–25,000; for decrease of punishment—$5,000–15,000; and so on. (*Corruption and Combat Corruption*, 2000: 62). However, these prices for bribes increase every year.

## PUNISHMENT IN RUSSIA

Unfortunately, crime control is still dominated by repressive approaches in contemporary Russia. The current punishment system in Russia stipulates the following types of criminal punishment: the death penalty (art. 59 of the Criminal Code of the Russian Federation [CCRF], 1996), life imprisonment (art. 57), deprivation of freedom (art. 56), limitation of freedom (up to five years, art. 53), arrest (up to six months, art. 54), corrective labor (up to two years, art. 50), compulsory labor (up to 240 hours, art. 49), fines (art. 46), deprivation of the right to hold a certain position or to conduct certain activities (up to five years, art. 47), confiscation of property (art. 52), and deprivation of military or special titles (art. 48). In addition, military personnel may be sentenced to serve in a special disciplinary unit (up to two years, art. 55) and there are various compulsory measures of education and supervision for minors (14–17 years, art. 90).

The last Criminal Code of the Russian Federation (CCRF) from 1996 contains very stern kinds of punishment: death penalty, life imprisonment, and deprivation of freedom for twenty years (through a combination of crimes, up to twenty-five years, or by combined sentences up to thirty years) (art. 56). In all previous criminal codes of Russia, including Stalin's period, there were no sanctions like life imprisonment or up to thirty years. Moreover, some kinds of probation and parole (deprivation of freedom with suspension of sentence) have been excluded from the new CCRF.

There has been a moratorium on the death penalty since 1997, but the Russian parliament (Duma) did not ratify this and more than eight hundred people wait for their fate. We see a tendency of more punishments that involve deprivation of freedom in the penal and sentencing practice: the quota of corrective labor without deprivation of freedom has decreased (from 26.4% in 1988 to 5.2% in 2003) and the quota of fines has decreased (from 16.8% in 1987 to 6.5% in 2003). The imprisonment rate (per 100,000 population) in Russia is the greatest in the world (more than 720–740 in 1999 without institutions of military justice (Abramkin, 1998; Christie, 2000; Barclay and Tavares, 2003). One in four adult men in Russia is a former prisoner. The overwhelming number of prisoners are not professionals but people who found themselves in prison because of poverty, unemployment, and homelessness. In 2003, 56.6 percent of prisoners were convicted with a sentence of more than five years.[11] The conditions in penitentiary institutions are terrible (Abramkin, 1998; Gilinskiy, 1998). Extremely harsh conditions exist in correctional institutions. The conditions violate basic human rights: overcrowding in the pretrial detention centers—those awaiting trial are compelled to sleep in shifts; bad food; the spread of tuberculosis; torture of those awaiting trial/under investigation in so-called press cells to procure confessions of guilt;[12] mass beatings; and so on. Life in these institutions (prisons and "correctional colonies") is unbearable; the possibilities for "correction" are nil. Thousands of prisoners die every year from hunger, tuberculosis, and suffocation from the lack of oxygen in overcrowded cells in pretrial detention centers. Thousands are HIV-positive. Thousands more have tuberculosis. It is deplorable. It is a shame, but I do not see any change in the future with respect to the Russian situation.

## RUSSIAN POLICE TODAY

The police of Russia, known as the militia, were set up a month after the state coup of October 1917 and continue as the militia to this day. The entire militia in Russia is under the direction of the Ministry of Internal Affairs, as are the internal army and specialized police forces (railroad, air, and river militia). The penitentiary service was transferred in 1998 to the Ministry of Justice, and the fire safety service was transferred to the Ministry of Extraordinary Situations.

The militia in the republics are directed by the republican Ministry of Internal Affairs, and in each territory, region, city, or district they are directed by the main board of internal affairs, as established by the constitution and law of each region.

The current directives, functions, and structure of the militia are laid down in the Russian legislation On the Militia, passed on April 18, 1991 (with following modifications). The militia is organized into two main subdivisions: the Criminal Militia and the Militia for Civil Safety (or Public Order) at the local level (On the Militia for Civil Safety, 1993). The Criminal Militia includes the Detective Service, the Service of Fight against Economic Crimes, the Service of Fight against Organized Crime, the National Center of INTERPOL, the Service of Own Security, scientific-technical specialists, operational investigators, and others who supply material for the criminal investigation. The Civil Militia includes the Duty Service, the Service for Securing Civil Order, the State Automobile Inspectorate, the Security Service, the Patrol-Duty Service, divisional inspectors, temporary detention guards, the prevention service, and others. The Criminal Investigation Service is a separate unit under the Ministry of Internal Affairs.

There are different data about the size of the Russian militia. The militia forces stood at about 540,000 and the internal army at about 278,000 in 1995 (*Everyone's Newspaper*, 1995, no. 51). The rate of police per 100,000 population in the Russian Federation was 1,224.58 in 1994 (Newman, 1999: 124). The staff of the system of the Ministry of Internal Affairs for the Russian Federation was about 1.5 million in 1996 (*Corruption and Combat Corruption*, 2000: 29).

We know there are in Russia powerful organized criminals, widespread terrorism, high levels of drug traffic, social violence, violent crime, corruption, and human trafficking (many people are missing [sixty to seventy thousand more every year] including twenty-five to forty thousand who go missing without leaving a trace, for which the police have no possibility of changing the situation for the better). Moreover policemen perpetrate many crimes themselves. There are so-called werewolves now: policemen who work as policemen and as criminals at the same time. It is a "new" Russian reality. Why?

The main police strengths were high professionalism, understanding one's goals and tasks, selflessness, and working for the achievement of a goal, not for personal profit. Unfortunately, in the last ten to twenty years these former strengths changed to weakness: deprofessionalism, corruption, and self-interest. Many professional policemen have left law enforcement. Corruption now permeates law enforcement at every level (as well as all state institutions and all public service).

All police services are organized such that there is a real possibility that an officer will take a bribe. Inspectors of the State Automobile Inspection (GAI) take a bribe for any breach of regulation of vehicular traffic. For example, "fixed rate" for drunk drivers was in 1985 30–50 rubles (about $5–8); in 2005, $200–500 (*Komsomol'skaja Pravda*, 2005).

To obtain a passport in a timely fashion is impossible without a payoff to the Service of Passport-Visa (PVS) (see, for example, the *Moscow News*, 2005, N26, p. 13). For example, the "fixed rate" for fast receipt of a foreign passport was in 1985 50 rubles (about $8); in 2005, $200 (*Komsomol'skaja Pravda*, 2005).

What are the causes of this omnipresent corruption in Russia, including police? There are many factors. The main factors ("causes") are the following:

- Russian traditions;
- the former Soviet corrupted "nomenclature" kept its position, and brought its corrupt habits to the "new" power system;
- privatization gave an economic basis for corruption;
- powerful Russian organized crime uses bribery as the main means of defense; and
- the highest strata of powers are corrupted; clearly, then, lower and ordinary officials will take bribes too (the Russian proverb is "the fish rots beginning with the head").

Besides, the salary of policemen is very low (for example, the average salary of a sergeant of police is about $150 a month; salary of a lieutenant, $250; salary of a lieutenant colonel, $ 300–350). At the same time a living wage is about $120.

Supervision of the Russian Ministry of Internal Security (MVD) (and police, the main part of MVD) changes very often. Every new minister of internal affairs replaces the staff of MVD and regional supervision. Of course, this prevents normal police activity (see in detail Avrutin, 2003a, 2003b). For example, the ministers of the Russian MVD have been:

V. Trushin (October 1989–September 1990)
V. Barannikov (September 1990–August 1991)
F. Dunaev (September 1991–December 1991)
V. Barannikov (December 1991–January 1992)
V. Erin (January 1992–June 1995)
A. Kulikov (June 1995–March 1998)

S. Stepashin (March 1998–May 1999)
V. Rushailo (May 1999–March 2001)
B. Gryzlov (March 2001–December 2003)
R. Nurgaliev (from December 2003 to present day)

Low salary, perpetual "perestroika" (modification) of the police system, low prestige of the profession, corruption, dangerous work, and numerous people leaving police service (e.g., 10,000 policemen left in May 1991; 11,000 in July 1991; 15,000 in September 1991; 127,500 in 1997; and 103,400 in 1998 [Avrutin, 2003a: 29, 77, 83]) make it difficult, if not impossible, to conduct police operations in a professional, law-abiding manner.

Unfortunately, a "considerable part of police staff do not realize the new mission of police in society" (Avrutin, 2003a: 177). The law On the Militia proclaims the police goal: defend everybody against crimes (art. 1). There is an analogous thesis in *The Conception of Development of the Police and Forces MVD RF* (1996), but this goal is clearly not realized.

Inasmuch as professionalism is absent, illegal methods of inquest and investigation, including fraud, falsification, and torture are fairly common. Torture by police is "ordinary" practice. Newspapers, television, and radio talk about police torture almost every day without results.

Another example is the December 2004 beating and torture by police of many people in Blagoveschensk, Bezeck, and Nefteyugansk. Perhaps it was the result of a tradition of militarization of Russian police and its ability to operate illegally, at will, with no repercussions. It is absolutely unthinkable in civilized society!

Some in the government recognize this issue. The first vice-speaker of Duma, Mrs. L. Slizka, spoke on July 20, 2005: "Our people fear police more than criminals!" Radio programs, too, including *Echo of Moscow*, advise that 76 percent of listeners answer: "We are afraid more of the police than criminals." It is an intolerable situation.

Our study in St. Petersburg (1999–2002) shows that the number of victims of crime averaged about 26 percent of respondents, but very few turned to police. An average of 72 percent did not report their victimization. The main reason for not reporting was the belief that "nothing would be done"—34–38 percent. Police cooperation with residents in solving public order problems was rated as very or quite poor by an average of 56 percent of respondents. Perceptions of change in police behavior for worse or better were fairly small, but concern must be triggered by the decrease in the proportion of people detained by police who felt police treated them fairly—from 42 percent in 1999 to 24.5 percent in 2002. With reference to assessments of whether the police acted legally on these occasions, the percentage of positive judgments decreased from 37 percent in 1999 to 25 percent in 2002.

Given this, it is not surprising that the prestige of police is very low. The scornful *ment* reflects the low prestige of contemporary Russian police (see, in detail, Avrutin, 2003b: 330–31). Moreover, Russian police are very militarized. It may be dangerous for the population. Police defend dignitaries and VIPs, but ordinary people are left to themselves.

There was and is a great turnover of personnel. As a result, about 25 percent of policemen work for less than three years. Only 53 percent of senior officers have higher education, including 45.8 percent of officers in the Criminal Investigation Department, 34.5 percent of district officers, and 67.2 percent of investigators (Avrutin, 2003a: 83–4).

Many policemen were killed in the line of duty: 3,318 persons from 1991 to 1998. Another 18,932 policemen were injured in the line of duty during this same time period (Avrutin, 2003b: 383).

Of course, Russian police carry out some functions. Police activity has attempted to control some criminal elements. However, the police themselves are too often the criminals. There are many honest, conscientious, courageous policemen, but they are not the norm in Russia.

## WHAT CAN BE DONE?

Gorbachev's perestroika opened the door to the West and the East to engage in international exchanges of information and training (Egorshin, 1994; Egorshin, 1999; Salnikov, 1999). Certainly, this process was slower for police, because this organization has some "secrets" and "special units." However, international contacts and connections increased, especially in the field of training and education for police.

There are exchanges between teachers of Russian police universities, policemen, and foreign colleagues. For example, the St. Petersburg's University of MVD RF (SPU) (SPU is one of the universities of the Ministry of Internal Affairs—in Russian, MVD means academy for policemen) has contacts with police schools and universities (academies) in Germany, France, the U.S., Great Britain, Finland, and other countries. Students of SPU often go to the London Police College. There is agreement about improving the connection between Russia and England and sending the best Russian students to British Higher Courses of Police Management. The SPU has close contacts with Illinois University (U.S.) as well as with the police and the educational institution of the state Rheinland-Pfalz (Germany).

The SPU organizes different joint international seminars and conferences, for example, "Basis and Methods of Police Activities," "Methods of Personal Safety of Policemen," "Fight on Corruption," "Fight on Economic Crime," "Fight on Computer Crime," and "Improving the Police Activity" (Salnikov, 1999). Similar international connections exist in Volgograd, Omsk, Nizhny Novgorod, Rostov, and other universities of the Ministry of Internal Affairs.

Some foreign educational institutions send books to Russian universities and colleges. Finnish colleagues translate books into Russian specially for use by Russian teachers, students, and police staff, for example, M. Laine (1994), *Criminology and Sociology of Deviant Behavior*, Helsinki: Training Center for Prisons Staff; J. Kivivuori (2001), *Crimes against Life*, Johan Beckman Institute; and A. Kinnunen, H. Niemi, and R. Siren (2001), *Crimes Related with Pay-cards*, Johan Beckman Institute. Russian police officers also go abroad for police training to Germany, the U.S., Denmark, and Finland. Unfortunately, such contacts and connections decreased after 1999–2000, when Russian police activities became more and more closed to the international community.

We repeat: police activity wholly depends on the social, economic, political, cultural, and other processes taking place in society. The Russian economic, social, and political situation determines the nation's problems, including inefficiency and corruption of police.

Some police understand these issues. For example, former minister of MVD general V. Barannikov said: "Stabilization of criminal situation is impossible without stabilization of economy and social sphere" (Avrutin, 2003b: 239).

One of the strategies that may help is "community policing" (Kury, 1997; Lab and Das, 2003; Skogan and Hartnett, 1997). The notion of community policing is not easy, especially for Russian police. There are many definitions of it (Lab and Das, 2003). Nevertheless, the main idea of "community policing" is *partnerships, cooperation between the police and community (population, citizens), to prevent crime.* The police are servants of the population (for taxpayers).

Contemporary Russia has a difficult time with this due to its history as a Communist state: in particular, the closed character of police activity is very difficult. Indeed, research of the police (militia) was, for decades, absolutely impossible. Only Gorbachev's perestroika opened the police to independent research. Today, *police (and other power structures) have become more and more closed.*

The idea of community policing is good, but alien to Russia. The police are a strange and malicious power for Russian people. Moreover, *Russian police (militia) do not make sure of the security of populations; rather, they are very corrupt and practice violence (including torture) on detained people.*

It is a pity, but the partnership between police (Russian militia) and the community is improbable in contemporary Russia. There are several causes for this:

- centuries-old fear of the population is present, especially from the time of the Soviet regime;
- the Russian militia does not deserve the trust today because of total corruption, inactivity, infringement including tortures, and so on; and
- contemporary Russian society is much separated and fragmented and civil society is absent; consequently the social basis for "community" is absent too.

## CONCLUSION

Certainly, the contemporary Russian system of the criminal justice and the police de jure is more democratic and more liberal than it was under the government of the Soviet Union. But there are de facto many negative manifestations and tendencies, particularly since 1999–2000.

- The number and rate of *violence* is very high. It is a result of the social and economic situation, social and economic inequality, and mass exclusion.
- There are new tendencies of *organized crime*: aspiration to legalization of criminal activity, transition to legal and semilegal activity, infiltration into legal business and the power structure, the politicization of organized crime, and the criminalization of policy and economy. Russia is going farther and farther along the road to the criminal state and the criminalized society.
- *Corruption* in contemporary Russia is an element of the political system, a mechanism of the political regime. Total corruption is the main Russian problem, because all other problems are insoluble until corruption is properly dealt with.
- *Criminal justice and police* are ineffective, unjust, corrupt, and depend on politicians.
- *Police* and other "*powerful structures*," including FSB, are very repressive, undemocratic, and irresponsible.

## NOTES

1. *Duma* is the old Russian term, from Russian *dumat*—to think, to brood.
2. *Kontora* is office; in this context it is the illegal agency of sex service.

3. *Ment* is the unofficial name for a police officer (as *cop* in the U.S. or *bobby* in England).

4. *Krysha* (roof) is a protection of business from criminal organizations.

5. *Tochka* (point) is a place for illegal drug selling.

6. President V. Putin began his career with the slogan: "Wet on terrorists in the toilet!" In criminal slang this means "to kill terrorists in the toilet."

7. In relation to Russia, "the cradle of terrorism," see O. Budnitsky (1996), *History of Terrorism in Russia (Documents, Biographies, Research)*, Rostov-on-Don: Phoenix.

8. For a more detailed description see D. Alexander and Y. Alexander (2002), and S. Aust and C. Schnibben (Hg.) (2002).

9. Maxim Gorky (1868–1936) is a famous Russian writer.

10. *Dedovshina* from *ded* (old man).

11. See http://www.index.org.ru/turma/st/uis-2003.htm.

12. A "press cell" is a cell that can be found in all institutions. In such cells prisoners selected by the administration beat, torture, and rape other prisoners to obtain information from them or to make them compliant to the needs of the administration.

## REFERENCES

Abadinsky, H. (1994) *Organized Crime*. Fourth ed. Chicago: Nelson-Hall Inc.

Abramkin, V. (1998) *In Search of a Solution: Crime, Criminal Policy and Prison Facilities in the Former Soviet Union*. Moscow: Human Rights Publishers.

Albanese, J. (1995) Organized Crime: The Mafia Mystique. In *Criminology: A Contemporary Handbook*. Ed. J. Sheley. New York: Wadsworth Publishing Company.

Alexander, D., Alexander, Y. (2002) *Terrorism and Business: The Impact of September 11, 2001*. Ardsley, NY: Transnational Publishers, Inc.

Antonyan, Y. (1998) *Terrorism: Criminological and Criminal Law Research*. Moscow: Shit-M (Russian).

Arlacchi, P. (1986) *Mafia Business: The Mafia Ethic and the Spirit of Capitalism*. New York: Verso.

Aust, S., Schnibben, C. (Hg.) (2002) *11. September: Geschichte eines Terrorabgrifs*. Deutsche Verlags-Anstalt.

Avrutin, Y. (2003a) *MVD of Russia, 1991–2001*. St. Petersburg: Universitet (Russian).

Avrutin, Y. (2003b) *Police and Militia in the Mechanism of Ensuring State Power in Russia: Theory, History, Prospects*. St. Petersburg: Yuridichesky Center Press (Russian).

Barclay, G., Tavares, C. (2003) International Comparisons of Criminal Justice Statistics 2001. *Home Office Statistical Bulletin*, December.

Berngard, A. (1978) *Strategy of Terrorism*. Warsaw.

Borodkin, F. (2000) Social Exclusion. *Sociological Journal* 3–4, pp. 5–17 (Russian).

Budnitsky, O. (1996) *History of Terrorism in Russia (Documents, Biographies, Research)*. Rostov-on-Don: Phoenix (Russian).

Cassesse, A. (1989) *Terrorism, Politics and Law*. Cambridge: Polity Press.

Chalikova, V. (1989) Terrorism. In *50/50 Experience from a Lexicon of New Think-ing*. Moscow: Progress (Russian).

Christie, N. (2000) *Crime Control as Industry: Towards GULAG's Western Style?* Third ed. London: Routledge.

*Corruption and Combat Corruption* (2000). Moscow: RCA (Russian).

*Corruption and Combat Corruption: Role of Civil Society* (2000). St. Petersburg: Norma (Russian).

*Crime and Delinquency 1991–2006*. Moscow: MVD RF, MJ RF.

*Das neue taschen Lexikon* (1992). Band 16. Gütersloh, Germany: Bertelsmann Lexikon Verlag.

Dmitriev, A., Kudryavtsev, V., Kudryavtsev, S. (1993) *Introduction to the General Theory of Conflict*. Moscow: CKI RAN (Russian).

Dmitriev, A., Zalysin, I. (2000) *Violence: A Socio-Political Analysis*. Moscow: ROSSPEN (Russian).

Egorshin V. (1999) *Detective, Let's Search!* St. Petersburg: Petrovsky Foundation (Russian).

Egorshin V. (1994) *Militia, Police, Sheriffdom*. St. Petersburg: Economics and Culture (Russian).

Erokhina, L., Buryak, M. (2003) The Problem of Trafficking in Persons according to Russian Experts' Estimates (Sociological Approach). In *Organized Crime, Terror-ism and Corruption: Studies, Surveys, Lawmaking, Statistics, Information*. Crimi-nology Almanac 3, pp. 36–42 (Russian).

Ferro, M. (1989) Terrorism. In: *50/50 Experience from a Lexicon of New Thinking*. Moscow: Progress (Russian).

Finer, C., Nellis, M. (Eds.) (1998) *Crime and Social Exclusion*. Oxford: Blackwell Publishers, Ltd.

Ganor, B. (2002) Defining Terrorism: Is One Man's Terrorist Another Man's Freedom Fighter? *Police Practice and Research: An International Journal* 3, no. 4, pp. 287–304.

Gilinskiy, Y. (2003) Contemporary Russian Corruption. In *Organised Crime, Traf-ficking, Drugs: Selected Papers Presented at the Annual Conference of the Euro-pean Society of Criminology, Helsinki, 2003*. Ed. S. Nevala and K. Aromaa. Helsinki: HEUNI, pp. 60–69.

Gilinskiy, Y. (2000) Challenges of Policing Democracies: The Russian Experience. In *Challenges of Policing Democracies: A World Perspective*. Ed. D. Das and O. Marenin. Newark, NJ: Gordon and Breach, pp. 173–94.

Gilinskiy, Y. (1998) The Penal System and Other Forms of Social Control in Russia: Problems and Perspectives. In *The Baltic Region: Insights in Crime and Social Control*. Ed. K. Aromaa. Oslo: Pax Forlag A/S, pp. 197–204.

Glonti, G. (2003) Human Trafficking: Concept, Classification, and Questions of Leg-islative Regulation. In *Organised Crime, Trafficking, Drugs: Selected Papers Pre-sented at the Annual Conference of the European Society of Criminology*. Ed. S. Nevala, K. Aromaa. Helsinki: HEUNI, pp. 70–80.

Gurvich, I., Rusakova, M., Pyshkina, T., Yakovleva, A. (2002) *The Commercial Sexual Exploitation of Children in St. Petersburg and Northwest Russia*. Stockholm: Save the Children Sweden.

Heidenheimer, A., Johnston, M., Le Vine, V. (1989) *Political Corruption: A Handbook*. New Brunswick, NJ: Transaction.

*Human Development Report in the Russian Federation, 1999* (2000). Moscow (Russian).

*Index on Censorship* (1999), nos. 7–8 (Land and Its Convicts).

Jacobs, J., Potter, K. (1998) *Hate Crimes: Criminal Law and Identity Politics*. New York: Oxford University Press.

Kabanov, P. (2000) *Political Crime: Its Essence, Causes and Prevention*. Nizhnekamsk (Russian).

Kangaspunta, K. (2003) Mapping the Inhuman Trade: Preliminary Findings of the Database on Trafficking in Human Beings. *Forum on Crime and Society* 3, nos. 1–2, pp. 81–103.

Kelly, R., Chin, K., Schatzbery, R. (Eds.) (1994) *Handbook of Organized Crime in the United States*. Westport, CT: Greenwood Press.

*Komsomol'skaja Pravda* (2005), 7–14 July.

Kury, H. (Hrsg.) (1997) *Konzepte Kommunaler Kriminalprävention*. Freibug i. Br.: Edition Juscrim.

Lab, S., Das, D. (Eds.) (2003) *International Perspectives on Community Policing and Crime* Prevention. Upper Saddle River, NJ: Prentice Hall.

Laqueur, W. (1987) *The Age of Terrorism*. Toronto: Little, Brown & Co.

Laqueur, W. (1977) *Terrorism*. London: Weidenfeld and Nicolson.

Lenoir, R. (1974) *Les exclus, un français sur dix*. Paris: Seuil.

Long, D. (1990) *The Anatomy of Terrorism*. New York: The Free Press.

Luhmann, N. (1998) The Globalization of the World Community: How to Understand Contemporary Society Systematically. In *Sociology on the Threshold of the 21st Century: New Perspectives in Research*. Moscow: Intellect (Russian).

Luneev, V. (1997) *Crime in the XXth Century: Global, Regional and Russian Trends*. Moscow: Norma (Russian).

Newman, G. (ed.) (1999). *Global Report on Crime and Justice*. New York: Oxford University Press.

*Novaya Gazeta* (2005a) July, N54 (Russian).

*Novaya Gazeta* (2005b) August, N55 (Russian).

*Novaya Gazeta* (2003) December, N93 (Russian).

*Questions of Statistics* (2004) N2. Moscow (in Russian).

Repetskaya, A. (2003) Criminal Exploitation of Human Beings in Eastern Siberia. In *Organized Crime, Terrorism and Corruption: Studies, Surveys, Lawmaking, Statistics, Information*. Criminology Almanac 3, pp. 29–35 (Russian).

Rose-Ackerman, S. (1996) Democracy and "Ground" Corruption. *International Social Science Journal* 149 (September).

Salnikov V. (1999) Education and Policy of Staff in Internal Affairs: Innovation and Problems of Reform. *Herald St. Petersburg*. University of Ministry of Internal Affairs of Russia, no. 1, pp. 14–17 (in Russian).

Satarov, G. (2003) Rusty Justice. *Native Notes* 2 (Russian).

Satarov, G. (2002) *Diagnostics of Russian Corruption: Sociological Analyses.* Moscow: INDEM (Russian).

Schnaider, G. Y. (1994) *Criminology.* Moscow: Progress-Universe (Russian).

Skogan, W., Hartnett, S. (1997) *Community Policing, Chicago Style.* New York: Oxford University Press.

Smith, D. (1975) *The Mafia Mystique.* New York: Basic Books.

Stoecker, S. (2000) The Rise in Human Trafficking and the Role of Organized Crime. *Organized Crime and Corruption: Studies, Surveys, Information.* Social and Legal Almanac 1, pp. 57–66 (Russian).

Sungurov, A. (Ed.) (2000) *Civil Initiatives and Corruption Prevention.* St. Petersburg: Norma (Russian).

Tsytsarev, S., Gilinsky, Y. (2004) The Roots of Violence in Modern Russia: A Psychocriminological Analysis. In *International Perspectives on Violence.* Ed. L. Adler, F. Denmark. Westport, CT, Praeger Publishers, pp. 225–40.

Vishnevsky, A. (2002) *Population of Russia, 2001.* Moscow: University (Russian).

Walmsley, R. (1998) *Prisons Systems in Central and Eastern Europe: Progress, Problems and the International Standards.* Helsinki: HEUNI.

Walmsley, R. (2002) *World Prison Population List.* Home Office. Finding 166.

Wewer, G. (1994) Politische Korruption. In *Politic-Lexicon.* München, Wein: Oldenbourg Verlag.

World Bank (2005) *World Development Report 2005.* The International Bank for Reconstruction and Development. Moscow: Ves' Mir (Russian).

World Health Organization (1996) *World Health Statistics.* Geneva: World Health Organization.

Young, J. (1999) *The Exclusive Society: Social Exclusion, Crime and Difference in Late Modernity.* London: Sage Publications.

## Chapter Seven

# Cross-border Crimes and Policing

## *Challenges and Lessons for Nigeria*

Abdul-Rahman B. Dambazau

Globalization, driven by modern technology, especially information and communication technology (ICT), and the free flow of capital around the world, has made the world much smaller in the sense that it has brought the world's political, economic, and social activities much closer, both in time and space. In time because most global activities are covered in real time, virtual, live, and so on, and in terms of space, physical boundaries no longer serve as obstacles to most of these activities, and things are done as if "next door." In this ICT era, for example, the spatial and temporal factors used in determining conventional crimes are of little importance, because individuals are able to attack or carry out criminal activities against their victims at a distance, while it is very easy for criminals to make deals or harass their victims within seconds.

By implication, therefore, one of the major consequences of globalization is the acute reduction of the importance of international borders as a means of control of most global activities. It reflects the reality of the extent to which borders are fading in relation to global or transnational activities. The fading of borders has also brought to the fore the activities of transnational organized crime groups. Although there is no universal definition of transnational organized crime, it is generally agreed that it involves conspiracy between two or more persons for criminal activities for the purpose of profit on a continuing basis. It is however widely recognized that organized crime groups possess certain attributes, such as hierarchy, limited or exclusive membership, violence, bribery and corruption, and monopoly of activities. According to Rider (1993), continuity in the activity from which organized crime groups seek to achieve profit is a primary characteristic of organized crime, therefore in an attempt to protect its investment and continued existence, organized crime employs violence and extortion. In an attempt to strategize in order to sustain their business and reduce risks to the minimum, organized crime groups diversify into legitimate and sometimes low-profile business activities, the result of which is usually operating in multiple jurisdictions as well as internationally, thereby making law enforcement difficult.

The question that comes to mind in discussing the topic of cross-border crimes is this: are there similarities and/or differences between transnational organized crimes and cross-border crimes? Are we referring to the same thing? First, not all cross-border activities are criminal. They involve both the legal and the illegal, the lawful and the unlawful, clean and dirty transactions, and so on. Second, the terms cross-border, transborder, and transnational are sometimes used interchangeably. It should be noted however that the nature of crimes; their structure, in terms of whether they are hierarchical or loose networks; and the "goods and services" involved determine the level of categorization. Third, cross-border crimes in West Africa are not characterized by the strict hierarchy and violence known in other regional organized crime groups, such as the Italian American Mafia, Japanese Yakuza, Chinese tongs and triads, the Colombian cartels, the Russian Mafia, and Jewish mobsters. Rather they are loose criminal networks, not necessarily involving conspiracy among the perpetrators (Albini, 1971). Fourth, most border-crossing crimes are sustained by corruption, threats, coercion, and actual violence against victims, and may also provide indirect support for other violent activities, such as terrorism, civil wars (Liberia, Sierra Leone, and Darfur are examples), and other forms of violent crimes (such as armed robbery), especially where arms smuggling is involved. Fifth, while cross-border crimes may be limited to immediate borders, transnational organized crimes always transcend national and continental borders. However, both transnational organized and cross-border crimes tend to thrive where government institutions and legitimacy are weak whereas the traditions of corruption are strong. What we have in West Africa, indeed in Africa, are criminal networks, which cannot be equated with any known organized criminal groups in other parts of the world.

Cross-border activities have tremendously influenced the development of cross-border policing, and indeed pose challenges to national, regional, and international security. One of the consequences of these challenges is the idea of regional integration. Africa currently has fourteen regional integration groups, with two or more in almost all the subregions. In West Africa, for example, the West African Economic and Monetary Union (UEMOA) and the Mano River Union (MRU) coexist with the Economic Community of the West African States (ECOWAS), which is the main regional integration grouping. Created in 1975, the ECOWAS currently consists of the fifteen West African states,[1] and the idea is to facilitate the free movement of persons and goods within the region. Cross-border crimes are of major concern in West Africa, and they impact not only the region but also the whole of Africa and other parts of the world, particularly Europe, the United States, the Middle East, and Australia.

Nigeria is a major player in ECOWAS, and as a matter of fact, is the most populous country not only in West Africa but in the whole of sub-Saharan Africa. With a population of about 140 million, it is often said that 40 percent of Africans around the world are Nigerians. Nigeria is also rich in oil and other natural resources. She ranks fifth in the world among producers of crude oil. Nigeria is also part of the world's experiences in cross-border crimes involving drug trafficking; human trafficking; advance-fee fraud; arms trafficking; smuggling of fake, adulterated, and expired drugs; armed banditry and car snatching; and money laundering.

This chapter aims to examine cross-border crimes and policing and the challenges these activities pose to Nigeria. It further examines the lessons learned as a result of the criminal activities and the policing response. In doing this, the chapter will identify and discuss in some detail cross-border crimes in Nigeria; examine the legislation relating to these crimes; analyze cross-border policing, to include identifying institutions involved, prevention and control measures, investigation, extradition, and prosecution; and examine the contemporary challenges and lessons learned.

## DESCRIBING AND DEFINING NIGERIA'S BORDERS

By definition, a border is the line of demarcation between two independent states, territories, and so on. While the terms border and boundary are often used interchangeably, according to Eskelinen et al. (1999) boundary can be understood as a line of physical contact between states and border as denoting the adjacent areas which line a boundary. A border can be defined on land, sea, or air. Nigeria is a land covering an area of 923,768 square kilometers (km), and has an estimated 4,049 km of land boundaries. A border in the context of Nigeria is that imaginary line of demarcation between her and Niger in the north, with a land boundary of about 1,500 km; Benin in the west, with land boundary of about 770 km; Chad in the northeast, with a land boundary of about 86 km; Cameroon in the east, with a land boundary of about 1,800 km; and a southern border of the 1,600 nautical kilometer–long coastline, beginning at the border with the Republic of Benin in the west and extending eastwards to the border with Cameroon. To describe the region further, one finds Benin sharing borders with Burkina Faso, Niger, Nigeria, and Togo. Cameroon, on the other hand, shares borders with the Central

African Republic (CAR), Chad, the Republic of the Congo, Equatorial
Guinea, and Gabon. Furthermore, Chad shares borders with Nigeria, Sudan,
CAR, Cameroon, Libya, and Niger, while Niger shares borders with Algeria,
Benin, Burkina Faso, Chad, Libya, Mali, and Nigeria. It is important to also
note that all the countries sharing direct physical borders with Nigeria are
French-speaking, even though the majority of the border settlements also
share similar cultures and traditions.

With the establishment of ECOWAS in 1975, Nigeria's borders have in a
way expanded, just like those of the fourteen other members of the community. The need to integrate the West African economies in which there would
be free movement of persons and goods led to a series of protocols,[2] aimed at
promoting regional economic integration in the transport, telecommunica-
tion, energy, commerce, and agricultural sectors and fostering trade among
the fifteen member states. Cross-border activities, including crimes and policing in Nigeria in particular and West Africa as a whole, can be attributed to
the fallout of the attempt to integrate the West African economies.

## CROSS-BORDER CRIMES IN NIGERIA

Cross-border activities involve all kinds of legal and illegal activities that take
place between the borders of two or more independent states. These activities
can be put under the broad categories of economic, political, and social. Although these categories are not necessarily mutually exclusive, and are interrelated in one way or another, this chapter is interested in those illegal activities which are recognized as criminal by either the domestic law of the
country where they exist or by international law. According to a United Nations Office on Drugs and Crime (UNODC) report, "perception surveys, as
well as international crime intelligence and seizures of contraband, suggest
that Africa may have become the continent most targeted by organized crime"
(UNODC, 2005). Cross-border crimes in West Africa are, according to the
UNODC, neither hierarchical nor organized, as in Mafia organized crime. Accordingly, they are loosely structured, project-based, nonpermanent criminal
activities that are difficult to detect, and are highly amorphous.[3] Although
cross-border crimes can be made synonymous to transnational crimes, not all
cross-border crimes have the characteristics of transnational crimes. Armed
banditry in northeast Nigeria, for example, is a cross-border crime dominat-
ing Nigeria's borders with Chad, Niger, and Cameroon, but it is not in the
same category as transnational organized crimes of drug trafficking or human
trafficking, which are also, to a large extent, shaped by cross-border activities. The dominant criminal activities in Nigeria that have a cross-border and,

to some extent, transnational character include drug trafficking; human trafficking; arms trafficking; money laundering; advance-fee fraud; armed banditry; smuggling of fake, adulterated, and expired drugs; and the smuggling of goods or contraband. Cross-border crimes are characterized by an offender crossing a police-force boundary to perpetrate a crime or commit an offense, which requires the police to cross boundaries to investigate it.

## Drug Trafficking

Drug trafficking is undoubtedly one of the most prominent cross-border criminal activities not only in Nigeria or the West African subregion but also in the world. Drug trafficking is also a transnational organized crime. Like all transnational crimes, it has no respect for borders, whether in the source, transit, or destination countries. Although Nigeria neither produces nor consumes illicit drugs, such as cocaine and heroin, it serves as a transit country for drugs, especially cocaine from South America and opium and heroin from Asia, to mostly Europe and the United States. The drug trafficking issue in Nigeria became a more serious problem sometime in the early 1980s with the execution of three convicted drug traffickers. It was in the later part of that decade that the National Drug Law Enforcement Agency (NDLEA) was established with the promulgation of an act to enforce laws against the cultivation, processing, sale, trafficking, and use of illicit hard drugs.

In West Africa, Nigeria features most prominently in the drug trafficking regime, including the statistics on arrests. According to the 2000–2004 compiled statistics, 92 percent of drug couriers intercepted with drugs through the subregion were West Africans, out of which about 56 percent were Nigerians.[4] Likewise, 2007 arrest data from law enforcement officials shows that holders of Nigerian passports account for about 44 percent of all West African drug traffickers arrested in Europe. According to a UN report, Nigerian networks dominate the air routes into Europe, the major destinations being Spain, the Netherlands, and Britain.[5] Virtually all the heroin trafficked through West Africa, with Nigeria as a major transit country, originates from Pakistan, India, and Thailand (Quist, 2004).[6] However, among the transit drugs in Nigeria cocaine dominates, accounting for 18,304 kilograms seized out of the total of about 31,000 kilograms of the drug seized in the period 1990–2007.

## Human Trafficking

Trafficking in human beings, particularly women and children, is of major concern not only in Nigeria, but also globally. It has been described as "a complex, multifaceted phenomenon involving multiple stakeholders at the institutional and commercial level"(UNESCO, 2006, p. 1). It is indeed a global business, which attracts markets for cheap labor and commercial sex. Nigeria is alleged to be one of the leading African countries involved in both internal and cross-border trafficking in persons. Unlike with drug trafficking, for human trafficking, Nigeria is a country of origin,[7] transit, and destination, but like drug trafficking, human trafficking knows no borders. Destinations for Nigerian victims of trafficking include Cote d'Ivoire, Mali, Benin, Equatorial Guinea, Cameroon, Gabon, and Guinea, all in West and Central Africa; Italy,[8] Belgium, the Netherlands, Germany, and the UK in Europe; Libya, Algeria, and Morocco in North Africa; Venezuela and Brazil in South America; and Saudi Arabia in the Middle East.

In 2003, Nigerian government promulgated an act (no. 24) establishing the National Agency for the Prohibition of Traffic in Persons (NAPTIP) and Other Related Matters, and vested it with the responsibility to enforce laws against traffic in persons and to investigate and prosecute persons suspected to be engaged in this crime. In fact, Nigeria is one of the few countries that passed the law against the crime after ratifying a related UN protocol. Generally, the victims of human trafficking in Nigeria are trafficked for the purposes of sexual exploitation, forced labor, and in some cases organ harvesting. Victims are lured through deception, false promises, physical force, coercion, fraud, and so on. The syndicates are usually small-scale, but with extensive criminal networks involving the recruiters, transporters, receivers, pimps, brothel keepers, and corrupt government officials (Fitzgilbon, 2003).[9] Between January 2003 and April 2008, NAPTIP recorded a total of 2,104 human trafficking victims (1,597 women and 507 children), and for the same period, 325 arrests were made, out of which 18 cases were successfully convicted.

## Advance-fee Fraud

Advance-fee fraud, also popularly known as 419 in Nigeria because it comes under section 419 of the Nigerian Criminal Code, is based on the payment of some fee, tax, kickback, or brokerage on the pretense that such payment is required as part of an official transaction in existing business deals.[10] Simply put, it involves obtaining prepayment for goods or services that do not actually exist or which the proposer does not actually intend to deliver.[11] Nigerian entrepreneurs remain prominent in this cross-border crime, and indeed it is their creation.[12] It starts by the entrepreneur somehow proposing a service that is clearly illegal, such as the laundering of illicitly acquired funds through the target's account, and if the target responds positively, he or she automatically becomes part of the illegal transaction. The scammers usually offer a share in a large sum of money that they want to transfer out of their country. They then ask the target to pay money or give them his or her bank account details to help them transfer the money through the target's bank. The money represents "fees," charges, or taxes for the release of the money.

Fraudsters involved in advance-fee fraud usually require the names and addresses of prospective victims and access to telephone, fax, and Internet facilities, and of course start-up capital is not required. The criminals do impersonate very important people or highly placed government officials in the society, claiming that some late relations left behind a large amount of money as inheritance, which requires laundering in collaboration with foreign partners in return for a specified percentage of the money as commission. Recently these fraudsters have acquired the name Yahoo Boys and have dominated various public Internet cafés or business centers.

## Arms Trafficking

In a recent opinion article on the control of the proliferation of small arms and light weapons (SALW) in West Africa, Efik concluded that "the incessant cases of political instability, deepening poverty, violent crimes of armed robbery, assassinations, militancy, oil bunkering . . . are all fueled by the effects of small arms and light weapons proliferation."[13] SALW use in Nigeria has increased the scale of lethality, the degree of intensity, casualties, and the extent of criminal destruction.[14] The weapons smuggled into Nigeria include AK-47 rifles, automatic pump-action shotguns, bazookas, pistols (Beretta and Browning), double-barreled shotguns, G3 rifles, general purpose machine guns, submachine guns, and carbine rifles.[15]

There is evidence of the impact of cross-border SALW flows in Nigeria. Proliferation of small arms and light weapons is not only a threat to Nigeria's national security, but also to international security. Trafficking in SALW is of major concern in cross-border criminal activities in Nigeria. Violent crimes of armed robbery; cross-border banditry, especially by Chadian rebels through the northeast; ethnic and religious conflicts; and militancy in the Niger Delta are part of the consequences of illegal arms trafficking. ECOWAS adopted Moratorium on the Importation, Exportation and Manufacture of Small Arms and Light Weapons in West Africa in 1998, which was transformed into a convention for the purpose of shifting the focus from mere "moral persuasion" in curtailing the spread of illegal weapons to the "enforcement" of the protocol.[16]

The extent of Nigeria's over 4,000 km of borders and large population of about 140 million (by World Bank estimate)[17] present serious problems by exposing the country to cross-border smuggling and trafficking in SALW. Among the sources of SALW trafficking in Nigeria are the conflict-ridden West African states of Liberia and Sierra Leone and, due to the rebellion and mercenary activities, Chad and Niger. Due to the peculiarities of the Niger Delta—its swampy geography, extensive access to international waters, and of course the illegal criminal activities of piracy, oil bunkering, and hostage taking—the region has become an important conduit for the trafficking of SALW.

## Money Laundering

The INTERPOL General Assembly adopted a working definition of money laundering as "any act or attempted act to conceal or disguise the identity of illegally obtained proceeds so that they appear to have originated from legitimate sources."[18] In identifying the offense of money laundering, the Money Laundering (Prohibition) Act, no. 7 of 2003, Laws of the Federation of Nigeria, defines it as the conversion or transfer of resources or property derived directly or indirectly from illicit traffic in narcotic drugs or psychotropic substances or any illegal act with the aim of either concealing or disguising the illicit origin of the resources or property. Inadequate official controls make Nigeria vulnerable to money laundering and corruption activities, both of which are vital to the expansion of cross-border crimes. Although the true nature of money-laundering activities in Nigeria is not known, according to UNODC, the "Nigerian money launderers operate sophisticated global networks to repatriate illicit proceeds from narcotics trafficking, financial fraud, and other crimes. Nigerian criminal groups are importing high value consumer goods purchased abroad with illicit funds and selling them at less than the market value back in the country."[19]

## Armed Banditry

Armed robbery or armed banditry is a major violent crime in Nigeria that also has cross-border influences: either trafficked arms or foreign criminals taking advantage of Nigeria's porous borders to infiltrate and carry out their dastardly acts. Referring to the northeast borders in Nigeria, Asiwaju noted the "unbearable problem of armed bandits operating from bases widely believed to be located in the adjacent border areas of the neighboring countries."[20] The bandits carry out their operations even deeper into parts of the northwest and north-central geographical zones of Nigeria. They use highly sophisticated weapons smuggled from the neighboring Republic of Chad to kill or maim their victims and forcefully take their property.

The Chadian armed incursions have turned the roads of northeast Nigeria in particular into killing zones in which lots of lives and property have been lost to the criminal activities of the bandits. It has been speculated that these cross-border bandits use the proceeds of their criminal activities to fund the rebellion against the government of Chad. It was for this reason that the Multinational Joint Task Force (MNJTF), made up of the military, police, paramilitary, and *gendermarie* of Nigeria, Chad, Niger, Cameroon, and Benin, was established to police the activities of the criminals.

## Illegal Importation of Fake, Expired, and Adulterated Drugs

A major area of concern relating to cross-border criminal activities in Nigeria has to do with the illegal importation of counterfeit, substandard, adulterated, and fake drugs into the Nigerian pharmaceutical market. According to the World Health Organization (WHO), counterfeit drugs concern medicine which is deliberately and fraudulently mislabeled with respect to identity and/or source; substandard drugs are genuine drug products which do not meet quality specifications. A product is regarded as adulterated based on the methods or facilities used for its production, whereby the quality or purity or sanitary conditions are not to the standard required by law. Fake drugs are those produced in order to mislead the public that they are genuine, even though they are not real. These categories of drugs and drug products are mostly imported from China, India, Taiwan, and Egypt into Nigeria. The perpetrators of this crime import either by land, through the countries sharing borders with Nigeria, or by sea or air. Although counterfeiting is a global problem, Asia is the center of a complex, global network which manufactures and distributes fake medicines, and India, according to a WHO Report, is responsible for about 35 percent of the world's fake drugs. India's dominance in this trade practice is also reflected in Nigeria's fake or counterfeit drugs market.

## Illegal Oil Bunkering and Smuggling

Oil is the mainstay of Nigeria's economy, and she is among the largest producers of crude oil in the world. The oil sector has been experiencing the problems of illegal bunkering of crude oil and the smuggling out of the refined products as part of cross-border illegal activities. The illegal bunkering and smuggling of Nigeria's crude oil is estimated to be as much as 35 percent of the country's oil exports. Accordingly, it is estimated that as many as three hundred thousand barrels of oil are illegally exported from Nigeria daily.[21] Refined products, particularly petrol and kerosene, are smuggled across Nigeria's borders to Benin, Niger, Chad, and Cameroon. Furthermore, it is instructive to note that oil bunkering links to wider patterns of organized crime, with cash, drugs, and weapons all being traded in exchange for illegal oil. Militancy in the Niger Delta has incorporated criminal activities, such as kidnapping for ransom, terrorism against oil installations, arms smuggling, and political violence, which are all consequences of the illegal bunkering of crude oil.

## CROSS-BORDER POLICING IN NIGERIA

On the opposite side of the criminal activities are the policing activities across Nigeria's borders aimed at the prevention and control of illegal cross-border crimes. Cross-border policing is a situation which requires the police or law enforcement agencies of one country crossing the boundaries or borders with neighboring countries in collaboration with the police or law enforcement agencies of those countries to investigate, arrest, extradite, and prosecute suspected cross-border offenders. Particular attention is paid to these cross-border criminal activities because of the fact that they obviously undermine good governance and security, with negative impact on the rule of law, economic activities and growth, human rights, and general societal and cultural advancement within West Africa.[22]

In Nigeria, policing activities relating to cross-border crimes involve not only the Nigeria Police Force, but also the military, the paramilitary, and the intelligence community. Immigration, customs, civil defense, NDLEA, NAPTIP, the military (army, navy, and air force), and other relevant agencies are all involved in cross-border policing. A lot of efforts have been made to stop the rising tide of cross-border criminal activities in Nigeria and West Africa as a whole. For example, in addition to the legislation in the individual countries on drug trafficking, joint efforts led to the establishment of the West African Joint Operations (WAJO) upon the conviction that "a decisive multilateral action is the answer" to curbing the drug trafficking trends.[23] Another example is the establishment of the West Africa Police Chiefs Committee (WAPCCO) for the purpose of addressing cross-border crimes, with the objective of strengthening cooperation among ECOWAS member states' police forces to prevent various forms of crimes affecting the subregion.[24] INTERPOL is yet another very useful outfit in curbing the trend of cross-border criminal activities in Nigeria, and the Nigeria Police take advantage of its operations in the subregion in fighting crime and arresting suspects or criminals engaged in these cross-border crimes. A couple of years ago, a Multinational Joint Task Force led by the military was established to fight cross-border criminal activities, particularly along the Nigeria, Chad, Cameroon, Niger, and Benin borders.

The initiatives of the Nigerian government against cross-border criminal activities for the purpose of cross-border policing activities include the establishment of joint anticrime patrols, involving immigration, customs, police, and, sometimes, the military and the adoption of various regulatory measures and the enactment of various laws, such as the promulgation of the following:

The National Drug Law Enforcement Agency (NDLEA) Act, no. 48 of 1989
The Money Laundering Act of 1995
The Advance Fee Fraud Act of 1995
The Anti-Corruption Act of 1999, which established the Independent and Corrupt Practices and Other Related Offences Commission
The Economic and Financial Crimes Act of 2002, which established the Economic and Financial Crimes Commission (EFCC)
The Trafficking in Persons (Prohibition) Law Enforcement and Administration Act 2003 (as amended)
The National Agency for Food and Drug Administration and Control (NAFDAC) Act 1993
The National Agency for the Prohibition of Traffic in Persons and Other Related Matters (NAPTIP) Act, no. 24 of 2003

## CHALLENGES AND LESSONS

### Nigeria's Porous Borders

Nigeria's borders are porous, and this is the reality on ground. The approximately 4,000 km border poses a serious challenge to border policing, thereby making the country vulnerable to cross-border crimes and other illegal activities. Presently, there are only fifty-nine border posts covering Nigeria's boundaries with her neighbors, and this translates to one border post per a distance of about 70 km. The most notorious border posts with regard to cross-border crimes are Idi-Iroko and Seme[25] in Ogun and Lagos[26] states, respectively, in the southwest; Warri in Delta State; Jibia and Maigatari in the northwest; and those in Adamawa, Borno, and Yobe in the northeast. In addition, Nigeria's coastline of about 850 km along the Gulf of Guinea is also very vulnerable to cross-border criminal activities, with links to Equatorial Guinea, Gabon, São Tomé, Congo, and the Asian countries. In addition to their porous nature, Nigeria's borders are plagued with problems of inadequate resources and expertise to effectively patrol them.

## Inadequate Funding and Resources

A major problem confronting cross-border policing activities is inadequate funding and resources. According to NAPTIP, in addition to inadequate budgetary allocations for the agencies, individual operators lack operational vehicles, communication gadgets, and other security equipment.[27] Cross-border law enforcement officials are also poorly trained to carry out their responsibilities, especially in the areas of collecting, compiling, analyzing, and publishing crime statistics. As a result of this situation, international criminal networks are attracted to Nigeria, and since the country cannot effectively monitor its borders, we see the rise in cross-border criminal activities.

## Corruption and Border Officials

Corruption is the most serious barrier to cross-border policing in Nigeria, and indeed in West Africa. In general, corruption undermines political, economic, and social stability while it threatens security and damages trust and public confidence in systems which affect people's daily lives. Corruption is rife massively in almost all the border posts, and for this single reason, cross-border criminal activities thrive. It is evident that corruption has made border controls in Nigeria very weak, while making border crossing relatively easy. These sharp practices have aided the growth of cross-border criminal activities as, for example, between 2003 and 2006 more than five thousand vehicles of different types were stolen from Nigeria and taken to the Republic of Benin through the poorly policed borders covering Lagos, Oyo, Ogun, Kwara, Niger, and Kebbi states.[28]

## Common Cultural Affinity of Border Communities

Nigerian borders, indeed all borders in Africa, were created by colonial powers without due regard to the social, cultural, historical, and political implications of the demarcation exercise of the Berlin Conference. It was an arbitrary delineation and demarcation. Most settlements along Nigeria's borders share the same language, customs, and traditions. Therefore the boundaries are merely an artificial creation without regard to the sociocultural realities of Nigeria and the neighboring settlements. Northern Nigeria, the Republic of Niger, and northern Cameroon, for example, have similar cultures, including a common language (Hausa). Likewise, southwest Nigeria and the Republic of Benin share common cultures, including the Yoruba language. Many of the cross-border criminal activities are made possible due to these common ethnic affiliations, in terms of language, beliefs, and so on, on either side of the borders. Moreover, in addition to the cultural affinity, Nigeria is the most populous country in the West African subregion, indeed in Africa, and it is not surprising that she produces greater numbers of transnational criminals than her immediate neighbors.

## Crimes without Physical Boundaries

A major challenge, especially to cross-border policing in Nigeria, is posed by those criminal activities that do not involve physical boundaries. They are borderless by their nature and characteristics, mainly because such crimes are executed by their perpetrators using modern technology, such as the Internet (cybercrime) or wire transfer (electronic fraud). Advance-fee fraud (419) and money laundering fall into the category of borderless crimes. These crimes span national boundaries and legal jurisdictions. Policing these crimes by means of conventional methods creates a big challenge for cross-border policing. A major initiative by Nigerian authorities is the establishment of a website to educate and inform individuals on scam letters and how to deal with them. Likewise, there are country-specific reports and instructions for victims of such crimes to seek redress. Furthermore, to combat the laundering of criminal proceeds, the EFCC is empowered to investigate, arrest, and prosecute such criminals.

## Poor Crime Intelligence and Statistics

In order to make a positive impact, cross-border policing requires timely, accurate, and adequate information on the nature, trends, and characteristics of cross-border criminal activities. Law enforcement officials on both sides need to share valid and reliable information on criminal activities. It appears however that law enforcement agencies on both sides of Nigeria's borders generally have very poor or nonexistent crime intelligence capacities. According to Salay (2005: 150), the "discrepancy between the officially reported drop in crime and public perception (in Nigeria) can be due to either under-reporting, taking into consideration the inefficiency, or weak record-keeping methods of the Nigeria Police (and also other law enforcement agencies)."

## Complicity of Multinational Companies and Financial Institutions

There are indications, especially regarding those involved in financial crimes, that they enjoy the support or complicity of major multinationals and financial institutions, particularly in moving criminal or stolen wealth from Nigeria to some destinations in Europe (especially Swiss banks) and North America. Some of the largest banks in the world are known to have been complicit in the laundering of dirty money. There is evidence, for example, that massive illegal transactions take place in the field of foreign exchange fraud, often involving international companies that collude to move large amounts of money to bank accounts abroad. All cross-border crimes are facilitated in one way or another by the perpetrators' ability to enlist the complicity, active or passive, of state officials.

## Collaborative and Cooperative Partnership

The need for synergy in terms of cross-border policing efforts to curb the menace of cross-border criminal activities is a necessity mainly because, while these crimes are more often executed in multiple jurisdictions, they also require the efforts of law enforcement officials on both sides of borders to effectively deal with them. Partnership among law enforcement agencies is a great challenge in the face of official corruption; inadequate funding and the fact that Nigeria is comparatively richer than her neighbors, therefore depended upon to carry much of the burden; the problem of uneven application of technology; and inadequate and unbalanced training. However, collaborative and cooperative partnership with nongovernmental organizations (NGOs), the law enforcement agencies, government departments, and embassies is a must if cross-border crimes are to be tackled successfully.

## Poverty and Ignorance

Poverty and ignorance are major factors in cross-border criminal activities in Nigeria, including the corruption involving law enforcement officials. While Nigeria is rich in resources, poverty is widespread. In fact, Nigeria is said to be one of the six poorest countries in the world, with per capita GNP of about US$280.[29] Poverty is the most visible cause of the vulnerability of women and children to both drug and human trafficking in Nigeria. By a 2000 estimate, 60 percent of the estimated population of 140 million people lives on less than US$1 per day.[30] Most of the victims of human trafficking, for example, are also victims of poverty and ignorance. Likewise many of the drug couriers in Nigeria are also victims of poverty and ignorance, a situation the drug barons take advantage of. One may conclude therefore that the roots of most cross-border crimes lie in extreme economic disparities, poverty combined with bad governance.

## Legal and Jurisdictional Differences

Nigeria is surrounded by French-speaking countries, which also means that the legal system of Nigeria and those of all her immediate neighbors are different. Likewise, the systems of law enforcement are different. To what extent does such a situation pose a challenge to Nigeria's efforts at preventing and controlling cross-border crimes? What this presupposes is that it is not only cross-border criminal activities that are the issue here, but also related issues of crossing boundaries of law enforcement, jurisdiction, administration of justice, and other community-related matters. When the commission of a crime starts in Nigeria with the connivance of citizens of the Republic of Benin, for example, and the perpetrators are arrested by Ghanaian police, how and where would they be prosecuted? Under which legal system should they be prosecuted, French or English? Asiwaju (2005: 54) observes that in Nigeria, "differences in the legal systems vis-à-vis the adjacent countries . . . have ensured the protection and safety for those who offend against Nigerian state and created as well as sustained havens for them in the adjacent foreign jurisdictions." It is about crossing not only the physical boundaries, but also the professional borders of policing, economic borders of trade and commerce, judicial borders of the administration of justice, and social borders of cultures and traditions. This is an example of a situation in which the issue of cooperation and collaboration for partnership becomes necessary in preventing and controlling cross-border crimes, including the support and understanding of INTERPOL, the governments of the countries concerned, and other relevant agencies. The challenge is even larger when one realizes that many of the cross-border crimes do not begin and end in West Africa, but go beyond the African continent, since most African countries only serve as transit. This situation underscores the need for the harmonization of laws and law enforcement practices for effective prevention and control of cross-border criminal activities.

## CONCLUSIONS

Globalization, with its attendant consequences, is a major factor to be considered in analyzing cross-border activities, including criminal and policing activities, in Nigeria. The opportunities created by the increasing power shift from nation-states to economic markets have been exploited by transnational organized crime groups, including cross-border criminal networks in Nigeria. These criminal networks are involved in cross-border criminal activities, prominently drug trafficking, human trafficking, arms trafficking, money laundering, advance-fee fraud, armed banditry, illegal importation (especially of fake, adulterated, and expired drugs), and illegal oil bunkering, to mention a few.

To deal with the situation, border policing structures have been put in place in which the combined efforts of the Nigeria Police Force, immigration, customs, civil defense, NDLEA, NAPTIP, and the military, in collaboration with their counterparts in the neighboring countries, are being used to prevent and control cross-border criminal activities. There are, however, challenges and lessons to learn accordingly, and they include the porous nature of Nigeria's borders; inadequate funding and resources; official corruption; the common cultural affinity of most settlements along Nigeria's borders, as borders remain mere geographical expression; crimes without physical borders; poor intelligence and statistics; complicity of multinational companies; poverty and ignorance; and the need for partnership and cooperation with governments, NGOs, and other law enforcement agencies.

## NOTES

1. The current ECOWAS members are Benin, Burkina Faso, Cape Verde, Cote d'Ivoire, Gambia, Ghana, Guinea, Guinea Bissau, Liberia, Mali, Niger, Nigeria, Senegal, Sierra Leone, and Togo.

2. ECOWAS protocols A/P1/5/79; A/SP1/7/86; A/SP1/6/88; and A/SP2/5/90.

3. United Nations Office on Drugs and Crime (UNODC) (Geneva), document on Transnational Organised Crime in West Africa, New York, 2005, p. 24.

4. Flemming Quist, "Drug Trafficking in West Africa 2000–2004 in an International Perspective," UNODC workshop on West African organized crime, Dakar, April 3, 2004.

5. Ibid.

6. Ibid.

7. Most of the victims are sourced from Edo, Delta, Kano, Akwa Ibom, and Lagos.

8. There are approximately twenty thousand Nigerian prostitutes in Italy alone, and 80 percent of Italian prostitutes of foreign origin are said to be Nigerians (see Osita Agbu, "Corruption and Human Trafficking: The Nigerian Case," *West African Review* 4, no. 1, 2003).

9. Kathleen Fitzgilbon, "Modern Day Slavery? The Scope of Trafficking in Persons in Africa," *African Security Review* 12, no. 1, 2003.

10. NgorNgor, Awunah Donald. "Effective Methods to Combat Transnational Organized Crime," in *Criminal Justice Processes: The Nigerian Perspective*. http://www .unafei.or.jp/english/pdf/PDF_rms/no58/58-13.pdf.

11. Etannibi E. O. Alemika, "Organized Crime: Nigeria," UNODC Seminar, Dakar, April 2004.

12. At an INTERPOL meeting in 2003, 122 out of 138 countries represented complained about Nigerian involvement in financial fraud in their countries. See UNODC (Geneva) document on Transnational Organised Crime in West Africa, New York, 2005, p. 24.

13. *This Day* (Lagos), January 15, 2008.

14. A. Ebo, "Small Arms and Criminality in Nigeria: Focus on Kaduna State," Background Paper for Small Arms Survey, Geneva, 2003.

15. Jeremy Ginifer and Olawale Ismail, "Armed Violence and Poverty in Nigeria," Centre for International Cooperation and Security, Dept. of Peace Studies, University of Bedford, 2005.
16. See Alex Vines, "Light Weapons Proliferation in West Africa," UNODC seminar, April 2004.
17. See World Bank, "Nigeria at a Glance," www.worldbank.org.
18. INTERPOL General Assembly, 1995.
19. UNODC, Nigeria country profile, April 2008.
20. Anthony I. Asiwaju, "Border Security and Transborder Crimes: The Nigerian Experience in Comparative Historical Perspective," in *Crime and Policing in Nigeria: Challenges and Options*, ed. Etannibi E. O. Alemika and Innocent C. Chukwuma, Lagos: CLEEN Foundation, 2005.
21. Etannibi E. O. Alemika, "Organized Crime: Nigeria," paper presented at UNODC Seminar, Dakar, April 2, 2004.
22. Prosper Addo, "Cross-Border Criminal Activities in West Africa: Options for Effective Responses," KAIPTC Paper No. 12, May 2006.
23. WAJO presently has its secretariat in Lagos, Nigeria. It had its first meeting in 2001 in Lagos.
24. Sixth WAPCCO meeting, Abuja, September 2004.
25. Apart from being linked by an expressway to Badagry and subsequently to Lagos and other parts of Ogun State by road, Seme is also connected by roads to Porto Novo, the Republic of Benin capital, as well as Cotonou. In fact, Seme's border is said to be a major highway for smugglers and armed robbers.
26. Lagos, a "mega-city" with a population of about 12 million, is the economic hub of Nigeria.
27. NAPTIP, Reference Letter NAPTIP RW/68/1, dated April 14, 2008.
28. Olapade Ajase, "How Porous Borders, Corruption Aid Smuggling Activities," *Guardian*, April 27, 2008.
29. http://www.worldbank.org/annualreport/2003/download_report.html.
30. UNDP (2005) Human Development Report, http://hdr.undp.org/reports/global/2005/pdf/HDR05_HDI.pdf.

## REFERENCES

Addo, Prosper, "Cross-Border Criminal Activities in West Africa: Options for Effective Responses," KAIPTC Paper No. 12, May 2006.
Ajase, Olapade, "How Porous Borders, Corruption Aid Smuggling Activities," *Guardian*, April 27, 2008.
Albini, J. L., *The American Mafia: Genesis of a Legend*, New York: Appleton-Century-Crofts, 1971.
Alemika, Etannibi E. O., "Organized Crime: Nigeria," paper presented at UNODC Seminar, Dakar, April 2, 2004.
Asiwaju, Anthony I., "Border Security and Transborder Crimes: The Nigerian Experience in Comparative Historical Perspective," in *Crime and Policing in Nigeria:*

*Challenges and Options*, ed. Etannibi E. O. Alemika and Innocent C. Chukwuma, Lagos: CLEEN Foundation, 2005.

Ebo, A., "Small Arms and Criminality in Nigeria: Focus on Kaduna State," Background Paper for Small Arms Survey, Geneva, 2003.

Eskelinen, H., J. Liikanene, and J. Oksa, eds., *Curtains of Iron & Gold: Reconstructing Borders and Scales of Interaction*, Aldershot: Ashgate Press, 1999.

Fitzgilbon, Kathleen, "Modern Day Slavery? The Scope of Trafficking in Persons in Africa," *African Security Review* 12, no. 1, 2003.

Ginifer, Jeremy and Olawale Ismail, "Armed Violence and Poverty in Nigeria," Centre for International Cooperation and Security, Dept. of Peace Studies, University of Bedford, 2005.

INTERPOL General Assembly, 1995.

Quist, Flemming, "Drug Trafficking in West Africa 2000–2004 in an International Perspective," UNODC workshop on West African organized crime, Dakar, April 3, 2004.

Rider, B., *Organised Crime in the United Kingdom*, Cambridge: Cambridge University Press, 1993.

Salay, P. (2005). Partnership Against Crime. In E. Alemika and I. Chukwuma, eds. *Crime and Policing in Nigeria: Challenges and Option*. Lagos, Nigeria: CLEEN Foundation. Retrieved July 7, 2009, from http://www.cleen.org/crime%20AND%20POLICING%20IN%20NIGERIA.pdf.

This Day (Lagos), January 15, 2008.

UNESCO, Human Trafficking in Nigeria: Root Causes and Recommendations, *Policy Paper Poverty Series No. 14.2 (E)*, Paris, UNESCO, 2006.

United Nations Development Programme (UNDP), Human Development Report, 2005, http://hdr.undp.org/reports/global/2005/pdf/HDR05_HDI.pdf.

United Nations Office on Drugs and Crime (UNODC) (Geneva), document on Transnational Organised Crime in West Africa, New York, 2005, p. 24.

UNODC, Nigeria country profile, April 2008.

Vines, Alex, "Light Weapons Proliferation in West Africa," UNODC seminar, April 2004.

World Bank, "Nigeria at a Glance," www.worldbank.org.

*Chapter Eight*

# Transnational Crime and the Law

## *An Overview of Current Practices*

## Anthony L. Sciarabba and Christopher G. Sullivan

Transnational crime is not a new phenomenon. The context in which it occurs has changed dramatically over the past fifty years. Innovations in transportation and communication, including the Internet, have undoubtedly changed the world, but to what extent? Globalization has created unprecedented business opportunities, with both positive and negative consequences. One result of this increasing globalization has been the creation of an environment conducive to transnational criminal opportunity. Transnational crime includes any illegal activity committed in a manner which crosses national borders. It can be argued that in many ways, terrorist and trafficking enterprises enjoy greater opportunities for growth, profit, and exploitation compared to legitimate enterprises. One reason for this is that they are exempt from and may successfully evade control and regulation. Additionally, the success of these organizations is, in part, made possible by corrupt individuals in the criminal justice and legal systems. Therefore, while transnational crime is not a new area of discussion, the effects of increased globalization combined with more traditional organizational aspects (i.e., corruption) on the topic of transnational crime is an area worthy of exhaustive discourse.

In addition to discussing the effects that globalization has had on crime, it is necessary to analyze the various legal models tasked with handling such issues. Currently, the popular legal models include civil law, common law, socialist law, and Islamic law. Each of these models will be examined, beginning with an overview of the legal model. Following this, a notable country that utilizes one of these legal models will be selected. Finally, the discussion will identify a transnational crime which is unique to each of the selected countries. This will include an overview of the crime and how the legal system of each selected country prosecutes and ultimately punishes transnational criminals. This chapter is designed with the idea in mind that in order to effectively discuss each model, it is necessary to see each model "in action." This allows a more refined, and, more importantly, a more practical examination of the various legal models operating in modern society.

## PROLIFIC EXAMPLES OF TRANSNATIONAL CRIME

When one hears of international and transnational crime, several types of criminal behavior come to mind. International terrorism is the first. The events of September 11, 2001, and the subsequent "War on Terror" are etched in the minds of every man, woman, and child living in the world today. There is justification for this effect. As acts of domestic and international terrorism increased in the 1990s and following September 11, 2001, there was an effort within the United States and throughout the international community to restructure criminal law to better deal with the unique threats presented by terrorism.

Interestingly, there is some disagreement as to the definition of terrorism within the international community. This is primarily due to the very diverse beliefs and ideas concerning crime and justice among the countries of the world. The quote "one man's terrorist is another man's freedom fighter" is a prime example of this fact.[1] The lack of consensus concerning the concept of terrorism is deeply rooted in cultural and traditional beliefs.

Terrorist activity, while prolific in nature, pales in its rate of occurrence when compared to rates of international drug trafficking. It is well known that significant amounts of illegal substances are consumed in the United States.[2] However, much of these substances is not grown in the country. As such, a significant amount of these drugs cross international borders, thus falling under the classification of transnational crime. Growing, transporting, and selling illegal substances for consumption is a complex and financially profitable criminal enterprise that shows no signs of diminishing. Drug trafficking is dependent upon stable long-term business relationships, which are complicated by similar issues which affect legitimate business trade. Because of its profit-driven nature, drug trafficking may be more organized than terrorist conspiracies and individual acts of terrorism. Drug trafficking gangs and cartels have emerged as significant transnational criminal enterprises. As such, domestic prosecution for international drug trafficking is difficult because violators operate outside of the borders of countries and often enjoy political and military protection. Additionally, criminal drug enterprises, such as the Eighteenth Street Gang, which operates throughout the United States, are operating under a horizontal organizational structure, therefore making any police investigation difficult and prosecution for heavy offenses nearly impossible. This reality parallels that of the prosecutorial difficulties associated with terrorism activity in that because of the unique transnational nature of such crimes, current lawmakers are playing a game of catch-up in dealing with such issues. As will be discussed, many countries report that transnational drug trafficking is a serious issue

In addition to terrorism and drug trafficking, the illegal trafficking of human beings is a major worldwide concern. Likely one of the most egregious acts violating the most basic and fundamental human rights, the issue of human trafficking has been examined and investigated by international law enforcement organizations as well as the United Nations. As will be discussed, many countries do report human trafficking as a serious issue. In this chapter, Cuba and Iran are identified by the United States Department of State as countries that have not taken the minimal steps required to combat such transnational issues.

As noted, further compounding issues of drug and human trafficking is corruption among police, judicial, and political figures. As will be discussed in the case studies of Italy, Cuba, and Iran, the damage from corruption serves as a double-edged sword. Complications caused by corruption not only hinder the prevention of such activity but inhibit the full implementation of some of the more prohibitive legal systems (i.e., socialist and Islamic legal systems).

As individual political systems around the world vary, so do their respective legal systems. Every nation has its own *unique* legal system. An integral part of a particular legal system is its criminal justice system and the methods and manners used to provide for the safety and welfare of its citizens and at the same time its ability to punish criminal activity. While the rules and principles used may evolve over time and address the specific and unique needs of the people of a particular nation, these rules may not always be effective. Issues of past colonization, war, famine, crime, and conflict over various issues, including natural resources, can lead to a breakdown in the social order. In a global world, these conflicts and pressures are often interrelated. For example, tribal warfare may be linked to illicit drug production which may be linked to terrorist financing which, in turn, may be linked to organized crime and domestic gang activities.

As the effects of globalization increase and become more apparent, national borders become less relevant and, as such, principles of international law become more critical. Identification of national interests can be complex and the use of international law to protect individual concerns becomes more critical. The complex structure of custom and cooperation, compliance, and enforcement of international law in the suppression of transnational crime grows in importance.

As globalization increases, local and national agencies of social control and security may not have the resources needed to address transnational criminal activities, acts of terrorism, and violations of international law. In the case study of Italy, we will see that successful prosecution requires cooperation, information sharing, and resolution of jurisdictional issues. In some cases, it requires formal international investigation and prosecution by external bodies, including the United Nations, INTERPOL, and Europol. However, due to the nature of such activities, more informal techniques may be preferred. Gerspacher and Benoît (2007) concur and contend that "[because these threats are] sophisticated, resistant, and highly motivated . . . , law enforcement and security providers have shifted from a bureaucratic and hierarchical approach toward a networking morphology. [As such], the emphasis is on the role of informal initiatives by members of the law enforcement community" (347). This assertion illustrates the necessity of briefly evaluating the role of law enforcement in the battle against transnational crime. Following this brief overview, the various legal systems operating in the world can be explored.

## POLICING TRANSNATIONAL CRIME

Before a discussion on the major legal systems occurs, it is necessary to provide a very brief overview of the role of law enforcement in the fight against transnational crime. Just as there are different legal systems operating throughout the world, individual nations will rely on different policing systems. One explanation for this is that the policing system of each nation is a product of the nation's history and political environment and its need for security and order.

Successful investigation requires cooperation and information sharing, and in the case of transnational crime, this cooperation can be extensive, spanning many diverse localities and countries. To date, several international organizations have been created for the purpose of addressing these critical needs. INTERPOL and Europol, which will be discussed in the following section, are two primary examples. As trends in transnational crime change, efforts by law enforcement must also change.

## INTERNATIONAL ORGANIZATIONAL EFFORTS

### INTERPOL

Of the major international organizations involved in the fight against transnational crime, the International Criminal Police Organization, or INTERPOL, is the most prolific. INTERPOL is the world's largest international police organization, with 186 member countries benefiting from its services. The organization was created in 1923 to facilitate cross-border police cooperation and to support and assist all organizations, authorities, and services whose mission is to prevent or combat international crime (INTERPOL Facts, 2007). It is comprised of a general assembly, executive committee, general secretariat, national central bureaus, and advisers. The General Secretariat (located in Lyon, France), its six regional offices (Argentina, Cote d'Ivoire, El Salvador, Kenya, Thailand, and Zimbabwe), and national central bureaus (NCBs), which are maintained by each member country, comprise the operating structure of INTERPOL. The activities of the organization are based on four core functions: (1) secure global police communication services, (2) operational data services and databases for police, (3) operational police service support, and (4) training and development services to police.

In addition to its core functions, INTERPOL, like many United States federal agencies (see chapter on the United States), has dedicated investigative and enforcement groups that have a single focus. These include money laundering, drug trafficking, human smuggling, cybercrime, and intellectual property crime. An increased amount of resources are available for the response to and investigation of terrorism. For instance, in September 2002, INTERPOL, in response to the obvious transnational nature of terrorism, expanded its organizational focus by developing a specialized division, the Fusion Task Force (FTF). As depicted in the earlier portion of this chapter, terrorist incidents have increased in recent times. As a result, INTERPOL developed the FTF, which is tasked with identifying terrorists and organizations and assisting in the sharing of such information to other INTERPOL member countries. As of November 2004, FTF is credited with developing over seven thousand terrorist profiles. Additionally, INTERPOL offers disaster victim identification (DVI) services, bioterrorism services (the Bioterrorism Prevention Unit, established in 2004), and initiatives that emphasize interorganizational cooperation (i.e., Project Geiger, an initiative between INTERPOL and the International Atomic Energy Agency [IAEA]).[3]

## Europol

Another international organization tasked with fighting transnational crime is the European Police Office, or Europol. This is the European Union (EU) law enforcement organization that is primarily concerned with criminal intelligence. Its mission is to improve effectiveness and cooperation between members of the EU in preventing serious international crime, including terrorism. Europol was established February 7, 1992, following the approval of the

Maastricht Treaty of the EU, and operates out of The Hague, Netherlands. Like INTERPOL, Europol identifies seven mandates in its battle against transnational crime:

- Illicit drug trafficking
- Illicit immigration networks
- Terrorism
- Forgery of currency
- Human trafficking
- Illicit vehicle trafficking
- Money laundering

Additionally, the organization provides support in cases involving crimes against persons and computer crime as long as the offenses are transnational in nature and involve an organized operation component.[4] Therefore, in a similar fashion to INTERPOL, Europol represents the governmental and institutional realization that transnational criminality poses not only serious threats to society, but significant challenges to the more standard and traditional criminal justice approaches of dealing with such acts. Other areas of the world are joined by agreement as well, such as the African Union (AU), the Organization of American States, and many others.

## TRANSNATIONAL CRIME AND THE LAW

Ultimately, following successful police investigative work and apprehension, criminal matters must be brought under the jurisdiction of a court with the authority to hear and adjudicate the issue in a manner consistent with the system of justice operating in that particular nation. This entails the adherence to nation-specific procedures that is required for successful prosecution. This presents unique challenges to individual domestic courts, where most transnational crime incidents are presided over under national law. Occasionally, however, domestic courts are incapable of prosecuting such cases.

International awareness and cooperation have led to the formation of international courts and specialized tribunals to prosecute serious transnational offenses as well as crimes against humanity, such as genocide. The Hague, for instance, serves as a prime example of this, as it contains over 150 separate international legal organizations. These include the International Criminal Court (ICC) and the International Court of Justice (ICJ), to name its most significant components. More recently, The Hague established specialized tribunals to address the issues of genocide and ethnic cleansing, including the

International Criminal Tribunal for the former Yugoslavia (ICTY), established in 1993, and the International Criminal Tribunal for Rwanda (ICTR), established in 1994.

The fight against transnational crime requires, by definition, a concerted transnational effort, which furthermore entails a need for increased understanding of not only the various international criminal justice agencies and organizations but of their respective legal systems as well. As such, a thorough examination of the various legal systems as well as an overview of select international countries and their legal systems are presented in the following discussion.

Every country in the world has a body of law which governs it. These laws organize the government, regulate interactions of individuals and groups, provide rules for the prosecution of persons accused of crimes, and define and provide for the punishment of crimes. Although individual legal systems do vary in mode of operation and theoretical orientation, they essentially originate from these traditional sources. These variations in practice do have the potential to impact judicial handling of transnational crime and criminality. This impact should not be viewed as being either positive or negative. It should be viewed as simply being different. Further complicating these differences is the concept of international law.

International law lacks many of the characteristics of national law. International law often includes customs, agreements, treaties, and alliances relating to the behavior of one country toward another. It also includes concepts and beliefs concerning the treatment of any person or group by a particular nation, either within its national borders or outside its national borders. It covers relationships between private parties and companies involved in trade and other forms of transnational behavior. Another aspect of international law is its substance. In some cases, general principles emerge that become so widely accepted internationally that they become part of the fabric of international law.

As an understanding of national legal systems is necessary to understand transnational crime and policing, an understanding of international law is important since opportunities for prosecution may be obvious or lie hidden within this overlapping maze of laws. According to Jost (2004), "International Law is a hard to grasp concept that inspires idealistic hopes for world peace among supporters and fears of loss of national sovereignty among skeptics. Its origins lie in what is called 'customary international law'—practices such as diplomatic immunity or freedom of the seas that came to be accepted as binding by nation states despite the lack of any international court or enforcement bodies" (n.p.). In most cases, it appears that compliance with international law is voluntary. For instance, when a state voluntarily enters into a treaty, it essentially promises that it will comply with the terms of the treaty. If, however, a state changes its mind, it can simply withdraw from or reject the treaty. Enforcement of international law is generally based on voluntary compliance. While individual criminal acts will generally be prosecuted by an interested nation under domestic laws, international law is involved in the extradition process, which may be influenced by other aspects of international law. For example, many countries refuse to extradite criminal suspects in capital cases when they might face the death penalty upon conviction.[5] In addition to capital cases, some countries may choose not to extradite a suspected criminal in felony cases. One recent example of this is the case of Serbian college student Miladin Kovacevic, who, after severely beating a college classmate at a local bar in Binghamton, New York, was sent back to his native Serbia by Serbian diplomats in an apparent attempt to avoid apprehension and prosecution.

The concept of extradition is defined as the surrender of one state or country to another of an individual accused or convicted of an offense outside of its own territory and within the territorial jurisdiction of the other, which being competent to try and punish him, demands the surrender.[6] While extradition between states within the United States is governed by the U.S. Constitution, extradition of individuals between the United States and other countries is governed by international treaties. Generally, these treaties will specify the parties or nations compacting, the offenses for which an individual can be extradited, limitations, and specific procedures to be followed. For example, the United States and United Kingdom Treaty of Extradition provides for extradition if the offense is punishable under the laws of both parties by imprisonment or other form of detention for more than one year or by the death penalty and shall be granted for any attempt or conspiracy to commit an offense or for the offense of impeding the arrest or prosecution of a person who has committed an offense for which extradition may be granted.[7] Additionally, specific provisions limiting extradition in death-penalty cases are contained in Article IV.

To effectively demonstrate these instances of international law, case studies of select countries will be examined and their respective legal systems and the handling of transnational crime specific to their areas will be highlighted.

## THE ROMANO-GERMANIC (CIVIL LAW) SYSTEM

Most countries in the world operate under Romano-Germanic or civil law traditions. They are used by the majority of the world's 192 countries. The basis for civil law can be traced back to the ancient Roman republic and the Justinian Code (*Codex Justinianeus*), which dates back to approximately the second century BCE. The single most significant characteristic of this system is that it is based on a written code and legal statutes. According to *Black's Law Dictionary* (1990): "The civil law is that body of law which every particular nation, commonwealth, or city has established peculiarly for itself. The system of jurisprudence held and administered in the Roman Empire, particularly as set forth in the compilation of Justinian and his successors comprising the Institutes, Codes, Digest, and Novels and collectively denominated the 'Corpus Juris Civilis' as distinguished from the common law of England and the Cannon Law" (n.p.).

Because the civil law system of justice is generally based on a written code and statutes, it is more easily adopted by nations interested in modernizing their legal structure. This appears to be especially true if countries were subject to colonial exposure to the civil law system. An example of this is Japan, whose legal system is based primarily on the German civil law system. Additionally, the Japanese legal system has been influenced by American law as well in that it contains elements of judicial review. Unlike the American legal system, the Japanese legal system does acknowledge the International Court of Justice (ICJ).

Generally, civil law nations have relied on the inquisitorial system of justice rather than the adversarial system of justice. In an inquisitorial system, the judiciary takes a more active role in the fact-finding process, whereas in an adversarial system, the judge acts more as a referee. Theoretically, the availability of a written code reduces the need for judicial interpretation of the law and the development of new legal concepts. Under the civil law system, the development of legal concepts is a task of the legislature. This may be beneficial in less-developed countries and localities that experience corruption at the judicial level, as the development of new legal ideas and concepts is essentially handed down by a group rather than a single individual.

The structure of the court in civil law systems is somewhat unique, as it operates on a structure of separation rather than hierarchy. The concept of separate courts for different criminal issues is a common finding in civil law countries. This can be found in the structure of French and Italian courts, as well as the German court system. Additionally, it is common for civil law–based countries to have tax and labor courts as well as administrative courts. With this type of separation of the courts, conflicts over jurisdiction can be expected. This can be especially troublesome in prosecuting transnational crime, in which many jurisdictions have the legal authority to preside over such cases. This is further complicated if more than one criminal issue is at stake (i.e., tax fraud and labor issues crossing national borders). In such cases, jurisdictions rely on rulings from specialized courts that are concerned with such issues. France, for instance, relies on the Tribunal of Conflicts, and in Italy, the Court of Cessation is used.

## Civil Law System Case Study: Italy

The Italian civil law system traces its roots back to both ancient Roman and Canonic times as well as more modern French principles. As a civil law system, the laws of Italy are found in both its penal code and other written legal statutes. Additionally, Italy's criminal justice system is adversarial in practice. This is counter to the traditional practice of a civil legal system. This adversarial nature, adopted in 1988, represents a modern shift from the more traditional inquisitorial practice. The Italian constitution, like other prominent constitutions, outlines basic legal prohibitions and procedural rules. These include the right to a fair trial, protection against ex post facto laws and punishment, and protection against the deprivation of one's freedom, to name a mere, but critical, few. The Italian penal code lists both serious offenses (*delitti*) and minor offenses (*contravvenzioni*). This is very similar to the two classifications used in the United States (*malum in se* and *malum prohibitum*). Since the Italian penal law is developed by Italian legislatures, such laws must not violate the rights of Italian citizens granted by the constitution. To protect against such violations, citizens of Italy rely upon the constitutional Court of Italy (Corte costituzionale della Repubblica Italiana). This Italian supreme court is tasked with hearing cases that concern potential conflict between written penal law and constitutional rights. The decisions of this court are final and are not eligible for any appeal. While similar in practice to the U.S. Supreme Court, it hears cases less frequently.

## Italy and Transnational Crime

A major transnational crime problem in Italy is organized crime. As of late 2007, organized crime activities in Italy profited an estimated $127 billion. Additionally, it is estimated that, via organized crime activities, such criminal acts account for approximately 7 percent of Italy's gross domestic product (Kiefer, 2007). The topic of organized crime is essential in the discussion of transnational crime because in recent times much of Italian organized crime has seized upon the opportunities of globalization. Formerly local and domestic organized crime groups are now international criminal enterprises capable of spreading their influence to a worldwide audience. To elaborate on this point, the Federal Bureau of Investigation (FBI) notes that the most well-known Italian criminal organizations are operating within the United States, with their members distributed throughout the country (Sicilian mafia,

Camorra mafia, Calabrian mafia, and the Sacra Corona Unita). According to the FBI: "We estimate the four groups have approximately 25,000 members total, with 250,000 affiliates worldwide. There are more than 3,000 members and affiliates in the U.S., scattered mostly throughout the major cities in the Northeast, the Midwest, California, and the South. Their largest presence centers around New York, southern New Jersey, and Philadelphia" (2008).[8]

The primary activities of these organized crime syndicates both in Italy and internationally involve drug activity, money laundering, and racketeering. Additionally, there is evidence to suggest that organized crime activities are expanding and profits are growing (Kiefer, 2007).

In recent times, Italy has been the focus of a concentrated effort in the battle against transnational crime. Interestingly, this focus is not due to major innovations in the battle against such issues, but is actually due to an overall lack of activity in this area. In a published interim compliance report from the 2006 Group of Eight (G8) meeting, the activities and actions of Italy in battling transnational crime clearly illustrate that corruption within the political and legal systems is prohibiting any possible success.

> Italy has not taken clear concrete steps in complying with its summit commitments on transnational crime, and corruption. Shortly following the G8 Summit in St. Petersburg on 2 August 2006, Italy ratified the UN Convention on Transnational Organized Crime.[9] However, since then Italy's progress in fulfilling its commitments have been limited. Italy has taken some part in the international fight against transnational crime. Italy participated in the FATF Vancouver Plenary, held from the 9 to 13 October.[10] Second, it contributed legal expertise to a FATF assessment team, which evaluated Iceland's anti-money laundering system based on the FATF Forty Recommendations plus the Nine Special Recommendations.[11] Nonetheless, it seems that Italy has not asserted its genuine support to a global anti-corruption network. Though it has signed the UN Convention Against Corruption, Italy has delayed its ratification.[12] In the 2006 Transparency International's Corruption Perception Index (CPI) for Western Europe and the European Union, Italy ranked far behind its G8 counterparts.[13] The CPI reported that Italy's low grade of 4.9 is suggestive of a "perceived serious corruption."[14] Thus among the economies of Western Europe, Italy's commitment to the twin pursuits of fighting corruption and improving transparency is uncertain. In order to register full compliance with its summit commitments, Italy must take focused action in improving its performance. (Kahn and Khazaeli, 2006, 101)

The occurrence of corruption within the Italian political and legal systems directly hinders any meaningful achievements in the fight against transnational crime issues. Within the Italian criminal justice system, corruption issues are joined with communication issues. Italian police agencies suffer from serious domestic communication problems. Friedrichs (2008) discusses how this issue has complicated investigations and subsequent legal action. He notes that Italian police agencies regularly rely upon INTERPOL to communicate police intelligence communications between individual agencies and departments. Friedrichs (2008) notes that, "in short, Interpol was necessary to guarantee a minimal information flow amongst Italian law enforcement agencies. To compensate for a fatal lack of internal coordination among its law enforcement agencies, Italy was forced to stick to Interpol as the privileged channel for the international exchange of information" (146).

With the recognized issues of corruption within the Italian criminal justice system, one cannot help but entertain the possibility that corruption issues may be linked to the reported communication issues among Italian police agencies. As such, the Italian criminal justice and legal responses to the transnational crime issues which plague Italy have been severely undermined. As a result, the expansion of Italian criminal organizations, combined with the inability of the Italian legal system, has undoubtedly helped transform the landscape of battling transnational crime on a global level.

## THE COMMON LAW SYSTEM

The common law system, unlike the civil law system, relies on judicial decision making, interpretation, and case law. Legal decisions are based primarily on legal precedent and the concept of stare decisis. While the legislature plays a role in this legal system, as it is responsible for passing new laws, legal decisions are the responsibility of individual judges. According to *Black's* (1990), "the common law comprises the body of those principles and rules of action, relating to the government and security of persons and property, which derive their authority solely from usage and custom of immemorial antiquity, or from the judgments and decrees of the courts, recognizing, affirming and enforcing such usage and customs; and, in this sense, particularly the ancient unwritten law of England. In general, it is the body of laws that develops and derives through judicial decisions as distinguished from legislative enactments" (n.p.).

The critical element of *Black's* definition is that under the common law the body of law is developed through judicial decision making and precedent rather than legislative choices, and that these decisions derive their authority from usage and custom. According to *Black's* (1990, n.p.), precedent is "an adjudged case or decision of a court, considered as furnishing an example or authority for an identical or similar case afterwards arising or a similar question of law." Stare decisis is a "doctrine that, once a court has laid down a principle of law as applicable to a certain state of facts it will adhere to that principle and apply it in all future cases where the facts are substantially the same, regardless of whether the parties or property are the same."

The principle of stare decisis also holds that prior legal decisions must stand until overruled by a higher authority within a particular judicial jurisdiction. A higher authority may be legislative or judicial. For example, in the United States, interpretation of constitutional matters falls solely to the judicial branch, and as such, the legislature (Congress or state legislature) cannot overrule the court. A judicial determination in nonconstitutional matters such as an interpretation of a provision of the Uniform Commercial Code can be overruled by legislative action (*Black's*, 1990). The use of precedent when making legal judgments is prevalent in common law systems, but virtually absent in civil law or Islamic law systems. The stare decisis doctrine does not exist in civil law systems based on Roman *ius civile*, where law making is a function of the legislature. A judge's role is considered to be passive to the implemented legal rules contained mainly in codes, laws, and statutes. The stare decisis doctrine, as will be discussed later, is also absent in Islamic law systems, where the law is derived from four principle sources: the Koran, the Sunna, consensus, and analogical reasoning (Powell and Mitchell, 2007 and Vago, 2003).

## Common Law Legal System Case Study: The United States

The English common law serves as the basis of the American legal system.[15] Many scholars trace the origin of the English common law to the Norman invasion of England in 1066. The Norman invaders, confronted with the practical task of governing England, elected to administer justice by relying on local custom rather than imposing Norman law. Royal judges who traveled in circuits and administered justice according to local customs met and discussed their decisions and eventually recorded them. While this system was attractive because it essentially left undisturbed local customs and traditions, it was not universal and provided little guidance for future decisions. It was difficult or impossible to determine what the law was on a particular matter in a particular location. To fill the need for a more universal and predictable system of justice, the principles of precedent and stare decisis emerged.

In the common law system, legal principles develop from individual cases, not from written codes. These principles of law must be adhered to within a particular legal jurisdiction until overruled by higher authority. In the United States, the judicial branch is the final authority in constitutional matters and the only recourse to such a determination would be to amend the Constitution.

In practice, most common law jurisdictions have extensive codification of common law principles. This is done for convenience, clarification, and modernization. Additionally, codification addresses emerging legal issues that cannot await the development of common law principles in the traditional manner. Most criminal law in the individual states of the United States is now codified. The codified principles are consistent with the common law from which they derive. The reliance on a system of codification does not imply strict adherence to tradition. For instance, American legal history contains examples of deviation. In 1794, Pennsylvania decided that not all murders were the same and ruled to divide murder into degrees, with first-degree murder being the more serious.[16] This was accomplished when Pennsylvania passed a law departing from the common law, and as such, "modernized" the crime of murder.

Prior to the Revolutionary War, the American colonies operated under and according to a written document. This may explain why there was a readiness to establish a nation based on a written constitution at a time in history when written constitutions did not exist. In addition to the charter granted by the King of England, the American colonies had the English common law. Following independence from England, the colonies were confronted with two problems: (1) the need for a national government and (2) the need for a legal system. To fill the need for a legal system, each individual colony adopted the English common law voluntarily through statutes and legislative actions. Therefore, the legal system in the United States is based on a written constitution and the English common law.

One characteristic of the common law legal system which bears directly on investigation and prosecution of transnational crime is the fact-finding process. As noted earlier, generally legal systems can be divided into adversarial and inquisitorial. Justice is administered in two parts or questions: law and fact. There are two approaches to determining the answers to these questions: adversarial and inquisitorial methods. The American legal system utilizes the adversarial justice process. Under this adversarial system, a prosecutor must develop his argument and then convince a judge. In contrast, under the inquisitorial system, the judge may participate in the investigation that leads to the final decision. According to *Black's* (1990),

> the adversarial justice system [is] the jurisprudential network of laws, rules and procedures characterized by opposing parties who contend against each other for a result favorable to themselves. In such a system the judge acts as an independent magistrate rather than prosecutor. According to the adversarial process, factual truth will emerge from fair and equally competent competition between the defense and prosecution. (n.p.)

Whether prosecution is brought in an adversarial or inquisitorial setting will have an impact on the role, actions, and burden of the police and prosecutor. For example, violation of a defendant's constitutional rights in an American prosecution will result in the exclusion of evidence obtained.[17] American criminal justice, therefore, is highly focused on the development of rules of criminal procedure and enforcing them against the government through the adversarial process.

Prosecution of transnational criminal acts (e.g., drug trafficking, money laundering, etc.) is usually based on national law and prosecuted by national rather than international courts. Certain crimes such as crimes against humanity and genocide, however, are now considered violations of international law and prosecution of these crimes may involve international participation in an international criminal court. A prosecution under international law, where relevant international law exists, is now possible. The first modern examples of such a proceeding were the Nuremburg trials, in which Nazi-party members were prosecuted by an international tribunal for crimes against humanity.

## The United States and Transnational Crime

We saw how the United States handles transnational crime in the chapter on the United States. Nevertheless, a good example of the complexities involved in the United States is the case of Manuel Noriega. As noted earlier, international law presents certain complexities in transnational prosecutions. The U.S. Court of Appeals for the 11th District outlines the history of the arrest and conviction of Manuel Noriega in the beginning of its 1997 decision denying Noriega's appeal.

> On February 4, 1987, a federal grand jury for the Southern District of Florida indicted Manuel Antonio Noriega for his involvement in cocaine trafficking. At that time, Noriega served as Commander of the Panamanian Defense Forces of the republic of Panama. Shortly thereafter, Panama's President Eric Devalle discharged Noriega . . . but Noriega refused to accept the dismissal. Panama's legislature then ousted the President but the United States continued to recognize Devalle as constitutional leader of Panama. After a disputed election, the United States recognized Guillermo Endara as Panama's legitimate head of state. On December 18, 1989 Noriega publicly declared that a state of war existed between Panama and the United States. Within days of this announcement, President George Bush directed United States armed forces into combat in Panama for the stated purpose of "safeguard[ing] American lives, restor[ing] democracy, preserv[ing] the Panama Canal treaties and seiz[ing] Noriega to face federal drug charges in the United States."[18] . . . Noriega surrendered to U.S. forces on

January 3, 1990 then was brought to Miami to face the pending federal charges.
. . . A Jury found Noriega guilty of eight counts in the indictment and not guilty
of the remaining two counts. The District court . . . sentenced him to consecu-
tive imprisonment terns of 20, 15, and 5 years, respectively. (1997)

In this case, the government secured the indictment prior to the apprehension
of Manuel Noriega. The indictment established probable cause to believe
Noriega committed the offenses alleged and served as the basis for an arrest
warrant and a request for extradition, for which a treaty between the U.S and
Panama existed. The legal issue was that Noriega purported to be the head of
state and immune from extradition and the United States did not recognize
him as the legitimate head of state of Panama.

The changing and expansive nature of drug trafficking has presented challenges not only to law enforcement, but to the American legal system. Over
the past several decades, the common law system has changed in order to
keep up with the evolving nature of drug trafficking. This includes extensive
legislation that increased the penalties of drug offenses. These more severe
penalties are not without controversy in public, legal, and academic circles.
Additionally, the use of extradition as a legal tool to prosecute transnational
offenders has also contributed to this change. Nevertheless, the example of
drug trafficking illustrates elements of the common law in action.

## THE SOCIALIST LEGAL SYSTEM

Another prominent legal system operating in the world today is the socialist
legal system. The foundations of this legal system can be attributed to the
early days of Communism in Russia, and more precisely, the introduction of
the Union of Soviet Socialist Republics (USSR). Unlike common law, socialist law relies on the work and decisions of legislatures.

Socialist legal systems have three unique objectives. Legal scholar Steven
Vago (2003) describes these objectives: "First, law must provide for national
security. Ideally, the power of the state must be consolidated and increased to
prevent attacks on the socialist state and to assure peaceful coexistence
among nations. Second, law has the economic task of developing production
and distribution of goods on the basis of socialist principles so that everyone
will be provided for 'according to his needs.' The third goal is that of education: to overcome selfish and antisocial tendencies that were brought about by
a heritage of centuries of poor economic organization" (14).

What is obvious in Vago's assessment of the objectives of the socialist legal system is the security of the socialist host nation. This includes the essen-

tial socialist ideals of rejection of personal economic opportunities as well as the rejection of the capitalist concept of separation of powers.

## Socialist Law Legal System Case Study: Cuba

Much of the Cuban legal system is based on Marxist legal theory.[19] Scholar Ray Michalowski (1993), in his observance of the Cuban legal system, notes the following:

> Thirty years of development guided by Marxist legal theory, and shaped by close ties to the former Soviet Union have added a clearly socialist character to the Cuban legal system. Key elements of Cuba's "socialist legality" are: (1) an emphasis on substantive rather than juridical measures of justice, (2) the use of law as a pro-active tool for socialist development, (3) limited use of formal legal mechanisms for the resolution of private disputes, (4) the use of informal "social courts" to resolve conflicts such as housing and labor disputes, (5) direct citizen involvement in the judicial and crime control procedures, and (6) a system of state-organized law collectives to provide low-cost legal services nationwide.

While elements of Spanish civil law and American common law are present in the Cuban socialist legal system, the bulk of the legal system operates in the socialist tradition.

### Cuba and Transnational Crime

Because of the socialist form of government, Cuba is less subject to many of the more common transnational crime issues faced by other capitalist nations. Drug trafficking in Cuba is somewhat restricted internally, but because of the geographic position of the island nation, traffickers regularly use its waters to move their products. In fact, Cuba instituted capital punishment in 1999 for drug trafficking offenses. While the issue of drugs remains something of a threat to Cuba, the issue of human trafficking is Cuba's largest transnational concern.[20]

Human trafficking poses a serious threat to individual human rights in developing and third-world nations. In Cuba, women, mainly underage girls, are regularly trafficked into the island nation for sexual purposes as there is a significant illegal market for such activity. Pedophiles from various countries travel to Cuba to engage in sexual activities with children. These children are trafficked into the country from various nations for the sole purpose of slavery, mostly sexual in nature. These trafficked individuals are joined by the sex slaves of Cuban nationality to form this underground market. In a 2007 U.S.

Department of State report titled *Trafficking in Persons Report*, Cuba is identified as a tier 3 trafficking nation in that it fails to comply with minimum standards intended to prevent trafficking. In its examination of Cuba's handling of human trafficking, the report notes that

> Cuba is a source country for women and children trafficked internally for the purpose of commercial sexual exploitation. Cuban adults and children also are exploited for forced labor, mostly in commercial agriculture; some are reportedly trafficked to the United States under circumstances of debt bondage. The extent of trafficking within Cuba is hard to gauge due to the closed nature of the government and sparse non-governmental or independent reporting. However, by all accounts, the country is a major destination for sex tourism, including child sex tourism. Cuba's thriving sex trade caters to thousands of European, Canadian, and Latin American tourists every year, and involves large numbers of Cuban girls and boys, some as young as 12. State-run hotel workers, travel employees, cab drivers, hospitality staff, and police steer tourists to prostituted women and children and facilitate the commercial sexual exploitation of these women and children. Sex trafficking of Cuban women to Mexico and Western Europe also has been reported. The Government of Cuba does not fully comply with the minimum standards for the elimination of trafficking and it is not making significant efforts to do so. Information about trafficking in Cuba is difficult to obtain because the government does not publicly release information, and attempts to engage public officials are regarded as politically motivated. (2007, 85–86)

While the trafficking of humans in Cuba presents a serious threat to the most basic of human rights, the inaction of the Cuban government is equally threatening. To be fair in this discussion, most trafficking which occurs in Cuba happens "underground," and the Cuban legal system does provide evidence of the official stance on human trafficking. This is also noted in the *Trafficking in Persons Report* (2007).

> Cuba prohibits some forms of sex and labor trafficking through various provisions of its penal code. Article 302 prohibits the inducement or promotion of prostitution and provides penalties of up to 20 years in prison; if the crime is committed across international boundaries, penalties may be increased up to 30 years. Article 316 bans trafficking in minors and carries penalties of up to 15 years' imprisonment. Cuba also has laws against forced labor and sexual exploitation. Despite these laws, which are sufficiently stringent, it is not known if any prosecutions or convictions of traffickers took place in Cuba during the reporting period. (86)

As evidenced in the discussion of Cuba, the socialist legal system is primarily concerned with aspects of national security and the strict prohibition of capitalistic legal features, including the separation of powers. While the socialist form of government can be viewed as being restrictive and rather isolated from outside influences, the Cuban socialist legal system has identifiable capitalistic attributes, including habeas corpus. In addition, Cuba is home to the more egregious crimes that violate human rights. The socialist form of government has pushed the trafficking underground but not entirely out of site of officials. With the trafficking of humans receiving the tier 3 designation from the U.S. Department of State, the lack of any prosecutorial action against offenders leads one to entertain the possibility that issues of corruption may be at work and may be acting as a barrier against any exercise of the criminal justice system in bringing to justice human traffickers.

## THE ISLAMIC LEGAL SYSTEM

Another very prominent system of law in the world today is based on the traditions of the very prominent religion, Islam. The Islamic legal system, as Badr (1978) notes, "arose with the birth of Islam in the Arabian Peninsula and Mesopotamia in the seventh century. As the Arab Empire expanded, Islamic, religious, and legal traditions became predominant in many Central Asian and Middle Eastern States" (187). The laws within the Islamic legal system are based on the Sharia, which outlines the way Muslims must live according to God.

The Islamic legal system differs in several ways when comparing it to the civil law, common law, and socialist law systems previously discussed. Vago (2003) outlines these differences and asserts,

Unlike other systems of law based on judicial decisions, precedents, and legislation, Islamic law is derived from four principal sources. They include the *Koran*, the word of God as given to the Prophet. This is the principal source of Islamic law. The second source is the *Sunna*, which are the sayings, acts, and allowances of the Prophet as recorded by reliable sources in the Tradition (*Hadith*). The third is *judicial consensus*; like precedent in common law, is based on historical consensus of qualified legal scholars, and it limits the discretion of the individual judge. *Analogical reasoning* is the fourth primary source of Islamic law. It is used in circumstances not provided for in the Koran or other sources. (17)

The reliance on religion as a framework for legal thinking is not unique to the Islamic legal tradition. It may be said that all legal systems are based, to some degree, on religious beliefs. Ancient legal systems relied heavily on religious dogma and included penalties for violations of religious practices as well as universal criminal acts. Early American legal systems, for example, would have to be described as theocratic in style. Escaping religious persecution, early colonists developed legal systems in which violations of religious practices, such as falling asleep in church, carried criminal penalties. In another more recent example, the Japanese devotion to the emperor as a deity was a powerful political and legal reality.

Today, theocratic influences on legal structure are most apparent in Middle Eastern countries. Ayatollah Khomeini overthrew the sectarian government of the Shah of Iran in February 1979. The Taliban created an Islamic-based government in Afghanistan following the withdrawal of Russian military forces in 1996. The Taliban became infamous throughout the world for its strict interpretation of the Sharia. Unlike the American Constitution, constitutions in some of these countries specifically include provisions requiring conformity to religious law. Today, in many Middle Eastern nations with devout religious populations and powerful clerics, governments exist which are, or appear, theocratic in practice. This is not to imply that seamless relationships exist between religion and state. It is common to see mainly Islamic countries adopt principles inherent in common and civil law systems.

## Islamic Law System Case Study: Iran

The Middle Eastern country of Iran utilizes the Islamic legal system, following closely the Sharia. Iran claimed its independence on April 1, 1979, officially declaring itself the Islamic Republic of Iran. The Iranian constitution (*Qanun-e Asasi*) was accepted December 3, 1979. The supreme leader is a religious figure, Ali Hoseini Khamenei. While Iran does have a president, currently Mahmoud Ahmadinejad, the supreme leader is considered chief of state. This position essentially declares the president the head of the government, thus making him the second most senior official in Iran.

The legal system of Iran is Islamic-based. The supreme leader, Ali Hoseini Khamenei, is tasked with selecting the head of the Iranian judiciary. The courts of Iran are divided into three distinct parts. The first is the public courts, which are tasked with hearing criminal and civil cases. The second, the revolutionary courts, are tasked with hearing cases of treason, crimes against national security, and any offense that is seen as attacking the foundations of Iran and Islam. The third court is the special clerical court, which is responsible for hearing cases in which religious clerics are accused of an offense. All judges holding positions in the Islamic legal system of Iran must be qualified and well versed in the teachings of Islam. The most senior members of the Iranian judiciary must be very proficient in Islamic teachings.[21]

Additionally, the judiciary is seen as being independent from the other branches of the government. In a similar fashion to the countries previously discussed (Italy, the United States, and Cuba), Iran has not accepted compulsory ICJ jurisdiction.

## Iran and Transnational Crime

Iran has been a focal point in the discussion of human trafficking. The country is seen as a source of, as well as a destination for, trafficked humans. In an assessment by the U.S. Central Intelligence Agency (CIA), Iran is designated as a country in which

> women and girls [are] trafficked for the purposes of sexual exploitation and involuntary servitude; according to foreign observers, women and girls are trafficked to Pakistan, Turkey, the Persian Gulf, and Europe for sexual exploitation, while boys from Bangladesh, Pakistan, and Afghanistan are trafficked through Iran en route to Persian Gulf states where they are ultimately forced to work as camel jockeys, beggars, or laborers; Afghan women and girls are trafficked to the country for forced marriages and sexual exploitation; women and children are also trafficked internally for the purposes of forced marriage, sexual exploitation, and involuntary servitude (2008).[22]

In a similar fashion to the socialist Cuba, individual rights are not seen by the government as being as important as the national security of Iran and the sanctity of the Islamic religion and its traditions. Additionally, also like Cuba, Iran has been designated a tier 3 nation with regards to human trafficking. In the annual *Trafficking in Persons Report* (2007), the U.S. Department of State highlights Iran.

> According to nongovernmental sources, Iranian women and girls are also trafficked to Pakistan, Turkey, Qatar, Kuwait, the United Arab Emirates, France, Germany, and the United Kingdom for commercial sexual exploitation. Media sources reported that 54 Iranian females between the ages of 16 and 25 are sold into commercial sexual exploitation in Pakistan every day. The Government of Iran does not fully comply with the minimum standards for the elimination of trafficking and is not making significant efforts to do so. Credible reports indicate that Iranian authorities commonly punish victims of trafficking with beatings, imprisonment, and execution. Lack of access to Iran by U.S. government officials prohibits the collection of full data on the country's human trafficking problem and the government's efforts to curb it. Nonetheless, sources report that the Iranian government fails to meet the minimum standards for protection of victims of trafficking by prosecuting and, in some cases, executing victims for morality-based offenses as a direct result of being trafficked. (120)

From this report, it is apparent that while Iran may have the crime rates within Iran among Iranian citizens under control, the same cannot be said about the trafficking of human beings. However, Iran does have severe laws which prohibit the trafficking of humans. These laws include capital punishment for convicted human traffickers. In summarizing the activity of the prosecution of human trafficking by Iranian courts, the *Trafficking in Persons Report* (2007) notes that "Iran did not make significant progress in prosecuting and punishing trafficking crimes over the reporting period [2007]. . . . The government did not report any prosecutions or convictions for trafficking crimes. Iran similarly did not provide any evidence of law enforcement efforts taken against government officials believed to facilitate trafficking" (120).

As evidenced, Iran is host to a substantial market for human trafficking. Innocent men and women, young and old, are regularly trafficked either into or out of the country. In some cases, as highlighted in the U.S. Department of State report (2007), Iranian officials are aware of and participate in this trade. This illustrates the possibility that corruption may be hindering both the prevention of such acts and the implementation of Islamic law in Iran. However, laws do exist that prohibit such behavior and these laws are consistent with Islamic law. This includes harsh penalties for any behavior that is inconsistent with the teachings of the Sharia. Additionally, the punishments for such offenses are also consistent with Islamic law. However, issues of administrative and official corruption within the Iranian judiciary hinder both the protection of individuals and the adherence to Islamic law.

## DISCUSSION: TRANSNATIONAL CRIME IN MODERN TIMES

As outlined in this chapter, transnational crime rates show no immediate signs of diminishing. Advances in technology, transportation, and science in general have greatly assisted the evolution of transnational crime efforts. The astounding profits of drug and human traffickers help keep this population of criminals on the same level as heavily funded law enforcement agencies.

Another important topic that deserves mention is the issue of supply and demand. Transnational criminal organizations operate essentially like businesses with regard to supply and demand. If there is a large demand for a product, the organizational response is to supply, thus quenching the thirst for demand. A result of this is profit. When discussing transnational criminal organizations, the same concept applies. For example, the United States is a primary consumer of illegal drugs, many of them either grown or manufactured overseas. With the demand of illegal drugs being so high among American citizens, drug cartels and gangs increase the available supply. This businesslike nature of criminal organizations presents serious problems for law enforcement agencies, which depend on taxpayer funds to fight crime.

Legal systems of the world, as discussed, often have laws prohibiting transnational crime. However, the existence of such laws does not necessarily translate into deterrence among transnational criminals. As noted by various professional sources, including the CIA and the U.S. Department of State, many countries currently have significant issues with regard to drug and human trafficking. This categorization includes countries from the United States, which features a common law legal system, to smaller countries including Cuba, which features a socialist legal system. Additionally, a country such as Iran, which features the Islamic legal system with its heavy emphasis on Islam, is home to significant human trafficking issues. Therefore, one assessment from the current issues is that regardless of the legal system in use, transnational crime remains an issue.

One essential aspect of nearly all of the case studies is the issue of corruption among police, judicial, and political figures. This was especially pragmatic in the Italian case study in which communication between individual police departments is currently being severely hindered by corruption issues. As such, Italian police agencies are forced to rely on Europol as a clearinghouse for police intelligence. The issue of corruption and its effects on society act as a poison to effective policing and, as outlined in this chapter, effective operation of the various legal systems in the world. A particular country can have a countless number of laws prohibiting certain acts. However, if corruption exists within the legal system, the amount of written laws becomes useless.

In addition to these two interrelated aspects, another very important mechanism in the fight against transnational crime is the international treaty. The establishment of treaties between countries is an effective method in the fight against transnational crime. In many locations, fugitive criminals can no longer seek refuge in a neighboring country. The United Nations Office on Drugs and Crime (UNODC) serves as a great example of a collective body built upon the obvious need to apprehend fugitive criminals involved in felony drug cases. In order to effectively carry out its mission, the member countries participating in the UNODC ratified a number of treaties designed to promote cooperation between countries during the extradition of fugitives. Some of the more prominent treaties established by UNODC include the Convention against Transnational Organized Crime, the Convention against Corruption, the Single Convention on Narcotic Drugs, the Convention on Psychotropic Substances, and the Convention against the Illicit Traffic in Narcotic Drugs and Psychotropic Substances. In addition to these drug treaties, the United Nations has adopted a number of treaties specifically designed to combat international terrorism. At the time of the writing of this chapter, the United Nations is continuing this fight against terrorism by establishing its fourteenth international antiterrorism treaty. The focus of this treaty includes the following components.

> This convention would complement the existing framework of international anti-terrorism instruments and would build on key guiding principles already present in recent anti-terrorist conventions: the importance of criminalization of terrorist offences, making them punishable by law and calling for prosecution or extradition of the perpetrators; the need to eliminate legislation which establishes exceptions to such criminalization on political, philosophical, ideological, racial, ethnic, religious or similar grounds; a strong call for Member States to take action to prevent terrorist acts; and emphasis on the need for Member States to cooperate, exchange information and provide each other with the greatest measure of assistance in connection with the prevention, investigation and prosecution of terrorist acts (2007).[23]

The use of treaties to fight transnational crime is certainly a positive legal mechanism. Criminal suspects can, in most cases, easily be deported to face charges. While this is true most of the time, certain complications arise when capital punishment is involved. This is because it is not an agreed-upon form of punishment in many countries. For example, difficulties arise during extradition cases between the United States and Mexico when capital punishment is a possible sentence that the criminal suspect faces following a guilty conviction in a U.S. court. This is because Mexico does not support the use of the death penalty.

In sum, as the fight against transnational crime continues, one cannot lose sight of the fact that the success of such a fight is nearly entirely dependent upon at least two aspects. First is the relationship between the demand by society for the supply of illegal goods, either drugs or humans. Second is the professionalism of the members of the criminal justice system. When these two aspects are left uncontrolled for, little if any success in the fight against transnational crime is possible. In addition, the use of treaties should be expanded to include developing nations. Many developing countries in which corruption is an issue can serve as operational headquarters for criminal and terrorist enterprises. If the governments of these nations sign international treaties, this allows for better cooperation between member nations and greatly increases the chances for criminal apprehension. Therefore, the effective operation of the major legal systems operating around the world requires, as a prerequisite, the control, establishment, and advancement of these interrelated aspects.

## NOTES

1. It is important to clarify this statement by noting that this view represents the political beliefs regarding terrorism. Social scientists however refute this assertion (see Schaefer 2001, 425, for an overview of this argument).

2. Interested readers can consult the latest results (2008) from the World Health Organization's (WHO) Mental Health Survey, available at http://medicine.plosjournals .org/archive/1549-1676/5/7/pdf/10.1371_journal.pmed.0050141-L.pdf.

3. For additional information and facts, readers are advised to consult http://www .interpol.int.

4. For additional information, consult http://www.europol.europa.eu.

5. See http://www.amnesty.org.

6. See U.S. Constitution, art. IV, sec. 2.

7. See article III of the United States Constitution.

8. See http://www.fbi.gov/hq/cid/orgcrime/ocshome.htm.

9. United Nations Convention against Transnational Organized Crime, UN Office on Drugs and Crime (Vienna). http://www.unodc.org/unodc/en/crime_cicp_signatures _convention.html.

10. Financial Action Task Force. Chairman's Summary: Vancouver Plenary (Paris), October 13, 2006. http://www.fatfgafi.org/searchResult/0,2665,en_32250379 _32235720_1_1_1_1_1,00.html.

11. Financial Action Task Force, *The Third Mutual Evaluation Report: Anti-Money Laundering and Combating the Financing of Terrorism: Iceland* (Paris), October 13, 2006. http://www.fatfgafi.org/dataoecd/54/38/37706239.pdf.

12. United Nations Convention against Corruption: Signatories. United Nations Office on Drugs and Crime (Vienna), 2006. http://www.unodc.org/unodc/crime_signatures _corruption.html.

13. G8 (Group of Eight) refers to an international annual meeting of the leaders of eight prominent countries situated throughout the world (the United States, United Kingdom, Russia, Canada, France, Italy, Germany, and Japan).

14. CPI 2006 Regional Results. Transparency International (Brussels), November 6, 2006. http://www.transparency.org/policy_research/surveys_indices/cpi/2006/ regional_highlights_factsheets.

15. It is important to bring to the reader's attention that the legal system of the United States is partially based on common law. In fact, it contains elements of both the civil and common law systems. For example, many of our laws are now codified.

16. *Pennsylvania Laws*, 1794, ch. 257, ss. 1–2.

17. The exclusionary rule was first articulated in *Weeks v. United States*, 232 U.S. 383 (1914). The rule was made applicable to the individual states of the United States in *Mapp v. Ohio*, 367 U.S. 643 (1961).

18. See *United States v. Noriega*, 746 F. Supp. 1506, 1511. (S.D.Fla.1990).

19. While much of the Cuban legal system is based on Marxist legal theory, American and Spanish influences are present as well.

20. https://www.cia.gov/library/publications/the-world-factbook/geos/cu.html.

21. Article 162 of section 11, Constitution of the Islamic Republic of Iran.
22. See https://www.cia.gov/library/publications/the-world-factbook/geos/ir.html.
23. See http://www.un.org/terrorism/instruments.shtml.

## REFERENCES

Badr, G. (1978). Islamic law: Its relation to other legal systems. *The American Journal of Comparative Law* 26(2): 187–98.

*Black's Law Dictionary*, 6th edition. (1990). Eagan, MN: West Publications.

Bureau of Justice Statistics. (2004). *Census of State and Local Law Enforcement Agencies, 2004.* U.S. Department of Justice.

Friedrichs, J. (2008). *Fighting terrorism and drugs.* Routledge Advances in International Relations and Global Politics. London: Routledge.

Gerspacher, N., and Benoît, D. (2007). The nodal structure of international police cooperation: An exploration of transnational security networks. *Global Governance* 13(3): 347–64.

INTERPOL Facts. (2007). Interpol: An overview. Available at http://www.interpol.int.

Jost, K. (2004). International law: Should U.S. policy give it more weight? *The CQ Researcher*, December 17, 2004.

Khan, A., and Khazaeli, S. (2006). *G8 research group—2006 final St. Petersburg compliance report.* Downloaded from www.g8.utoronto.ca/evaluations/2006compliance _final/14-2006_g8compliance_crime.pdf.

Kiefer, P. (2007). Organized crime takes lead in Italy's economy. *New York Times*, October, 23, 2007. Downloaded from www.nytimes.com/2007/10/23/world/europe/ 23italy.html?ref=europe.

Michalowski, R. (1993). Cuba. World Factbook of Criminal Justice Systems. Office of Justice Programs, U.S. Department of Justice. Downloaded from http://www.ojp .usdoj.gov/bjs/pub/ascii/wfbcjcub.txt.

Powell, E., and Mitchell, S. (2007). The International Court of Justice and the world's three legal systems. *The Journal of Politics* 69(2).

Schaefer, R. T. (2001). Sociology, 7th ed. New York: McGraw-Hill.

U.S. Department of State. (2007). *Trafficking in persons report.* Downloaded on June 8, 2008, from http://www.state.gov/documents/organization/82902.pdf.

Vago, S. (2003). *Law and society*, 7th edition. Upper Saddle River, NJ: Prentice Hall.

# Index

# About the Editors and Contributors

**Abdul-Rahman B. Dambazau** is a serving officer in the rank of major general in the Nigerian Army. He holds a bachelor's degree in criminal justice (1982) from Kent State University, Kent, Ohio, and a PhD in criminology (1989) from the University of Keele, United Kingdom. Commissioned as an officer in the Nigerian Army in 1977, he began his military career as a military police officer having had his basic training at the U.S. Army Military Police School, Ft. McClellan, Alabama, in 1979. He served in various capacities as a commander in military police units, as a special investigator, and as a training instructor. Dambazau was also the registrar of Nigeria's Military University for a period of six years (1993–1999). He attended the National Defence College, New Delhi, India, from January to December 2003, at the end of which he was awarded the Colonel Pyar Lal memorial gold medal for the best thesis on national security and strategy. On return, he was deployed to the then–National War College, Nigeria (now National Defence College), to serve as a directing staff member, and thereafter the director, of Higher Military Organization and Operations, between 2004 and 2006. In 2006, he was appointed the principal general staff officer (PGSO) to the Honourable Minister, Ministry of Defence, the position he held until he was appointed the chief of army standards and evaluation (CASE), an inspectorate department of the army. It was from the position of the CASE that he was appointed the general officer commanding, Second Division, Nigerian Army (August 2007–present). Abdul-Rahman Dambazau is also an academic of high reputation in the field of criminology and criminal justice. He lectured part-time in criminology at the Ahmadu Bello University, Zaria (1995–1999). He has published a number of books (*Law and Criminality in Nigeria*, 1994; *Issues in Crime Prevention and Control*, 1996; *Criminology and Criminal Justice*, 1999; 2007). He has published a number of scholarly articles in academic and professional journals. His current interest in the field of criminology is in the area of transnational organized crime, particularly as it relates to Nigeria. He is married with children. His hobbies include research, golf, and listening to music.

**Dilip K. Das** served as police chief before joining academia. He is the founding president of the International Police Executive Symposium (IPES, http://www.ipes.info), which brings police researchers and practitioners together to facilitate crosscultural, international, and interdisciplinary exchanges for the enrichment of the profession. Professor Das also serves as the founding editor-in-chief of *Police Practice and Research: An International Journal*, which is affiliated with IPES. His publications include more than two dozen books and numerous articles. He is a professor of criminal justice and a human rights consultant to the United Nations.

**Emilio E. Dellasoppa** is professor of sociology and politics at the Law School and the Social Work School of the State University of Rio de Janeiro, where he has taught since 1995. He was also professor at the Public Security Course for police officers at the State University of Rio de Janeiro and at the Military Police Academy.

He teaches graduate courses in research methods and sociology of law, and was visiting researcher at the Center for the Study of Violence at the University of São Paulo in 2002 and visiting professor at the Institute of Social Science of the University of Tokyo (2002–2003). During 2002–2003 he was a member of the project Public Security and Police Reform in the Americas: Coping with New Challenges of Crime and Violence, at the Georgetown University School of Foreign Service, Center for Latin American Studies. He has been since 1997 coordinator of the Latin American Sociological Association (ALAS) working group Violence and Human Rights. He was a member of the Latin American Council of Social Sciences (CLASCO) working group Violence and Society and was granted a CLACSO/Asdi Senior Researcher Fellowship in 1999 for the research project "Strategies and Rationality in the Civil Police of the Rio de Janeiro State." As a member of Globalisation Économique et Droits dans le Mercosul (GEDIM), he was project coordinator of the project Organized Crime in Brazil: Present Situation and Penal Control Tendencies under the GEDIM/Management of Social Transformations (MOST)-UNESCO research "Organized Crime Control in the Mercosul Area." Presently, he is a member of the Foro Iberoamericano de Seguridad Ciudadana.

His main areas of interest are urban violence and police institutions in Brazil and organized crime in the Mercosul area. His research has focused on demographic methods for comparative studies on violence and crime, transitions to democracy, human rights, police institutions and police reform, and citizen security. He is author of *No Justice for the Enemy: Political Violence in Argentina 1943–1983*. His literary output includes several chapters in books, such as *Brazil's Public Security Plans: Rationality vs. the Politics of "Muddling Through"* (edited by John Bailey and Lucia Dammert); *Policing Corruption: International Perspectives* (edited by Rick Sarre, Dilip Das, and H. J. Albrecht); *Funk'n Rio: Leisure, Music, Gangs, Violence and Socialization of the "Young Wave"*; "Brazil: Developing Nation-State," in *Crime and Crime Control: A Global View* (edited by Gregg Barak); and *J'ajuste, mais je ne corrige pas: Youngs, Violence and Demography in Brazil*. Dr. Dellasoppa received an engineering degree from the University of La Plata (Argentina) and a PhD in political science from the University of São Paulo, Brazil.

**John A. Eterno** is the chairperson, and associate dean and director of graduate studies in criminal justice at Molloy College. He received his PhD in criminal justice from the State University of New York at Albany and has two master's degrees, one in criminal justice and the other in human relations. Dr. Eterno is a retired captain from the New York City Police Department (NYPD), where he had extensive hands-on experience in precinct patrol, conducting research in both the Personnel Bureau and in the Police Commissioner's Office of Management, Analysis and Planning. Notably, Dr. Eterno's research with NYPD led to the 1994 reestablishment of physical standards for police officer candidates. In recognition of his work and commitment to law enforcement, he received the prestigious Hemmerdinger Award for his research on physical standards and the Enterprise Initiative Award for his research on mapping. Dr. Eterno is the managing editor of *Police Practice and Research: An International Journal*. He is widely published including a recent book entitled *Policing within the Law: A Case Study of the New York City Police Department* (2003). You can also find book chapters and peer-reviewed articles by Dr. Eterno featured in such publications as *Professional Issues in Criminal Justice, Police Practice and Research: An International Journal, Justice Research and Policy, The International Journal of Police Science and Management, Policing: An International Journal of Police Strategies and Management, Women and Criminal Justice*, and *Criminal Law Bulletin*.

**Yakov Gilinskiy**, PhD, is professor in the Department of Criminal Law at St. Petersburg's juridical Institute of the Academy of the General Prosecutor's Office of Russian Federation and head of Department of Criminal Law, the Russian State University of Education, St. Petersburg. He is the author (or coauthor) of over four hundred articles, book chapters, and books (in English, French, German, Hungarian, Italian, Norwegian, Polish, Russian, and Japanese).

**Steve James** is associate professor in the School of Social and Political Science at the University of Melbourne, Victoria, Australia, where he teaches courses in law enforcement and illicit drugs policy. His PhD in criminology from the University of Melbourne was a longitudinal study of police performance measurement. He coedited the Melbourne University Press volume *Violence and Police Culture* and has published on policing and drug law enforcement issues in *Policing and Society*, *Police Research and Practice*, *Australian and New Zealand Journal of Criminology*, and *Current Issues in Criminal Justice*. He was for ten years a member of the Victoria Police Ethical Standards Consultative Committee.

**Anthony L. Sciarabba** is a research assistant in the Department of Criminal Justice at Molloy College in Rockville Centre, New York. He also serves as the associate managing editor of *Police Practice and Research: An International Journal*. Currently, he is involved in field research, evaluating a "weed and seed" initiative in Far Rockaway, New York, for the Community Capacity Development Office of the United States Department of Justice.

**Christopher G. Sullivan** is an associate professor in the Department of Criminal Justice of Molloy College. He joined the faculty in 1998 and served as chairperson from 1999 to 2006. Sullivan has served on a variety of college committees, including faculty development, priorities and planning, and contract. A graduate of the John Jay College of Criminal Justice in 1972, Sullivan received a master's degree in criminal justice from Long Island University, C. W. Post. In 1985, he received his juris doctor degree from St. John's University Law School and was admitted to practice law in New York the next year.

Sullivan joined the New York City Police Department in May 1970 and retired September 1997, having attained the rank of lieutenant special assignment. As a New York City police officer, Sullivan worked in various patrol assignments, taught as a Police Science instructor at the police academy Commanding Officer In-Service Training Unit, and ultimately retired from the Personnel Bureau, where he served as special counsel to the chief of personnel. Prior to retirement, Sullivan was responsible for the development of legally defensible personnel programs and initiatives, such as enhanced physical standards, increased appointment age, performance evaluation systems, drug screening, and college education requirements for appointment to the position of police officer and promotion to supervisory ranks. Sullivan is a member of the New York State Bar Association, NYPD Holy Name Society, and Criminal Justice Educators of New York.

**Arvind Verma** has served in the Indian police for seventeen years in the state of Bihar, holding several senior-level positions in the organization. His first degree was in engineering mathematics from the Indian Institute of Technology–Kanpur and he earned his doctoral degree in criminology from Simon Fraser University in Canada. His doctoral work was concerned with analysis of criminal justice data using a variety of mathematical techniques, such as fuzzy logic, topology, and fractals. He has served as the managing editor of *Police Practice and Research: An International Journal* and he has also been an advisor to the Bureau of Police Research and Development in India. His current research interests are in data analysis and visualization, criminal justice in India, and comparative policing. His recent publications include a book titled *The Indian Police: A Critical Review* and journal articles "Anatomy of Riots: A Situational Prevention Approach," "Measuring Police Performance in India: An Application of Data Envelopment Analysis," and "The State and Coercive Power in India and Visualization of Criminal Activity in an Urban Population."

**Ian Warren** is lecturer in criminology in the School of History Heritage and Society at Deakin University in Victoria, Australia. Dr. Warren has a law degree from the University of Melbourne, and his PhD from Victoria University dealt with the comparative regulation of boxing. He combines enduring interests in law enforcement and the regulation of violence with sports history. He has collaborated with Dr. James previously in research on police culture and violence, and his work has been published in a number of edited Australian criminal justice volumes.

**Kam C. Wong** is visiting professor of law, City University of Hong Kong, School of Law; chair and professor, Xavier University, Cincinnati, Ohio; BA (Hons.), JD (Indiana); diploma (NITA V, Northwestern); MA, PhD (SUNY–Albany); vice-chair, Hong Kong Society of Criminology (1999–2002), vice-president (1999–2002); associate fellow, Center of Criminology, University of Hong Kong; and vice-president (2001–2002), and president (2002–2003) AAPS (Asian Association of Police Studies). He has published seventy books/articles, and his articles have appeared in *Criminal Law Bulletin*; *Georgetown Journal of Law and Public Policy*; *Columbia Journal of Asian Law*; *British Journal of Criminology*; *Journal of Information Law & Technology (JILT)*; *Pacific Rim Law & Policy Journal*; *International Journal of the Sociology of Law*; *Australian Journal of Law and Society*; *Australian* *and New Zealand Journal of Criminology*; *John Marshall Journal of Computer and Information Law*; and others. His latest books are *The Impact of USA Patriot Act on American Society: An Evidence Based Assessment* (2007) and *The Making of USA Patriot Act: Legislation, Implementation, Impact* (2008) (in Chinese). He is working on two new books, *Policing with Chinese Characteristics* (2008) and *Police Reform in China* (2009).